A Free
HUMANITY

Paul the Apostle saw that law keeping was robbing people of their freedom in being in relationship with the Trinity. It prompted him to write a response to what freedom as humanity looks like when lived in relationship with Father, Son, and Spirit. Luciano has taken the Apostle's thoughts and has offered us a picture of the free humanity that emerges from the new humanity that is ours in Christ. With the same patience, simplicity, and joy of his experienced mind in his previous book, *A New Humanity*, Lombardi encourages us to live in the freedom with which Christ has set us free.

C. Baxter Kruger,
Author of The Great Dance *and the international*
best seller The Shack Revisited

As I read Luciano Lombardi's commentary, *A Free Humanity*, I was highly conscious of the valuable contribution this work is in biblical studies at this time. I am very appreciative of his exegetical excellence and the ability to make Galatians accessible to the reader, yet with depth.

Luciano's earlier commentary on Ephesians enlivened the vision of the Church being "the new humanity" Jesus intends us to be. This volume amplifies the Spirit enabled calling believers share to be faithful witnesses of the freedom Christ provides rather than descending back into the downward cycle of human effort and law keeping. The commitment Paul showed to ensure the Galatians were a transformed, grace centred community of Christ followers is highly applicable to those who currently serve in Christian leadership. Engaging *A Free Humanity* has provided a fresh determination to "Stay in the freedom that Christ freed you with…". This is a freedom worth standing for, individually and as a community of Jesus' disciples.

Rev. David Wells MA, DD.
General Superintendent – The Pentecostal Assemblies of Canada
President – Pentecostal Charismatic Churches of North America
Vice-Chair – Pentecostal World Fellowship

A Free Humanity is a book that has come at just the right time. In the midst of our important debates about personal freedoms and rights, Luciano (Luc) turns our attention to the way the Bible reframes our perspective. Using an easy to follow approach, Luc takes readers through the book of Galatians and stirs us to see how freedom, human responsibility, and faithful Christian devotion to Jesus and his Church are inseparable."

Our culture defines freedom as "the power or right to act, speak, or think as one wants" (Oxford Dictionary). As alluring as this sounds, the application of this definition erodes relationships and communities whenever there are competing "freedoms" or "wants". Simply put, this definition does not work! In his book *A Free Humanity*, Luciano Lombardi explores the Biblical view of freedom found in the book of Galatians. This freedom empowers by reminding us that true freedom is found in the framework of community. It is in our submission to community with God and each other that we truly find our way out of the prison of self-interest and into the beauty of who we were truly created to be. If this is the freedom you are looking for, this book is for you!

A Free HUMANITY

A WALK THROUGH THE LETTER OF GALATIANS

LUCIANO LOMBARDI

A FREE HUMANITY
Copyright © 2022 by Luciano Lombardi

Scripture quotations marked (NLT) are taken from the Holy Bible, New Living Translation, copyright ©1996, 2004, 2015 by Tyndale House Foundation. Used by permission of Tyndale House Publishers, Carol Stream, Illinois 60188. All rights reserved. Scriptures marked (KJV) taken from the Holy Bible, King James Version, which is in the public domain.

Printed in Canada

ISBN: 978-1-4866-2259-7
eBook ISBN: 978-1-4866-2260-3

Word Alive Press
119 De Baets Street Winnipeg, MB R2J 3R9
www.wordalivepress.ca

Cataloguing in Publication information can be obtained from Library and Archives Canada.

CONTENTS

PREFACE

Back in 2013, when I was writing my previous book, *A New Humanity*, my hope was that I would have completed at least two more volumes by this time. Little did I know how busy life would get and that more and more commitments would fill my days and challenge me in writing other books.

Regardless, my hope is that this present volume continues the vision of the Apostle Paul regarding our humanity, and who we are created to be and what we are destined to live out.

When I wrote *A New Humanity*, I sketched out at least five volumes addressing the theme of humanity from the letters of Paul. These are subjects I have taught at Master's College and Seminary since 2001. This second volume on Galatians is a sequel to that earlier book, which addressed the freedom that comes when we live in the new humanity given to us through the loving action of the Trinity.

For those who have read my first volume, I hope this second offering continues to reveal what the Trinity destined for us, living in the love and acceptance of the Father, Son, and Spirit, and as a result living in love and harmony with one another.

For those who are new to my writing, I hope this volume encourages you to seek out my first book as well to complement what you will read here and give you a rounded view of what we are called towards as followers of Christ. For those thinking about putting their faith in Christ, both volumes will give you the perspective of who you are and what God desires for you. My hope is that this will move you to trust Jesus, who introduces us to the character of God as revealed in the Christian Scriptures.

As I write this preface on this third day of 2022, the reality of the past two years of living in a pandemic only strengthens my resolve to focus on what it means to love one another and how that is accomplished in a world that is so often at odds with itself. More than ever, God's community is called to live out the new humanity in fresh ways where love is the focus and redemption the goal.

We have the opportunity to lead our world into the freedom of love and acceptance. The only way we can do that is to stay focused on the Spirit's help, guiding us to what Christ has accomplished for us in the will of the Father who loves us. The Triune God of grace is our hope!

I want to say to the many students, friends, and pastors who kept asking when this volume would be available, "It's finally here!"

For my colleagues and their unending support in creating an environment where I have been able to think through my thoughts and put them through the rigor of conversation, thank you for always being willing to listen!

To my wife and children who put up with my constant "whining" about not having time to write, I want to say, "Thank you for your patience and support, but more importantly for your love that is constant and always encouraging! I love you!"

Thank you to those at Word Alive Press for your patience with me and your willingness to help me put out my next book. You helped me convey what I felt was important in this book and made it even better than my original manuscript. Thank you!

I pray that what I have discovered in this volume will give you a continued foundation for living a life of faithfulness to Christ. May the richness of the presence of the Trinity cause you, and those around you, to thrive regardless of what is going on in our present world.

—Luciano Lombardi
This third day of January 2022
Mississauga, Ontario, Canada

INTRODUCTION

A Small Flashlight and Two Candles

Never in our wildest dreams did my wife and I think we would start out the way we did. After our beautiful wedding, we looked forward to heading down to tropical Jamaica. Tired from all the planning and celebration, we anticipated some well-deserved days on the beach relaxing under the hot Caribbean sun. This would be our first vacation together on our own as a couple. There would be nothing better than this.

Or so we thought.

After five beautiful days in sunny, laidback Negril Beach, we started hearing some buzz around our resort that a hurricane was brewing south of us and there was a possibility it could hit the island. The locals didn't look too worried. They assured us that a hurricane hadn't hit Jamaica in the past fifty years.

But as the day progressed, the locals started getting anxious. Some of them were worried that they may not be spared a direct hit this time around. The next morning, we woke up to notice that several of the guests from our resort had left for home. Planes had been sent in from their respective countries to retrieve them. British, Australian, and American vacationers had left early that morning to board their planes.

We started getting worried. After lunch, we noticed that the hotel staff had left for home as well. As the wind picked up, we stood outside our second story balcony and watched the storm come in off the ocean.

At about two o'clock that afternoon, the wind got stronger and the palm trees bent from its force; we went inside when we noticed some of the tops breaking off.

By four o'clock, the storm hit the island in full force. The rush of the wind was like a jet engine. Fearing that the windows in our room might break, we propped the mattress against the glass, hoping that if the glass broke the mattress would keep the glass from blowing into the room.

We could hear the terracotta roof tiles lifting off and crashing on the cement walkways below. Fearing that the roof might cave in, we huddled under the frame of the bathroom door.

As we huddled and prayed, we heard the voice of a little girl crying in the hallway. Worried that she was out there without any protection or cover, we opened the door and saw a couple with their young daughter crouched in the corner. The roof over their room had been ripped off by the storm and they were exposed to the elements and flying debris.

We quickly brought them into our room and shut the door. Together we waited out the storm for a couple of hours.

At about six o'clock that evening, the wind suddenly stopped. It was like someone had turned off a switch. We ventured down to the main floor and met the other hotel guests in the front foyer. Some employees had stayed at the hotel, braving the storm, and they had prepared supper for us!

I remember our feeling of relief as we gathered in the restaurant of the hotel and had our meal. We shared stories of what had happened and were thankful that no one had been hurt.

As we chatted out in the courtyard of the resort after our meal, I saw a small plane flying above us. I recall wondering why someone would have risked heading out on such a dangerous day. Then it dawned on me: weather planes will fly into the eye of a hurricane where the winds are calm to measure both the path and intensity of the storm.

No sooner had I mentioned this to my wife than the wind started picking up again. The hotel manager moved us to rooms on the first floor since our rooms on the second level had damaged roofs and windows.

The storm grew in intensity again, stronger than the first round we had experienced that afternoon. The rest of the hurricane lasted all through the night.

By morning, the worst of it was over, but the hotel and resort had suffered some severe damage. We had no power, no running water, and no air conditioning. For the next five days, we survived by the good graces of the hotel staff who continued to cook for us and by gathering rain runoff from the roof to clean ourselves and flush our toilets.

Those of us who remained at the hotel stayed together, making sure we weren't alone at night out on the beach. We had heard that there was looting in town by the locals, and it was recommended that we not venture away from the resort. We shared each other's stories and became a family during those five days. We ate our meals together and looked out for one another.

It's a daunting feeling to think you might not make it through a crisis. A severe storm like the one my wife and I survived that fateful week in 1988 could have easily taken our lives. We were so very grateful to come through it unscathed.

As I think back on that adventure, I recall how the hotel staff left a small flashlight, two candles, and a set of instructions in our room on the day the hurricane hit. It makes me laugh all these years later to think that these small things could in any way have helped us. They were so insignificant compared to the category-five storm that hit us, one that would live in infamy among Jamaicans. On our way home, we bought T-shirts with "We Survived Hurricane Gilbert" written on them. We had certainly earned them!

That flashlight and two candles reminds me of what the King James Version translates as *"the weak and beggarly elements"* (Galatians 4:9).[1] At times our attempt to hold fast to observances, to stem the tide of evil in our world, is like trying to fight a category-five hurricane with a small flashlight and some candles. Anyone in their right mind would know that they're no match for a storm that carries with it gusts of 250 kilometres per hour.

The analogy works well for us who try to use the law to combat evil, which is a ridiculous notion. That which has plunged our world into darkness cannot be eradicated by our attempts to follow the law. The law in our hands is no match for stemming the tide of evil in our humanity. Evil is far too strong and entrenched for us to root it out on our own.

That's why Paul was so upset with the believers he wrote to in the region of Galatia in the first century. The good news he had brought to them was that Christ had freed them from the evil that had held them in bondage. Evil had alienated them from God, but now Christ had brought them close to the Father again, restoring them to their true humanity—their new humanity.[2]

It was impossible for them to do this on their own. They lacked both the capacity and awareness. They were like walking dead people, wandering the world like animals feeding their flesh and living a broken existence. The resurrection power of Jesus had brought them back to true life. They had nothing to do with it; it was all His doing.

Paul found out later that they had gone back to their old ways of observing the law in order to stay in relationship with the Father. This was lunacy! How

---

[1] In the Greek, this is written as "ἀσΘενῆ καὶ πτωχὰ στοιχεῖα." It's in reference to things people do based on observances that have no inherent power to help our fallen humanity. My own translation of this phrase, shared in Chapter Nine, is written like this: *"Why do you turn back again to weak and empty systems?"*

[2] See Luciano Lombardi, *A New Humanity: A Walk through the Letter of Ephesians* (Bellville, ON: Guardian Books, 2014), 35. What Jesus has done is restored us to relationship with the Father. This relationship results in a true reflection of humanity lived in relationship with the Triune God of Grace. When human beings live in proximity to relationship with God, they live the humanity God had created them to live.

could they go back to something that in the first place hadn't held the power to free them? It was like choosing to crawl back into a six-by-six-foot prison cell after experiencing the freedom of living on the outside.

Paul wondered if someone had actually cast a spell on them. How could anyone go back to a place of bondage after being set free? I can't imagine me and my wife attempting to catch a hurricane simply for the thrill of experiencing it again. If we did, I'm sure our extended family and friends would think we were out of our minds.

And yet the Galatians did go back to their old observances. They were enticed into thinking that the *"weak and beggarly elements"* were still needed. Somehow what Jesus had gone through during His life, death, resurrection, and ascension wasn't quite complete enough for them. They still needed the law to belong, the same laws that had brought hostility and separation to humanity.

The reality is that some people just don't want to change. They stubbornly continue with what they know, blinded to the wonderful thing that stands before them. For the Galatians, they had been bullied back into observing the law.

I want you to know that you're not stuck with a flashlight and two small candles while the storm rages around you. You have none other than the Creator of the universe by your side—and He has the power to tell the storm to shut up! He is able and has shown himself worthy to eliminate the tide of evil that threatens to swallow you up. You are not helpless anymore. Christ is by your side, with you, His Spirit in you! There is no more need for impotent observances that keep you in bondage.

All you need is Jesus. His life is now your life. He brings freedom to your humanity so you can live free of evil. You're no longer confined to rules and regulations that stifle your humanity. After all, as Paul writes in Galatians 5:1, it was for freedom that you were set free.

Don't go back to the bondage you were in before. My hope is that as you read this book, Paul's vision of free humanity will capture your heart and imagination and set you free from evil's hold on you. After reading it, I hope you will be more convinced than ever that the law can never help you obtain what Jesus has given to you: a free humanity!

Chapter One

FREEDOM FROM EVIL

Galatians 1:1–5

Paul, a messenger [sent] not by other men or chosen by man but commissioned by Jesus Christ and God the Father, who raised Jesus from the dead, along with my missionary team,[3] to God's communities[4] in Galatia: grace and peace from God our Father, and our LORD Jesus Christ, who gave himself over to our fallen human existence so that he could rescue us out of the present evil age. This is in keeping with our God and Father's well-known desire that transcends the ages. Amen.[5]

PAUL'S CENTRAL FOCUS

Paul wrote this letter after having travelled with Barnabas and John Mark through south Galatia. It had been their first missionary journey and they'd begun to experience the openness of the Gentiles to the good news that Jesus had created a new humanity. They had much success in bringing some Jews and many Gentiles to Christ, yet there was also much pain, as for the most part Jews did not accept their message. Their time in each city was cut short due to word that Jews were plotting against Paul and his fellow missionaries.

---

[3] Paul elsewhere referred to his missionary team, who travelled with him, as *"brothers who are with me"* (Philippians 4:21, NLT). I lean toward believing that Paul directed this letter to those in south Galatia whom he had encountered during his first missionary journey, and that he wrote the letter just after his trip to Jerusalem with Barnabas. Paul's autobiography at the beginning of Galatians 2 is a description of the Jerusalem council mentioned in Acts 15, which Paul and Barnabas attended. James Dunn writes that "the weight of considerations probably favours the view that Gal. ii.1–10 is Paul's account of the Jerusalem council" (Dunn, *The Epistle to the Galatians: Black's New Testament Commentaries* [London, UK: A&C Black Limited, 1993], 8).

[4] As I did in my Ephesians commentary, I will translate ἐκκλησίαις as "God's community." The word is most often translated as "church," and I think we have so enculturated this into our western evangelical context that we need to go back to its original intent. Leslie Newbigin emphasizes that the term *ecclesia* was borrowed by the early church, with the word having originally been used to refer to municipal gatherings called by a town's clerk, gatherings at which all participants were required to be present. The universal intent of the term emphasized the open invitation of all to belong (Newbigin, *The Open Secret: An Introduction to the Theology of Mission* [Grand Rapids, MI: Eerdmans, 1995], 16).

[5] I have translated the letter in its entirety to offer another version of what Paul is writing so that the reader can compare it with other translations.

On their return to Antioch in Syria, whether before or after their attendance at the Jerusalem council, Paul wrote a pointed letter to the new community of believers established during his travels through south Galatia. The first sentence is so forward that it almost sounds defensive: *"Paul... not by other men... but commissioned by Jesus..."* The tone lends one to think he felt the need to defend both his status and his mission. No doubt, those Jews who were upset by what Paul preached had sent word throughout the Jewish community about him.

Never for a moment questioning his own Jewish heritage, Paul based his position and credibility on his calling, which came directly from God the Father through the resurrection of Jesus. It was because of the resurrection[6] that Paul was involved in such missionary activity. Fourteen years after his encounter with Jesus on the road to Damascus, Paul's entire focus centred on Christ and the mission on which the Father had sent him to bring the good news to both Jews and Gentiles.

Unfounded were the accusations of these instigators, many of whom had personal agendas to undermine Paul. On the contrary, Paul had encountered the Messiah, who happened to also be the Son of God. Such a revelation turned into a calling for him to bring the good news of Christ to the Gentiles.

This good news was the fulfillment of the promise God had given Abraham, that through him all the nations of the world would be blessed.[7] God would restore fallen humans by cleansing them and putting in them a heart of flesh and causing His Spirit to dwell in them.[8] Out of all the divided nations and kingdoms, one new humanity would emerge, defined as God's people. This renewal for Paul rang true with what Jesus had done.

Paul's birth name, Saul, spoke of a privileged existence, being a man with the education of a Jewish Pharisee. Saul had seen the world through the Torah and the Jewish laws and persecuted any Jew who endangered such a view.

When Jesus appeared to him, everything changed. His privileged religious status was no match for the reality of the appearance of the light that opened his mind and heart to something he had never known before: God is connected to all people and his desire is to restore all people.

---

[6] See Paul's account in Acts 17, 23, and 24:26.

[7] *"This is my covenant with you: I will make you the father of a multitude of nations! What's more, I am changing your name. It will no longer be Abram. Instead, you will be called Abraham, for you will be the father of many nations"* (Genesis 17:4–5, NLT). *"I will certainly bless you. I will multiply your descendants beyond number, like the stars in the sky and the sand on the seashore. Your descendants will conquer the cities of their enemies. And through your descendants all the nations of the earth will be blessed..."* (Genesis 22:17–18, NLT)

[8] These are promises that God gave to Israel (Ezekiel 36:22–27, Jeremiah 31:33–34). Such transformation would spill out from Israel to other nations.

This plan was different and much more expansive than anything he had perceived through his Jewish training. He had thought God only cared about his own people, and his hope had been that God would come and vindicate his nation and restore its grandeur. He'd believed that the only way to make this happen was to adhere to the Torah and its laws. His hate towards others who disagreed with this notion had been fuelled by a very narrow understanding of God's plan. He had been hurting the very humanity God sought to rescue.

Jesus's revelation to Paul showed him that God is connected to people. He came to realize that when he was persecuting those who followed Christ, he was hurting God in the process.[9]

Having been taught by other men to persecute humanity, Paul vowed to never be deceived in such a way again. This new perspective given him by Jesus became his focus. No man, organization, nationality, or human influence opened his eyes; it was Jesus, the Son of God, who revealed it to him and God the Father who so willed it. The reality of Paul's encounter with the Son of God inspired him to share the good news that this new humanity is available to both Jew and Gentile.

The language in Galatians 1:3 is a reference by Paul to God the Father and God the Son, Christ Jesus, who is in and has been forever in relationship with the Father.[10] As in other letters, Paul continues to reference God in a deeply familial and relational way. This is how Jesus appeared and spoke in terms of his relationship with the Father.

Inherent in this relationship is the source of grace and peace. These qualities are fundamental to the Triune God Paul will reference in the next verse.

FALLEN HUMAN EXISTENCE

As Paul continues into the next sentence, we find the foundational truth that would forever convince him that God's desire for the recovery of humanity is made evident in what Jesus did for the human race.

In Galatians 1:4, most translations mention that *"Jesus gave his life for our sins"* (NLT). In my translation above, I write that *"Jesus gave himself over to our fallen human existence."* The reason for this phrasing is due to the impact of what Paul states about what Jesus had done.

---

[9] *"Saul! Saul! Why are you persecuting me?"* (Acts 9:4, NLT)

[10] The words of Jesus to His disciples in the gospel of John: *"I and the Father are one"* (John 10:30, my translation), *"Believe me that I am in the Father, and the Father in me"* (John 14:11, my translation), *"All that the Father has is mine"* (John 16:15, my translation), and *"Father, glorify me with the glory I had with you before the world was created"* (John 17:5, my translation).

In this verse, most translations are poorly represented by the English word "sin." Sin is commonly used to refer to "missing the mark" or "disobedient acts" that go against God's commands.[11]

What Paul is referencing here, by using the Greek word ἁμαρτιῶν, is much deeper than an isolated incident of sin, so as to change the meaning of his intent altogether. When Paul says that Jesus gives Himself over to our ἁμαρτιῶν, he is saying that Jesus offers Himself over to the very experience of our fallen humanity in an environment where people live at a distance from God, where the reality of not having a relationship with God has covered humanity with a deep darkness that prevents people from perceiving their true identity.[12] In such a context, sin is not only present in our actions but is the very essence that permeates everyday life. It is the social context in which we are born and the culture to which we have become accustomed.

One might ask, how can that be derived from what Paul writes? The reason is that for Paul, being a Jew, concepts are connected to narrative. Sin is not just a definition that dropped out of the sky and into the Galatian letter. The concept of sin emerges from the biblical narrative, which tells the story of how humanity fell into such an existence. In this broader use of the term, Paul is referencing not a definition but a narrative that speaks to the meaning of the word sin. The word references the story,[13] and the story behind the concept of ἁμαρτιῶν is humanity's plunge into darkness.

---

[11] A simple definition of this word won't suffice in helping us understand the impact of Paul's statement. The use of ἁμαρτιῶν in its plural form builds a picture of the human condition that Jesus has come to embrace and rescue. Author N.T. Wright points out, "Once we get the goal right (new creation, not just 'heaven') and the human problem properly diagnosed (idolatry and the corruption of vocation, not just 'sin') the larger vision of Jesus' death begins to come into view" (Wright, *The Day the Revolution Began* [San Francisco, CA: Harper One, 2016), 79.

[12] G.B. Caird and L. D. Hurst point out that for Paul "sin can be depicted as the human race's failure to be what God intended—Sin is more than doing wrong acts: it is the loss of a perfection God meant the human race to have, a coming short of the highest standard of which it is capable. The full extent of the loss was apparent to those who, like Paul, had seen in Christ the image and glory of God (2 Cor. 4:6) and who, under the influence of his Spirit, had begun to recapture the lost reflection (2 Cor. 3:18)" (Caird and Hurst, *New Testament Theology* [Oxford, UK: Oxford University Press, 1995], 94–95). See also, from W. Gunther: "...there is the subjection of all men to the power of sin from which they can be redeemed only through God's once-and-for-all act of reconciliation in Jesus Christ" (W. Gunther, "Sin," *New International Dictionary of New Testament Theology, Volume Three* [Grand Rapids, MI: Zondervan, 1971], 581).

[13] G.B. Caird points out the fallacy that a word and its meaning in the Bible corresponds to the same image every time it occurs. He points out that Paul uses multiple meanings for different uses of the same word. There are also moments when he references a concept without using the common word that reflects the concept at hand. Words reference narratives so that a writer need not go into detail about the narrative that the word represents, because of the common understanding among readers (Caird, *The Language and Imagery of the Bible* [Philadelphia, PA: Westminster Press, 1980], 42).

In light of this, the use of the words *"gave himself over"* identify a profound reality. Jesus takes on the state of our sinfulness, offering to live in our darkened existence so that by doing so He can rescue us. Where we are unable to free ourselves, He, as the Son of the Father, can free us.[14] We know that He isn't bound by any sin that will inevitably overtake Him.

Paul tells us that He gave Himself. This is the opposite of what we are capable of. We had no choice but to inherit sin.

So begins the theme of freedom in this letter. Such a freedom is described as *deliverance.*

In the Exodus story, the concepts of deliverance and freedom are profoundly imaged by the passing over of the angel of death and the freeing of the Hebrew slaves from the oppression of Egypt (Exodus 11:1–9, 12:31–42). God does this for Israel, and it lives forever as a stamp on their psyche, both individually and as a nation.

In the words of author N.T. Wright, whenever "Paul and other biblical writers talk about people being set free from slavery, they are echoing the Passover story, and the Exodus narrative."[15] In this letter, it is evident that Jesus gave Himself over to the sin of humanity so that sin would not destroy it.

The Exodus is echoed in the deliverance that Jesus offered the believers in Galatia and, by implication, the entire human race.

So profound was this reality for Paul that anything that drew one away from the Messiah was a deviation from what the Father and Son had planned for humanity. The Son had entered our very broken existence so that He might free us from our bondage to evil. He rescued us from our fallen state. No matter what we have done, He didn't hesitate to enter into it so that He might redeem what we have lost.

In this act of the Son, we see the very heart of the Father whose desire is to restore us.[16] This desire stems from His eternal love. He not only wanted us here; He has made provision that we be with him.

This became Paul's central belief after his encounter with Jesus. He began his corrective letter this way so he could orient his readers towards what is central to our human existence and place in God's community.

---

[14] *"The light shines in the darkness, and the darkness cannot overcome it"* (John 1:5, my translation).

[15] N.T. Wright, *The Day the Revolution Began: Reconsidering the Meaning of Jesus' Crucifixion* (San Francisco, CA: Harper One, 2016), 235.

[16] Gregory A. Boyd writes that "the cross is the summation, culmination, and perfect expression of the central theme of Jesus' whole ministry, which is about putting on display ('glorifying') the loving character of God" (Boyd, *The Crucifixion of the Warrior God: Interpreting the Old Testament's Violent Portraits of God in Light of the Cross, Volume One—The Cruciform Hermeneutic* [Minneapolis, MN: Fortress Press, 2017], 188).

THE FATHER'S DESIRE TO FREE US

The freedom Jesus achieved for us is based on the desire of the Father from ages past. The quick doxological statement in Galatians 1:5 outlines Paul's awareness that the Father had planned for this deliverance from the outset.[17]

It is related to a cosmic conflict that is narrated in the Hebrew Scriptures. Evil has undermined the creation and the Father's goal, and His cooperation with the Son and the Spirit, is to deliver creation from its broken, fallen state and restore it to its proper form and function.[18]

This verse presents the essence of our salvation as a human race. The core desire of the Father, for which He is well known, is to deliver us from our fallen human existence. This action speaks of His divine character of love, which is eternally present in the relationship of the Father and the Son.

Evil led humanity astray, plunging it into a distorted existence alienated from God. Having gone astray from its intended purpose, God—in His love as Father, Son, and Spirit—rescued it through the work of the Son and the Spirit, breaking the bond of evil. With this rescue came forgiveness, embrace, and res-toration—and freedom in which the Spirit enables fallen humanity to become renewed to live out its true role in creation. Later in the letter, Paul will make this point clear (Galatians 5:1, 5–6, 24).

The portrait of the Father at the beginning of this letter is one who, out of His infinite love, seeks to rescue humanity from its brokenness.[19] His eternal desire is to bring it back to its rightful place in creation.

The Exodus and the Exile narratives in the Old Testament point to such an end. Unlike the sensational interpretations of condemnation and destruction of our world by an angry God, Paul presents a Father who wants to recover what the enemy has taken.[20] This is the deep desire of the Father. It's not a

---

[17] One needs to pay attention here to the echo of Ephesians 1 and the awareness of the Father as to what evil would do to undermine creation before he even began creating. His response of love was to set a plan of rescue in motion even before the hijacking of the world by evil began.

[18] Wright puts to rest the misguided Western theological premise that Jesus's work addresses the "works contract" dilemma. Having historically read this narrative into the Bible, the actual purpose of Jesus's work is missed entirely, that being the rescue of humanity from idolatry and alienation and a return to its true image-bearing role in the creation devoid of evil altogether. This is pointed out by Jesus as the focus of the prayer taught to his disciples—"*Your kingdom come; your will be done on earth as in heaven*" (Mathew 6:10, my translation). See: Wright, *The Day the Revolution Began*, 74.

[19] Gregory Boyd writes that "the dominant way divine judgment is understood throughout Scripture is that it is restorative, not retributive, in nature, as a multitude of scholars have argued" (Boyd, *Crucifixion of the Warrior God*, 783).

[20] As Wright has written, "The great scene in the end of the book [Revelation] is the joining together of the 'new heavens and new earth.' Being there in the presence of God and the Lamb will give back to the redeemed the role marked out for them from the beginning in Genesis and reaffirmed as Israel's vocation in the book of Exodus" (Wright, *The Day the Revolution Began*, 78).

reaction to an infraction, but rather a planned and anticipated rescue of cosmic proportions.

It is significant that Paul mentions this as the chief and overriding intent of God the Father, and not the punishment of the human race motivated by his anger towards its evil behaviour. He desires to rescue His creation from the hold of evil. It is a liberation, not a condemnation.[21]

The image of God that Paul paints in this letter isn't characterized by the behaviour of pagan deities. He is thoroughly unlike any other god, both in substance and character. Creation is a focus for Him. It is the object of His actions. His actions are destined to vindicate humanity.

These five verses put this in clear perspective. As one reads on, it's important to focus on the foundational elements of Paul's argument regarding faith, the law, and the Spirit's role: the action of the Son in giving Himself over to our fallen humanity and the intent of the Father in His desire to deliver us from evil.

In the following section of the letter, Paul points out that anything that would distort this good news of deliverance is both at odds with the Father's intent and what he and his missionary team had been communicating abroad. Paul hadn't risked his life and spent his own funds to promote a kind of good news that put one into slavery. The good news he delivered to the Galatians was what he and they had experienced in the freedom Jesus brought to those who put their trust in Him.

Fundamental to this reality is the depth of love the Trinity has for creation. In their love for humanity, the Trinity has been on a cosmic rescue operation. The revelation of Jesus in Paul's day is a focal point of this love and governs how we as followers of Christ continue in relationship with the Father, Son, and Spirit. Paul will spell this out in detail as he tackles the dilemma the Galatian believers found themselves in.

How we view the Trinity, and their cosmic activity, is paramount to how we live our lives. Deliverance is key and gives us an indication as to the direction the Father desires for us to walk as we put our faith in Christ. We must always be oriented towards the good news that fallen humanity has been rescued by the Trinity, which we can only comprehend because the Trinity has revealed it to us.

---

[21] This is well argued by John Macleod Campbell: "the atonement retrospectively finds us in the condition that we are in through God's grace and prospectively raises us to a new condition" (Campbell, *The Nature of the Atonement* [Grand Rapids, MI: Baker Books, 1996], 50). Campbell also argues that the Scriptures demonstrate God as the subject of the atonement, not the object: "the Scriptures… do not represent the love of God to man as the effect, and the atonement of Christ as the cause but—just as the contrary—they represent the love of God as the cause, and the atonement as the effect. 'God so loved the world, that He gave His only begotten son, that whosoever believeth in Him, might not perish, but have everlasting life'" (Ibid., 46).

The action of God towards us finds its clarity in Christ and the Spirit, who leads us into a life of freedom. Hoping to achieve this clarity through our own attempts to free ourselves from evil is lunacy; it's the equivalent of trying to fight a category-five hurricane with two candles and a flashlight.

In the verses that follow, Paul will describe his astonishment that the Galatians were trying to do that very thing, bypassing the freedom that comes by trusting in Father, Son, and Spirit.

Chapter Two

FREEDOM FROM DISTORTION

Galatians 1:6–10

I am puzzled[22] as to why you have so quickly turned away from he who has called you in the grace of Christ to a different good news which is not good news. There are only those that are making you all hot and bothered by perverting the good news of Christ. Even if we or an angel from heaven were to announce to you something different than what we announced to you, let them be condemned. As we already mentioned, I'm saying it again, if anyone announces to you another good news than what you received, let them be condemned. Does it sound like I'm looking for the approval of others or of God? If it's the approval of others I was looking for, then I would not be a servant of Christ.

CHRIST IS THE FOCUS OF BELONGING

It was unthinkable for Paul that anyone would deviate from the core of the good news he had just described in Galatians 1:4–5. Christ's work of delivering humanity from the evil of this present world, and transforming fallen humanity to its ideal condition, beats any other means of redemption. All religious attempts by humanity to redeem its condition and environment fail. There is no match for the freedom that comes from the will and love of the Triune God—no moral improvement strategy, no pattern of structured worship, no adherence to a system or set of propositions, no twelve-step program—that can accomplish what the Father has acquired for us through the work of His Son and Spirit.

---

[22] The Greek verb θαυμάζω is predominantly used in the New Testament as an expression of amazement in reaction to the signs and wonders of Jesus and His teaching. This is one of the very few instances where the word is used to describe a reaction that doesn't make sense to the author (W. Mundle, "Miracles, Wonder, Sign," *New International Dictionary of New Testament Theology, Volume Two* [Grand Rapids, MI: Zondervan, 1971], 621–625). To capture what Paul felt at this point, I chose to use the word "puzzled." It is a moment of shock for him to realize that the Galatians have traded the good news of being delivered from evil with trying to ward off evil by following the law.

Imposing a version of the good news that causes us to focus on the law is to exclude Christ altogether.[23] This is why Paul was flabbergasted that the Galatians would sacrifice their freedom in Christ, their deliverance from evil, their transformation by the Spirit, for a way that put their redemption in their own hands.

The distortion of this good news of freedom is a critical departure from what God has done for us and to us. Any good news that puts its administration into the hands of people distorts the intent of what Paul wrote in Galatians 1:1–5.

In his earlier life as a Pharisee, Paul focused on the Torah and the conformity of his co-nationals to the Torah. His religion was one of falling in line, keeping the tenants of the Jewish faith, observing its 613 laws, and remaining in the community of God's people. The function of such a view resulted in his belief that faithfulness to the Torah kept one in covenant with God while not keeping the Torah caused one to break covenant with God.

The Jewish understanding—that keeping Torah would result in one's sustained inclusion with the people of Israel[24]—does not reflect what Paul came to know through his encounter with Christ: that relationship with God is a result of deliverance from evil by the work of Christ. It is not a function of the law. The law doesn't have the power to obtain deliverance for us,[25] and this will be Paul's argument as he reflects on the purpose of the law in Galatians 3.

In addition to this, Paul's encounter with Christ resulted in him understanding that the Gentiles also had the opportunity to be in relationship with God. This would have been his view as a Jew, being knowledgeable of the Hebrew Scriptures

---

[23] James D.G. Dunn writes, "Paul insisted that *pisteuein eis Christon* was a full response to the gospel of Christ. To insist on anything more as equally fundamental was to diminish and deny the fundamental character and role of faith" (Dunn, "The Christian Life from the Perspective of Paul's Letter to the Galatians," *The Apostle Paul and the Christian Life*, eds. Scot McKnight and Joseph B. Modica [Grand Rapids, MI: Baker Academic, 2016], 4.

[24] This is known as the concept of covenantal nomism and it was first established by E.P. Sanders in his early published works, and later by scholars such as James Dunn (*Unity and Diversity in the New Testament: An Inquiry into the Character of Earliest Christianity* [London, UK: SCM Press, 2006]) and Stephen Westerholm (*Justification Reconsidered: Rethinking a Pauline Theme* [Grand Rapids, MI: Eerdmans, 2013]). This was to combat the idea of works righteousness, imposed on the Jewish Christian narrative in the New Testament by early reformation writers. The thought here is that Jews did not believe that works of the law is what included them in covenant with God; rather, they believed that it *kept* them in covenant with God. It was God's election of Israel, and law-keeping, that put them into God's community. If Gentiles were to be included, then the requirement would be that they'd have to keep the law. Paul experienced otherwise in his encounter with Christ.

[25] In fact, law-keeping puts one in a vicious circle of trying to be faithful to the law only to be condemned by one's own failure (cf. Romans 7). There will be much more to say about this when we get to Galatians 2–3.

that make a point of emphasizing that God has called on Israel to be a light to the nations[26] and a pathway to restoring relationship with Him. In his pharisaic mind, this would not have been possible unless Israel remained faithful to the Torah and in covenant with God. The way for Gentiles to be included was to embrace such faithfulness to the Torah. [27]

Paul's reaction in this passage shows that he now saw the matter in a very different light.

THE GOOD NEWS IN ITS PUREST FORM

For Paul, it was a foreign concept for the efficacy of the good news to be in the hands of the people. Although that may have been his understanding prior to his encounter with Jesus,[28] it was not his perspective as the Apostle to the Gentiles.

In its purest form, the gospel is our deliverance from evil by Christ, according to the will and desire of the Father. This deliverance restores us to our new humanity, as Paul outlined in his Ephesian letter,[29] allowing us to live in peace and freedom with God and one another. By recovering this relationship, humanity can trust in Christ both for what He has done for humanity and what He continues to do for it.[30] Jew and Gentile now keep relationship with the

---

[26] Walter C. Kaiser Jr., *Mission in the Old Testament: Israel as Light to the Nations* (Grand Rapids, MI: Baker Books, 2012). See Chapter Six, "God Calls Israel to be a Light to the Nations."

[27] E.P. Sanders mentions the following: "Many Jews, and all the Jewish Christians whose views are known to us, expected Gentiles to be brought into the people of God in the messianic period. There was, however, no accepted *halakah* governing the conditions of their admission.—The Jewish Christians, who considered the end to be near, however, had to make practical decisions. The normal requirement for entering the people of God was to make full proselytization, and some Jewish Christians obviously thought that the same condition should be maintained even in the last days" (Sanders, *Paul, the Law, and the Jewish People* [Minneapolis: Fortress Press, 1983], 18–19. Sanders considers this the view of the "false brethren" whom Paul mentions in Galatians 2:4.

[28] Wright has written, "The majority of Pharisees until A.D. 70 were Shammaites whose legendary strictness in this period was not simply a matter of the personal application of purity codes but, as we see in the case of Saul of Tarsus, had to do with a desire to purify, cleanse and defend the nation against paganism" (N.T. Wright, *The Challenge of Jesus: Rediscovering Who Jesus Was and Is* [Downers Grove, IL: InterVarsity Press, 1999], 56). Wright also identifies Pharisees, such as Saul, as an "unofficial and self-appointed pressure group—spying out offenders against Torah" (Ibid., 57).

[29] In my previous book, I wrote that "by taking Jew and Gentile and making them, in himself, one new humanity and so restoring peace. He did this so that he might reconcile both Jews and Gentiles into one body by putting to death hostility and division through his work on the cross" (Lombardi, *A New Humanity*, 45).

[30] Such is the notion of Paul's words in Romans 3:21–22, which says, *"Apart from the law, a righteousness of God has been revealed—through faith in Jesus Christ in all and to all those who believe"* (my translation).

Triune God by trusting in what the Father has done for us in Christ and leaning on the Spirit to remain free of evil.[31]

Paul addressed the Galatians' distorted gospel, which came about when rival missionaries offered them a version of the good news that didn't reflect the freedom procured for humanity through the sacrifice of Jesus. This opposing good news, made by "imposters,"[32] was a syncretism of following both the Torah and salvation through Christ.

The result is hypocritical, as seen in Galatians 2 when Peter distances himself from the Gentiles as false brothers appear in the Syrian Gentile church of Antioch. These false brothers gave primacy to Jewish laws of custom, such as not eating at the same table with Gentiles, which opposed the inclusion of Jews and Gentiles into one people through the sacrifice of Jesus. Rather than demonstrating inclusion, this news resulted in segregation.

This was the recurring sin of Israel in the Old Testament as they alienated the Gentile nations around them. Jesus would recover the intended vocation of Israel by being the true light to the nations and offering the Gentiles a return to their true humanity.[33]

What we encounter in this period of the early church is a difference of opinion about what forms the basis of the gospel. Rival missionaries of Jewish background preached something very different than Paul, and their critique of the good news was centred on their belief that Gentiles, like Jews, had to stay connected to Christ by keeping the Torah. Paul's response was that the Torah had no place in drawing Gentiles to Christ and that claiming so was a distortion of the good news.[34]

Paul argued that faith in Christ was the pathway for both Jew and Gentile alike. He was completely convinced that anyone who deviated from the faith-focused good news they had heard from him and his missionary team should

---

[31] This will be Paul's argument in Galatians 5.

[32] The Greek word Paul uses in Galatians 2:4 is ψευδαδέλφους, meaning "false brothers."

[33] Paul addresses this misguided nationalism in Romans 9–11, where he builds a case for Israel making it in the end even though more Gentiles were coming to Christ than Jews. He especially cited Jewish "misguided zeal" as contributing to their sense of belonging and nationalism, warning Gentiles not to make the same mistake in light of their condemnation of Jews (N.T. Wright, *The Climax of the Covenant: Christ and the Law in Pauline Theology* [Minneapolis: Fortress Press, 1991], 240).

[34] James D.G. Dunn points out, "What was at stake here, in Paul's view, was whether this new faith in/commitment to Jesus (the) Christ meant that gentile believers were converting to Judaism. Was belief in Jesus (the) Christ simply a first step to becoming a Jew? Paul was clear that the answer was no! It was the incomers (to Galatia) insisting that the Galatians' belief in/commitment to Christ was only the first step to becoming a full proselyte which so infuriated Paul" (Dunn, *The Apostle Paul and the Christian Life*, 4).

be cursed. The word used by Paul is translated as anathema, which is "related to the Hebrew word *herem* used of that which is devoted to God, usually for destruction."[35] Paul felt this deviation from the true good news was so dangerous that he called for the destruction of all those who would take part in such activity.

Why is Paul so adamant that anyone promoting such distortion be damned to eternal annihilation? The matter rests ultimately on where control lies in the conquering of evil and sin in creation. The Bible makes it clear that people haven't been able to thwart the impact of evil on them and the world. No other god, nation, individual, or religious system has been able to break this hold. Only God has made the advance against evil, crushing its hold on us. Adding anything to the good news, besides our simple acceptance and embrace of it in our lives, puts humanity in the position of God. Such has been the idolatrous reaction of humanity since the fall in Genesis.[36]

In Paul's day, such idolatry was evidenced in the worship of the Roman emperor, who referred to himself as Father of the Empire and keeper of peace among all his territories. His evangelistic message was, essentially, "Pledge your devotion and allegiance to me and I will give you peace and prosperity."[37]

This type of idolatry also exists in the use of the Torah to keep one from evil. There is false hope in this view, making the keeper of the law the cause of one's acceptance and belonging rather than the desire of God the Father that we be part of His family.

Paul addresses such exclusivism in Romans 2, pointing out how the Jewish Christians pointed their fingers at the sin of the Gentiles while ignoring their own condition, which was masked by their law-keeping. He demonstrated that this behaviour *"despises the riches of his [God's] goodness, forbearance, and patience"* and ignores the fact that *"God's goodness leads to complete transformation"* (Romans

---

[35] Frank E. Gaebelein, *The Expositor's Bible Commentary, Volume Ten* (Grand Rapids, MI: Zondervan, 1976), 429. This volume includes James Montgomery Boice's work on Galatians.

[36] N.T Wright mentions, "The human problem is not so much 'sin' seen as the breaking of moral codes—though that, to be sure, is part of it, just as the headaches and blurry vision really were part of the medical problem—but rather idolatry and the distortion of genuine humanness it produces" (Wright, *The Day the Revolution Began*, 74).

[37] Upon the emergence of the emperor cult, where worship of the emperor was encouraged and became a religious devotion of its own, the emperor boasted of his own "gospel" or "good news" more in terms of a propaganda to solicit devotion from his subjects across the Empire. The notion that a man could be a saviour of sorts, or a god who behaves as father, was challenged by the story of Jesus and the emergence of Christianity (Karl P. Donfried, "The Imperial Cults in Thessalonica and Political Conflict in I Thessalonians," *Paul and Empire: Religion and Power in Roman Imperial Society*, ed. Richard A. Horsley [Harrisburg, PA: Trinity Press International, 1997]).

2:4, my translation). More to the point, it boasts of human achievement and status rather than God's grace and faithfulness.[38]

Like the two candles and flashlight from the analogy of my wife's and my honeymoon, human self-reliance, regardless of whether they're Jew or Gentile—or an emperor, commoner, or landowner, slave or free—cannot keep one in fellowship with the Trinity. Fellowship is accomplished by Christ on the part of the Triune God to draw us and keep us close. The Triune God comes down and draws us up into relationship with the Father, not we through our own actions or ethnic status. The capacity for relationship with God is given by God through the work of Christ and the presence of the Spirit, not through our actions or pedigree—or, in the case of the Galatians, keeping the legal requirements for belonging to Christ.

Such a position distorts who God is and renders Him akin to pagan gods, who demanded offerings. The Father and our Lord Jesus Christ gave themselves for our restoration and belonging.

Paul combated these false notions by reminding the Galatians that Jesus was crucified. His giving of Himself is what not only causes us to belong but allows us to continue to belong in fellowship with the Trinity.

THE FALSE HOPE OF LAW-KEEPING

While these imposters in Galatia equated law-keeping with belonging, the keeping of commands and regulations today produces in us false confidence.[39] It feels good to keep a set of laws, as it affirms our own goodness.

Of course, everyone wants to be viewed as good. Paul himself attests to the fact that the law, in and of itself, is good.[40] The problem is that the law, in the

---

[38] Matthew J. Thomas points out the common view of the law in the early patristic period. He identifies five major headings of objection to Torah-keeping in this period: "1. The arrival of the new law and covenant in Christ replaces those of the Mosaic law. 2. The prophets in OT Scripture testify regarding Messiah and new covenant with the cessation of previous works. 3. The universal nature of the new covenant meant for all nations evidenced in the Gentiles receiving grace apart from becoming Jews. 4. The new birth or circumcision of the heart brought by Jesus which renders Israel's laws as unnecessary. 5. Abraham and the patriarchs, who were accepted by God and whose righteousness confirm that the Mosaic law and circumcision were not given for humanity's justification" (Thomas, *Paul's 'Works of the Law' in the Perspective of Second-Century Reception* [Downers Grove, IL: InterVarsity Press, 2020], 272–273). The evidence of this important work gives us a sense of what was passed down from the apostles regarding works of the law.

[39] Faith of any kind in the first century had a communal quality. In our present Western mindset, faith has a very personal and individualistic focus. Focusing on ourselves and keeping the law shifts our sense of belonging and makes us feel falsely self-confident.

[40] Romans 7:14 says, *"We know that the law is spiritual."* E.P. Sanders wrote that "it is not doing the law in and of itself, which in Paul's view, is wrong.—It is completely wrong, however, when it is made an essential requirement for membership" (Sanders, *Paul, The Law, And the Jewish People*, 20).

hands of fallen humanity, quickly creates a false confidence of control. The result is that we focus on obedience while God is looking for relationship. Law-keeping distracts us from the true focus, which is our connection to God. We will look at this further when we get to Galatians 3.

The point is that such a legal focus is a house of cards. It provides a sense of security absent of the safety of true connection with God. We put our focus on our moral uprightness and fitness—but as soon as one command is disobeyed, the entire house of cards comes crashing down.[41] When that happens, evil has us right where it wants us: defeated, disillusioned, and broken.

Communities that focus on legalism create a false vision of the good news that distorts the freedom God the Father gives us. It allows evil to still reside among us and obscures all notions of grace and deliverance.

It's tempting, in our western individualistic mindsets, to seize the opportunity to affect our own salvation. Hijacking the terminologies of repentance, and faithfulness, we put stock in our own ability to remain faithful in relationship with Christ by improving our moral character and elevating ourselves to acceptability before God.[42]

For the Galatians, the allure was to be able to control their continued inclusion among the people of God when in fact their legalism was causing their exclusion from the riches of the Father's grace. For this reason, Paul speaks of it as a return to slavery.[43]

Galatians 1:10 addressed the danger of pleasing ourselves with what we want to hear. This comes in the form of the imposters Paul references in his letter, and their desire to control how one stays in God's community. He points out that pleasing these imposters would result in ceasing to be a servant of Christ. To argue against it, he bears witness to what Christ Himself communicated to Paul at his own conversion.

---

[41] Compare this to Romans 7, where Paul points out the lethal mix of law of God and the law of sin and death at work within us, undermining our attempt to observe the law of God. This gives us false hope and leads to self-condemnation. The reality is that even though the law is good, it was not meant to restore us. Sadly, we are accessing the wrong entity to free us from our brokenness. It is the law of the Spirit of life that frees us from the law of sin and death, and this only comes from Christ, which is why Paul was so adamant about this being the centre of the one and only good news!

[42] Wright points out that "popular modern Christian thought" has made the mistake of "moralizing our anthropology (substituting a qualifying examination of moral performance for the biblical notion of the human vocation) with the result that we have paganized our soteriology, our understanding of 'salvation' (substituting the idea of 'God killing Jesus to satisfy his wrath' for the genuinely biblical notions of deliverance from evil and idolatry and restored to our true vocation in the creation" (N.T. Wright, *The Day the Revolution Began*, 147).

[43] *"Stay in the freedom that Christ freed you with. Don't get caught again in the shackles of slavery"* (Galatians 5:1, my translation).

Serving Christ is demonstrated through drawing humanity's attention to Christ and not to their own pathways to freedom. Requiring believers to keep the law distorts the pathway to freedom Christ gave us.

Remember that evil is a hurricane, and the law is two candles and a small flashlight. Only the creator of heaven and earth has the power to stop the hurricane and calm the sea.

The only real restoration of our humanity, and deliverance from evil, is through Jesus the Son. He is the one who reaches into our fallen humanity, takes it on Himself, and does the will of the Father by freeing us. Anything added to this distorts the gospel and makes it bad news that keeps us enslaved in darkness and brokenness, leaving us out of communion with the Triune God.

The reality is that this legalism is no match for the onslaught of evil that pushes on, in, and against us. For this battle, we need the ongoing presence of the Spirit in our lives to empower us with the life of Christ and remain steadfast in our relationship with the Father while evil continues to do war with God and Christ's community.[44]

In the next section of the letter, Paul will offer a narrative about how law-keeping played no part in his coming to Christ. In fact, law-keeping had caused him to persecute his co-nationals and hurt Jesus. Paul uses his own conversion story and calling to give evidence to the reality of the good news he preached. This good news is that through Jesus, Gentiles and Jews are now brought into one family of God and kept in relationship with the Trinity by their trust in Jesus Christ, not by law-keeping.[45]

Gentiles coming to Christ through Paul's mission were experiencing the Spirit without being taught anything about law-keeping. This proved to the early Jewish Christian community that God was doing something new and real. Rather than squash it by forcing Gentiles to become Jewish, they needed to acknowledge that Gentiles were being included apart from law-keeping.

---

[44] Gordon D. Fee mentions that "Paul [in the Galatian letter] gives a rather full-orbed view of life in the Spirit in his experience and understanding. Christ life, individually and corporately, begins, is carried on, and comes to eschatological conclusion by means of God's empowering presence, the Holy Spirit" (Fee, *Pentecostal Commentary Series: Galatians* [Dorset, UK: Deo Publishing, 2011], 7).

[45] Matthew Bates points out that "Paul does not primarily call us to 'faith' ('belief' or 'trust') in some sort of atonement system in order to be saved (although mental affirmation that Jesus died for our sins is necessary), but rather to 'faith' ('allegiance') unto Jesus as Lord" (Bates, *Salvation by Allegiance Alone* [Grand Rapids, MI: Baker Academic, 2017], 39). Allegiance is a proper response to the work of Christ, who came as king to bring peace and deliverance from evil.

There were some among the Jewish Christians who had a hard time with this, especially those who drew Peter astray in Antioch, and those who visited the Galatian believers and drew them astray with the law-keeping good news they continued to teach and impose.

Chapter Three

FREEDOM OF AN AUTHENTIC STORY

Galatians 1:11–24

I want you to know, my family members,[46] that the good news I brought to you is not of human origin. I didn't receive it from anyone, nor did anyone teach it to me, but rather Jesus Christ opened my eyes to it.[47] You know how I behaved before [as a Pharisee] in the Jewish religion; how I went to the fullest extent to persecute God's community, working[48] to destroy it. I was far ahead of anyone my own age who sought leadership[49] in the Jewish religion, and much more zealous for our fathers' traditions. But God's pleasure and his grace called me from my mother's womb to reveal his Son in me and bring the good news to the Gentiles. I didn't quickly seek out human approval and I didn't go to Jerusalem to those who were Apostles before me, but I went to Arabia and then came back to Damascus.

Three years later I went up to Jerusalem to consult with Peter and stayed with him for fifteen days. I didn't see any of the other Apostles

---

[46] The Greek word here is ἀδελφοί. It originates from the word *delphys*, meaning a womb, and the prefix *a* is a connective denoting "from the same womb." As W. Gunther stipulates, "In Gk. Literature *adelphos* is used for a physical brother or close relation, and metaphorically for companion, friend, fellow-man" (Gunther, "Brother, Neighbour, Friend," *New International Dictionary of New Testament Theology, Volume One*, 255). There is also evidence of this word being used to refer to a "brother" in the faith of eastern cults. I chose to translate it as "my family members" to catch the sense of people having the same origin—in this sense, origin in the faith. See also: Robert J. Banks, *Paul's Idea of Community: The Early House Churches and Their Cultural Setting* (Grand Rapids, MI: Baker Academic, 1994), 49–52.

[47] Paul uses the Greek word ἀποκαλύψεως, which has connotations that speak to revealing what previously was hidden or secret (W. Mundle, "Revelation," *New International Dictionary of New Testament Theology, Volume Three*, 310–315). I chose to translate it as "open my eyes," since it reflects Paul's reference to his Damascus encounter with Jesus and how his eyes were opened to the truth.

[48] The use of the phrase καὶ ἐπόρθουν αὐτὴν comes with the sense of ongoing destruction, which is in the imperfect indicative form. Paul was in the process of working toward destroying God's community rather than having already destroyed it.

[49] The phrase ἐν τῷ γένει μου in Galatians 1:14 translates literally as "among my countrymen." I chose to make it more specific, as no doubt Paul compares himself to others of his Jewish community who pursued both religious and political stature.

except James, Jesus' brother. About what I'm writing to you, as God is my witness, I am not lying. Then I went to Syria and Cilicia. The communities of Christ in Judea would not be able to point me out in a crowd; all they knew was what they heard; that the one who was persecuting us now shares the good news that he once tried to destroy. It was God within me that they revered. [50]

A RADICAL SHIFT

No doubt there were many rumours floating around regarding who Paul was and his connection to the communities of Christ in Palestine, Syria, and Asia Minor. The questions in the minds of sceptical followers of Christ must have been palpable. How did someone so opposed to Christ become his ambassador and chief evangelist to the Gentiles?

Paul provides an autobiographical sketch that answers this ambiguity in the early Christian community. His goal is to give an authentic account of what he experienced, to lend credibility to his apostleship and what he taught and communicated to the Galatians, both in the beginning of his encounter with them and in his present letter.

Paul is careful to help his readers realize that what he had been teaching wasn't something he was taught, neither in his past life as a Pharisee nor in his present life as an Apostle. It came to him by direct revelation from Christ.

He refers to his encounter with Jesus on the Damascus Road, as narrated by Luke in the book of Acts. This is a one-time revelatory encounter with Christ that changed Paul's life. This is different than the multiple revelations he refers to in 2 Corinthians 12:1.[51] It's a defining moment which changes the course of his future.

His encounter with Jesus challenged everything he knew about God, religion, himself, and the world around him. He heard for the first time the true heart of the Father, spoken to him through the Son. Jesus told him how his destructive activity toward those who followed Him had been directed to Him

---

[50] I'm choosing here to stay away from using the word "glory" and "glorified," as they have essentially lost their meaning in our present context. The root of it lends itself to the weight of God and who He is. Thus, the use of the word revered.

[51] Ronald Y.K. Fung writes, "…thus making the revelation of the gospel not immediately a part of Paul's initial experience of encounter with Christ, but subsequent to it. The entire context suggests that the revelation here is to be closely connected with the revelation of v. 16…" (Fung, *The New International Commentary on the New Testament: The Epistle to the Galatians* [Grand Rapids, MI: Eerdmans, 1988], 54).

personally. It was beyond Saul's[52] comprehension to think these lax law-keepers and followers of a wayward rabbi could in any way be connected to God. In fact, the crucifixion of Jesus was, for Saul, evidence of God's condemnation. Jesus's death was more of a curse confirming his inauthentic ministry as a false messiah than the Messiah all the Jews had been expecting.

All the physical qualities of this encounter speak loudly regarding the impact they made internally on Saul's mind and heart. Imagine the horror of coming to the knowledge that the very thing he was doing in support of God was contrary to how He works. Jesus Himself challenged Saul's rash conclusion that He was a failed messiah and cultic rabbi.

Jesus appeared to him in a very anthropomorphic way, consistent with how God appeared to Abraham and Moses, in human form and with bright lights. There was no doubt in Saul's mind who this was. Luke has him calling out to Jesus, questioning, "Who are You, Lord?" (Acts 9:5) This indicates that Saul knew the lights were of God, although he was confused as to who was appearing to him on God's behalf. The clarity to follow soon communicated to Saul that this was Jesus of Nazareth appearing to him with God-like authority.[53]

In Galatians 1:13–14, Paul assumes that the reader will know that he was previously Saul of Tarsus, a zealous Pharisee who was bent on forcing compliance among his co-nationals to Jewish law.[54] Paul emphasizes how invested he was in religious nationalism. He was a prodigy, excelling at the training and rites of passage for a religious leader. He was even more zealous for the traditions of the law than his fathers before him.[55]

---

[52] Remember here that Paul is the name Saul used in the Gentile world. It was common in that day for Jews to have distinct Gentile names. In his article "The Name of Paul" (*Tyndale Bulletin*, 36, 1985, 179–183), Colin J. Hemer refers to the name Paul as a cognomen, a nickname passed down from father to son. For the purposes of this book, I will use Saul for the period before his encounter with Jesus, and Paul for the period after his encounter with Jesus.

[53] Luke, in Acts, uses the ἐγώ εἰμι construct—"I, I am"—which is consistent with the Septuagint translation in terms of how God identifies himself to Moses in Exodus when Moses asks Elohim (the generic Hebrew term for God) for a personal name.

[54] Paul emphasizes how, in his pre-conversion life, he took part in a resistance movement bent on cleaning up Jewish practices among Jewish communities of God. This most likely was inherited by the Maccabean tradition of revolt against any entity or behaviour that threatened the Jewish way of life and religion (Craig Keener, *Galatians: A Commentary* [Grand Rapids, MI: Baker Academic, 2019], 14).

[55] The translation of περισσοτέρως is "exceedingly abundantly," coming from the word group of the root περισσεύω, meaning "to be present in abundance." T. Brandt points out, "Just as the Apostle Paul was exceedingly (*perissos*) zealous in the persecution of the church (Acts. 26:11) and the traditions of the law (Gal. 1:14), he pursued with the same zeal the saving work of Christ…" (Brandt, "Fullness, Abound, Multitude, Fulfil, Make Room," *New International Dictionary of New Testament Theology, Volume One* [Grand Rapids, MI: Zondervan, 1971], 730).

Young, committed, zealous, and protective of his nation, Saul was a combination of a religious leader and patriotic protector. In our very polarized culture at present, we're quick to understand how difficult it is for someone like Saul to convert. So inbred were his beliefs and values that it took an encounter of cosmic proportions to change his mind and direction.

We should take comfort from Paul's story that God the Father is continually seeking to intervene in the life of individuals with the hope of setting them on the path of working with Him rather than against Him. Although we suffer the consequences of evil, it doesn't hinder God's plan to redeem those who are distant from Him. God is actively involved in bringing freedom, even to a harsh and hard critic of Jesus like Saul of Tarsus.

GOD FREES THE EYES TO SEE HIM AS HE IS

The use of the words "But then" at the beginning of Galatians 1:15 indicate the radical turn that God brought into Saul's life. His zeal for Judaism was challenged by the appearance of Jesus. Looking back on it all, Paul recognized that God's calling had been on him from birth.[56] He viewed this as the extent of God's grace in his life, the purpose having been to show Paul that God had always been with him, even when he had been working against Him.

From this reality, Paul furnishes his view that humanity, both those who are faithful and unfaithful, are connected to God.[57] That Jesus would point out how Paul's behaviour was hurting Him personally speaks of their relationship even though Saul had neither acknowledged one nor legitimized His identity as Messiah. This would develop into a full-blown view of humanity as the object of the Father's love and fuel Paul's passion to see Gentiles come to Christ.

Paul's phrase at the beginning of Galatians 1:16—"*to reveal his Son in me*" (my translation)—is akin to the way the Apostle John wrote about the incarnation of Christ and the impact of that incarnation on our fallen human condition. He stated in John 1:4–5: *"In him [the Word] was life, and his life was the light of humanity. The light shines in the darkness and the darkness cannot overcome it."*

This declaration by the beloved disciple of Jesus is both one of cosmic and micro proportions.

---

[56] Keener points out, "The dominant Greek version of Isa. 49:1 uses precisely the same words for *from my mother's womb* and the indicative form of *called*" (Keener, *Galatians: A Commentary*, 24).

[57] Paul's address to the Athenians on Mars Hill in Acts 17:24–28 shows us how his view of humanity's connection to God had shifted from his view as Saul of Tarsus.

The light enters creation[58] in a cosmic sense and shines in the darkness of human existence. In the same way, the light of the presence of Christ also shines in the individual. Paul speaks of this micro sense of Christ's light in his autobiography in the Galatian letter.

The revelation[59] of the Son to Paul raised his internal awareness of Jesus and drove out the dark perspective he had of God, himself, and the world around him. The Triune God[60] made Himself known to Paul through the revelation of the Son, and that revelation produced an external awareness of vocation whereby Paul received clarity over how his natural zeal could instead be directed toward sharing the light through communicating the good news to those outside the nation of Israel.

The darkness of his hatred for those who rejected His Jewish faith couldn't snuff out the direct light of Christ he received that day on his way to Damascus.

This is consistent with Galatians 1:4–5, where Paul describes Jesus giving Himself over to our fallen humanity. Like the Apostle John, Paul's eyes were opened to the magnitude of the life of Christ revealed in us. This light cannot be extinguished.

This is part of the good news that Paul shared in his missionary efforts. The unprecedented light of Christ shone in the Gentile communities as the people were awakened to the good news of Christ. What's significant in all this is that John's description of the inability of darkness to extinguish the light assures its bearer that darkness will not steal it away. Even the darkness within us cannot overshadow this light.

As Paul defends the authenticity of the good news he shared, he points out that he didn't need human approval to affirm this discovery. It was real, authentic, and transformational. No human instrument was involved to distort what he had received from Christ.

Paul uses this part of his story to combat what the imposters had told the Galatians about how he came to Christ. They were telling the Galatians that Paul had received this revelation from the Jerusalem Apostles who had also commissioned him to share their own law-keeping good news. Paul's biography tells the opposite story to confirm the genuineness of the Galatians' own

---

[58] By creation, I am referring to the world and humanity in it.

[59] This is the same word used in Galatians 1:12.

[60] Ronald Y.K. Fung writes, "Paul's consistent use of—Christ's divine sonship in the unique, ontological sense (Rom. 1:3f.; 1 Cor. 1:9; 15:20–28; Gal. 4:4; 1 Thess. 1:10) suggest that the term should be similarly understood here" (Fung, *The New International Commentary on the New Testament*, 16). Paul is claiming that he received insight into the unique nature of Jesus's sonship.

experience and its direct origin from Christ Himself. He will remind them of this at the beginning of Galatians 3.

We can draw an important pastoral moment from Paul's conversion and the words of the Apostle John in his gospel. The light that has shone in us, revealing the Son there, confirms our own transformation from darkness into light. For all the times we may feel that darkness is still advancing and wreaking havoc on us, it doesn't have the ability to overpower the light of Christ. The Son revives in us the life of the Trinity that lay dormant and unknown to us. Both on a cosmic and micro level, this light continues to move us forward to our true humanity. Evil does not have the power to stop it.[61]

The lie we believe is that our behaviour has made God distant. Yet that is far from the truth. God was with Paul from the moment of birth. Despite his wrong-headed idealistic notions and murderous rampages, the Father was still with Paul, having put his stamp on him.

The Father has been with you too! Like Paul, He was there when you felt you were furthest from Him, and that same light that brings the world daylight shines in us and restores us to the glory of our humanity which the Father gave us from the beginning.

This is what Paul was preaching: the light of Christ shone brightly into the hearts of Jews and Gentiles alike! The dim light of our efforts to rid ourselves of the darkness and keep us in the light (the two candles and flashlight) are feeble and frail attempts to replicate what only shines brightly through the revelation of God's Son in us. It is His light that drives the darkness away.

NOT OF HUMAN ORIGIN

The concern for Paul was that the imposters had somehow convinced the Galatians that he was in accord with their version of the gospel. Based on what he says back in Galatians 1:11–12, they were most likely telling others that Paul had learned his gospel from the same place they did, back in Jerusalem

---

[61] Baxter Kruger wrote a fictional story of a burned-out suicidal theologian named Aidan who was caught up for three days on the island of Patmos with the Apostle John. In their conversation, John reminds Aidan that separation from God is a lie of *Ophis*, the Greek word for serpent, who convinced humanity that we somehow lost connection with God and that we must find him on our own. John tells Aidan, "This is Ophis' chief trick—blind us to how close the Lord is, closer than breath: we're in him and he's in us. Ophis deceives the nations by one lie—separation… Our joy—his face lit up like the rising sun—is to tell the truth, let the light shine—and persevere the tribulation of enlightenment" (Kruger, *Patmos: Three Days, Two Men, One Extraordinary Conversation* [Jackson, MS: Perichoresis Press, 2016], 1229).

under the discipleship of the authorities in the Christian community of Judea.[62]

We will learn later that those authorities the imposters invoked were of the same opinion as Paul, that the Gentiles could remain in their faith without observing the law. They didn't need to be forced into becoming Jewish.

The imposters were distorting Paul's own story of conversion, and so he sets the record straight in this focused narrative of how he became the Apostle to the Gentiles.

There was a period of three years during which Paul went into territories not accessed by the other Apostles who were leaders in Judea. You will recall that in Acts 6, these Apostles had made the decision to not be involved with administering food to the local church community. This way, they could devote themselves to prayer and teaching.

The individuals they picked to be deacons, all Greek-speaking Jewish Christians, became travelling evangelists, venturing outside Judea to preach the good news of Christ to other Jews and Gentiles. For the most part, the Apostles in Jerusalem stayed put in Judea.

Paul's decision to travel to Arabia and Damascus right after his encounter with Jesus proves the point that he had no contact with Jerusalem, and subsequently they had no influence on him. Paul took this time in foreign lands to work out on his own the implications of what he had experienced in having seen Jesus.[63]

Some may wonder what Paul was doing in Arabia and Damascus those three years. Where in Arabia did he go? We know very little on this point. In Acts 9, Luke wrote about Paul's conversion in a much more concentrated fashion. He adds that Paul preached in Damascus after his conversion (Acts 9:19–22). Paul, in Galatians, mentions that he went immediately into Arabia and then back to Damascus for the much longer period of three years. It appears that Luke didn't know these details about Paul going to Arabia.

---

[62] Richard N. Longnecker writes that "the issue in Galatia had to do with where Paul got his message and how he received certification as an apostle, with his opponents claiming that he was dependent on and subordinate to the apostles at Jerusalem" (Longnecker, *Word Biblical Commentary, Volume 41: Galatians* [Grand Rapids, MI: Zondervan, 1990], 33).

[63] James D.G. Dunn writes, "That after his conversion Paul spent three years in Damascus and (significantly) Arabia suggests a lengthy and penetrating rethinking of his priorities and goals. It was evidently also of importance to him to insist that he did not consult with anyone whom the Jerusalem authorities would recognize, nor did he return to Jerusalem during that time (1:16–17)" (Dunn, "The Christian Life from the Perspective of Paul's Letter to the Galatians," *The Apostle Paul and the Christian Life*, 5).

As well, Damascus was part of Arabia, depending on where the border was drawn at any given time.[64] It would be a good assumption that Paul spent some significant time in solitude working out all that had happened to him, and after his contemplative sojourn in Arabia[65] he returned to Damascus which is where Luke picks up the narrative.

Luke describes Paul being lowered out of Damascus in a basket by night to evade those who were plotting to kill him (Acts 9:24–25). These were probably Greek-speaking Jews who felt threatened by the Pharisee who had converted to become a follower of Jesus and preach a "lawless" message.

Paul's visit to Peter and James in Galatians 1:18–19 is probably the same as Luke's record of Paul having gone to Jerusalem to meet with the Apostles (Acts 9:26–28). He also mentions that Barnabas was with him and provided Paul with direct access to the Apostles.[66] Paul specifically mentions that he only met with two of the Apostles, Peter and James the brother of Jesus.

The important detail about Paul's account here in Galatians is that it identifies the fact that Paul didn't go to Jerusalem to get instruction from Peter and James. Rather, he went in a consultative manner to compare their stories and encounters with Jesus. It was more about sharing information than going to be instructed

---

[64] See both Richard Longnecker and Craig Keener, who point out that by mentioning Arabia Paul was probably referring to the Nabatean Kingdom, of which Damascus would have been a part. This would have resulted in him not travelling that far from Damascus at any given point during his sojourn there.

[65] N.T. Wright mentions, "Paul was stopped in his tracks, just as Elijah had been. Elijah, dejected and depressed, went off to Mount Sinai to meet his God afresh, to learn about the still small voice as well as the earthquake, wind, and fire. Saul of Tarsus went off, probably to Sinai (he says 'Arabia', which is where Sinai is) most likely for a similar private wrestling with the God whom he worshipped" (Wright, *Paul for Everyone: Galatians and Thessalonians* [London, UK: SPCK Press, 2004], 9). Wright believes that Saul of Tarsus patterned his calling after the major prophets, specifically Elijah.

[66] Joe Morgado Jr. points out that Luke and Paul have different intentions in what they record. Luke chronicles the history of the beginning of the Christian movement. Paul provides a polemic to those who have been lied to by other leaders about his conversion story and teaching. Luke no doubt misses pertinent details that Paul felt important to establish in terms of the uniqueness and divine origin of his conversion and calling. Luke mentions that Barnabas had accompanied Paul to Jerusalem, whereas Paul doesn't mention Barnabas until Galatians 2:1 when he writes that he went up again to Jerusalem with Barnabas and Titus. Essentially neither story is meant to provide every exhaustive detail that occurred; rather, they appropriate the intention of each writer (Morgado, "Paul in Jerusalem: A Comparison of His Visits in Acts and Galatians," *Journal of Evangelical Theological Society*, series 37, volume 1, Mar 1994, 55–68). Ronald Y.K. Fung adds that "the most satisfactory solution to the apparent discrepancy between the two passages is to take Paul's 'at once' seriously and literally, and to treat the same word in Acts 9:20 (NEB. 'soon') as meaning 'immediately following his return to Damascus'" (Fung, *The New International Commentary on the New Testament*, 68).

for the purpose of authority and accountability. His swearing of an oath to God regarding his account of his Jerusalem visit shows the importance of the accuracy of this event for Paul amid the false narrative promoted by the imposters.

Consistent with Luke's account in Acts 11:30, and Acts 13–14, Paul mentions in Galatians1:21 that after that Jerusalem visit he spent time in Syria (no doubt in Antioch, which we will see in Galatians 2) and Cilicia. Neither territory is in proximity to Jerusalem. Given the limited time he spent in Jerusalem, Paul mentions that Judaeans on the street wouldn't have been able to recognize him. He simply hadn't spent that kind of time in Jerusalem, even though they no doubt would have heard about his conversion to join the followers of Jesus. These Judaeans would have been part of the Jewish-speaking Christian community. Paul says they gave thanks to God for his conversion, marking their acceptance of his transformation from persecutor to preacher of the good news.

This part of Paul's story highlights the divine origin of his teaching, the point being that what happened to him began at his encounter with Jesus. Jesus was the focal point of God's community made up of Jews and Gentiles who pledged their allegiance to Him.[67]

Looking at the good news from the vantage point of our present day, it's so important that we understand that we would have no faith in Christ if the Son hadn't come, the incarnation hadn't happened, and the life, death, resurrection, and ascension of Jesus had been merely a myth. These occurrences are the necessary foundation to the story of God's community through the centuries. Any deviation, addition, subtraction, or omission would put the entire message of the good news in jeopardy.

To know the history of God's community since the time of Jesus is to know that there has been no shortage of attempts at additions and alterations to its message. The Spirit continues to preserve our focus on Christ through the inspired words of Paul, which affirm both the source and sustainer of our faith. That same Spirit continues to work in us as God's community, challenging us regarding this important reality.

We all have a story about when Jesus captured our hearts and minds as we were overcome by the good news of His death and resurrection. This direct

---

[67] N.T. Wright further writes, "It is some comfort to know that these problems were endemic in Christianity from the beginning. But it is more important still, in recognizing the problem, to know how to go about tackling it. If Paul is to be our guide, the first rule seems to be: tell the story clearly. Don't fudge the background out of which the problem has come. Learn to prize both the independence which grows out of a fresh view of Jesus, and the convergence between different teachings of the gospel. But keep your eye on the main issue, which must always be God's glory" (Wright, *Paul for Everyone*, 12–13).

experience is the authentic impact of the reality of Jesus in our lives. His having drawn us into relationship with the Father resulted in bringing us into the protective and nurturing community of the Triune God of grace. In that place of shelter, no darkness can overtake or consume us. In this place we become our true selves, reflecting the new humanity Jesus brought us. That humanity lives in complete and utter dependence on Christ.

No human can take credit for this experience. No candles and flashlight could provide such insight. It came directly from Jesus and the efforts of the Father and Spirit in affirming us and keeping us connected to Him. The radical change in us is affected through the work of Jesus.

There will be those who seek to rob us of our authentic experience by attempting to conform our experience to their structure and system. Being steadfast in our place with the Father, Son, and Spirit will dispel the temptation to let others redefine what happened to us. Paul gives us such an example by bringing clarity in response to the imposters' distortion of his story.

No one can take away what Christ has done in you. No darkness can overcome the light of Christ revealed in you. For Paul, the transformation resulted in his bringing the good news to the Gentiles. I encourage you to take a moment and recount how your own transformation has benefited the world around you, allowing you to bring the good news of Christ that draws back the veil of darkness in others.

I think of my grandfather, who functioned during the Nazi occupation of southern Italy as a "black shirt"[68] in fascist Italy. He went to a Pentecostal service to spy out the pastor and congregation on suspicion that they were rebelling against the fascist state. In that service, he was moved by the preaching and worship. He remembered how kind and loving this pastor was in taking care of the spiritual needs of all those living in their town, and through this individual the light of Christ shone in his heart, illuminating the truth of Christ and bringing him into relationship with the Father, Son, and Spirit.

My grandfather experienced the empowering presence of the Spirit through that Pentecostal pastor and his caring community. He was so impacted by the encounter that he declared to his wife and children, "From now on, this will be our church, and these will be our fellow brothers and sisters in Christ."

The light of Christ entered his heart, and also into my father's heart. It was the same light I experienced when they shared the good news with me. I now continue to carry that light in my ministry as a pastor, Bible college professor,

---

[68] Those who supported the leadership of Mussolini were enlisted as militia. They wore a black shirt that told their community they were the eyes and ears of the dictator.

and mentor to many ministry leaders. The fascists couldn't extinguish the light of Christ that continues three generations later.

Just as it was with Paul, the main character in my story is Jesus, who works through His faithful followers to shine His light of life in and through me. He has done the same for you!

What is your story of the light shining in your life? Take confidence in knowing that the light hasn't been snuffed out; it remains to connect you to the Triune God of grace and form you into your new humanity!

Chapter Four

FREEDOM OF CONSENSUS AMONG LEADERS

Galatians 2:1–10

Then after fourteen years, I went back to Jerusalem with Barnabas, this time taking Titus with us. A revelation prompted me to go up and present to them the good news that I preached among the Gentiles. I did it privately with those in leadership there so that I would not get ahead of myself and discredit what I had fought hard to build[69] [in terms of Christ's communities among the Gentiles]. But not even Titus, being of Greek background, felt compelled to submit to the distorted news of law-keeping.[70] 4 The pressure came from the imposters who were smuggled into the meeting, listening in on us to rob us of the freedom we have in Christ Jesus and enslave us again. We didn't give them the time of day so that the true good news would stay with you. The leaders in Jerusalem did not add anything to what I had shared because regardless of who they are, credibility comes from God, not people. Instead, they saw that [God]entrusted me with the Good News to the Gentiles,[71] just as Peter was entrusted with the Good News to the Jews. The same God appointed both of us. Having sensed the degree of grace God had given me, James, Peter, and John, known as the foundational leaders, extended their hand of fellowship to us, so that we would continue in our mission to the Gentiles, and they focus on the Jews. The one thing they did ask us to remember was the poor—of which we agreed to do.

---

[69] The phrase μή πως εἰς κενὸν ἢ ἔδραμον conveys the care with which Paul addressed the Apostles in Jerusalem. Paul had intended to do it privately so as not to rattle the Jewish Christian community and so discredit what he, Barnabas, Titus, and others had accomplished so far in the emerging Gentile mission. The literal translation is *"perhaps in vain I was running, or had run."* My attempt in the translation is to provide more of the context of Paul's carefulness.

[70] Paul uses the word περιτμηθῆναι, which translates into "circumcised," to represent a preoccupation with law-keeping versus the grace and faith in Christ that Paul preached. Titus, being a Gentile, would have been representative of the type of people in the Gentile territories who were coming to Christ.

[71] Paul will again use the Greek words for circumcision and uncircumcision to represent the groups of Jews and Gentiles. I chose to translate these words to represent those groups for the sake of clarity.

FREEDOM TO TREAD CAREFULLY

The shift in Galatians 2 is to a more recent narrative that will be familiar to the readers of the letter.

Paul moves to a part of his story that is fourteen years removed from his first visit to Jerusalem. During that time, Paul and his missionary team built a Gentile movement of Christ communities through Asia Minor.

Luke narrates in Acts 13–14 the first missionary journey of Barnabas and Paul. They were commissioned by Christ's community in Syrian Antioch, supported by that community's resources and prayers. They made their way through Asia Minor preaching primarily among the Gentiles the good news of deliverance from evil and restoration to true humanity, although they also preached to Jews in the region.

The results were remarkable for two preachers with a Jewish upbringing. The Spirit was made evident in their preaching and Gentiles put their faith in Christ. Signs and wonders followed them as Christ was made known in that part of the Roman Empire.

However, as they ended their journey back in Antioch, there was evidently still a clash of views in the early Christian community concerning the good news and what it represented in terms of its requirements on Jew and Gentile alike.

Throughout their first journey, Barnabas and Paul experienced opposition from Jews regarding what they preached. The Jews reacted against the teaching of Jesus as God's Son and His resurrection. They identified it as blasphemy, challenging their monotheistic Jewish belief.

Paul's teaching on the law also created a stir. In some communities, their lives were threatened by these Jewish nationalists. In others, it was the pagan or political leaders who were upset by the signs and wonders that delivered people from bondage to evil and enslavement to their pagan cults.

Returning to Antioch, the Jewish backlash they experienced turned into controversy over the good news by Jewish Christians who were a part of their community. As they shared with their fellow Christ-followers in Antioch about what God was doing among the Gentiles, it was made clear to Paul that a visit to Jerusalem was in order.

The phrasing of Galatians 2:2—*"A revelation prompted me to go up"* (my translation)—indicates that a divine nudge probably came from God. He didn't only speak directly to Paul, as in his conversion experience, but through Christ's community in Antioch.[72]

---

[72] Herman N. Ridderbos writes, "Paul's declaration that he went to Jerusalem based on, and in agreement with, a revelation, tells us that he took this important step neither arbitrarily nor by

Several scholars believe that this journey to Jerusalem coincides with the Jerusalem council called by the Apostles to discuss the matter of requiring Gentiles to observe the law in addition to their conversion to faith in Christ.[73]

Paul makes a point in this passage about how thoughtful he is with the approach he took at the Jerusalem meeting. He carefully presented to the Apostles the good news he had shared with the Gentiles. He did it privately, so as not to create the kind of opposition he'd experienced openly by Jews in the Gentile regions. No doubt his meeting with Peter, many years earlier, had given him confidence that they would give him a fair hearing.

A problem arose when others secretly made their way into the meeting, most likely unbeknownst to the Apostles, to circumvent Paul and Barnabas. These individuals were from the same group of imposters that had led the Galatians astray from their faith in Christ.

The maturity of the Apostle Paul rings loud and true in this narrative. The grace of the Lord Jesus Christ had tempered the heart of this once volatile individual. Paul was careful to respect his apostolic counterparts and he worked hard not to upset the Jewish Christian community or endanger what he, Barnabas, and his Gentile missions team had founded in their ministry.

---

way of experiment, but in the strength of divine commissioning and empowerment. Nor is it in conflict with this view that he also went on assignment from the church at Antioch (Acts 15:1). It is even possible that the revelation did not come to him personally (cf. Acts 13:2, 4)" (Ridderbos, *The New International Commentary on the New Testament: The Epistle of Paul to the Churches in Galatia* [Grand Rapids, MI: Eerdmans, 1984], 80). Compare this to the words of Gordon D. Fee: "Given the presence of Barnabas and Titus and Paul's free appeal to such 'revelation' as something that could be verified or tested, I would lean toward the latter. If so, this is another one of those side notes in Paul that indicate the presence of the 'charismatic' Spirit in the life of the early church— such a prophetic utterance would have been understood as a community event, which, properly tested, would have been acted upon as a community sending of the three brothers" (Fee, *God's Empowering Presence: The Holy Spirit in the Letters of Paul* [Peabody, MA: Hendrickson Publishers, 1994], 373). We see this even later in Acts 21 and onwards regarding the vision that one member of Christ's community had of Paul being put in chains when he arrived in Jerusalem on his third journey there to bring the people a collection from the Gentile communities in Asia Minor and Macedonia.

[73] According to James D. G. Dunn, "The majority of commentators favour the second alternative: that the Gal. ii visit is the same as the Acts xv visit (Gal. ii = Acts xv). The decisive consideration is that the central issue, key participants and principal agreement are so close that the two accounts must be variant versions of the same episode—Most of the variant details can be accounted for in terms of the different perspectives of Luke and Paul in their writings" (Dunn, *Black's New Testament Commentary*, 88).

Titus's purpose at that meeting, no doubt, was to present evidence of what the Gentile mission had produced.[74]

The attempted sabotage of the meeting with the Apostles in Jerusalem was handled without incident. Paul pointed out to the Galatians that they hadn't given in to their desire to control the meeting. In fact, neither had they swayed the Apostles. It was a lame attempt to circumvent what for Paul was an appointed moment by God.

The lesson in this story is that no matter what evil design attempts to thwart God's purposes, His plan prevails. The Spirit was breaking open the structures of the early church, which had been confined to its Jewish origins and expressions, so that Gentiles could also come to Christ and join the one true family of God.

Some Jewish believers were threatening to stifle this Spirit-led Gentile expansion, but God's purposes prevailed in the ministries of the Jerusalem Apostles and Paul's missionary team. Paul shares this to remind the Galatians that Jewish Christian agitators were trying to undermine the work he was doing among them only to be frustrated by how the Spirit transformed their lives.

Like in Paul's context, some of us are stifling what the Spirit wants to do in our communities and culture. The deterrent is present in those who want to keep everything the same, as if the structures they've assumed over the years are what control the moving of the Spirit. Their candles and flashlights have become a false representation of what keeps us close to Christ. In a very real sense, they have replaced the Spirit altogether.

I have seen firsthand how some children of first-generation believers try to preserve the freedom of Christ, imparted to them by their matriarchs and patri-archs, by putting that freedom into neat systems of structure and observance. This keeps our communities from growing and forces us into patterns of conformity that block the movement of the Spirit, as opposed to letting the Spirit do what He wants to do through us. The deception is that those who hinder the Spirit's move-ment think that their behaviour will promote the Spirit's activity.

Leaders need to tread carefully in such scenarios, being sensitive to the desire for the Spirit to move while at the same time challenging the structures that hinder His movement. The takeaway from Paul's words in this passage is that

---

[74] Craig Keener writes, "Some suggest that Paul brought Titus to Jerusalem as an example of the fruits of the mission; if Titus was his child in the faith (cf. Titus 1:4), Titus was his convert or mentee, possibly from Antioch or possibly a convert among the Galatians (like Timothy, Acts 16:1–3), which would explain their knowledge about him.—Then again, Antioch's current leadership may have chosen Titus along with others; Luke mentions that Paul, Barnabas, "and some of the others" were part of the Antioch delegation (Acts 15:2)" (Keener, *Galatians: A Commentary*, 71).

remaining true to the freedom of the good news, putting no restrictions on conduct, allows the Spirit to do His work of drawing and convincing those who are at a distance. There will be those who challenge such freedom, but we are called to remain steadfast in what we have experienced and trust that the Spirit will do His work.

We are called on as leaders to not let individuals with ulterior motives undermine what God is doing among the majority. Paul demonstrated at the Jerusalem meeting that he was a true shepherd of those God had entrusted into his pastoral care. He protected them from those who sought to undermine the freedom Christ had brought to them.

Paul hoped that by sharing this story with the Galatians, they would be encouraged to abandon the false gospel and return to their freedom in Christ.

From Paul's account, the meeting went very well. The Apostles in Jerusalem had nothing more to add to their presentation, and in fact they welcomed Paul and Barnabas, acknowledging the good news they were preaching to the Gentiles by shaking their hands in a gesture of fellowship. Through this act, they recognized Paul was their equal. Although his view of this was inconsequential, since in his estimation God was the one who gave his words and will credibility.

There is a lesson in this for us all, in that God is the one who confirms His word in us. The confirmation of others is simply an acknowledgment of what God has already approved and commended.

This momentous event established the growth of the community of Christ beyond the Jewish world. It was a moment of growth begun by Christ and fuelled by the Spirit's presence in God's communities spread across Judea, Syria, and now Asia Minor.

FREEDOM TO CARE FOR EVERYONE

Like the Spirit breaking the small Jewish Christian community out of its immediate geography of Judea in the Acts 6 controversy, the same Spirit breaks open the discipleship structures that held the faith within the framework of Judaism through Paul's efforts in Syria, Arabia, Cilicia, and beyond.

The lesson for our day is to consider how our structures hold back the spread of the good news to other people. The imposters put structure before relationship, tradition before people, nationalism as a banner of community rather than gather around the love of Christ. Out of his encounter with Jesus, Paul the Apostle put people before politics, relationship with God before nationalism. The good news had freed Paul to care for people rather than enforce structures and tradition.

It's clear in the example of the New Testament Christian community that God will blow open structures to allow His good news to reach others. It's delicate to manoeuvre through such tension without causing further issues. This whole ordeal had real people on both sides of the issue.

The capacity for Paul to keep in mind the well-being of all involved is evidence of the peace of God that was his in Christ. His careful handling of the meeting with the Apostles in Jerusalem is proof of the authenticity of his encounter with Jesus and the goods news he preached.

Paul's goal wasn't to blow up the Jewish Christian community to give the Gentile Christian community primacy; his focus was on the health of both communities. His credibility is evident in the Jerusalem Apostles' acknowledgment of the emerging Gentile phenomenon. They gave him their partnership in the mission of Christ to go into the world and make disciples: they to the Jews, and he and his missions team to the Gentiles.

When the Jerusalem Apostles asked Paul and Barnabas not to forget the poor, which most likely referred to the poor among them in Jerusalem and Judea,[75] Paul complied because he truly cared about the Jewish Christian community. In fact, he was already collecting money for famine relief in Judea. He encouraged the Gentile churches scattered abroad to return their gratitude to the Jewish Christians for introducing them to Christ—and a tangible way of doing this was offer famine relief.[76] Paul told the Galatians he was zealous in his response since it was consistent with how he already felt about the believers in Jerusalem.

What we see in this narrative is the form by which we can gauge true authentic Christian love sourced from the good news of Christ. When our behaviour, in the midst of controversy, seeks to care for all those involved and withstands the advances of anyone trying to sabotage unity, we have true authentic Christianity.[77] When a person's behaviours seek to alienate dissenters and push

---

[75] Herman N. Ridderbos writes, "By *the poor* Paul is recognizably referring to the poor at Jerusalem (cf. Rom. 15:26). Again and again, we learn that the Gentile churches took up collections for the church at Jerusalem (Rom. 15:25ff., 1 Cor. 16:1ff., 2 Cor. 8:1 ff., 9:1 ff., Acts 11:29 ff., 12:25 ff., and 24:17)" (Ridderbos, *The New International Commentary on the New Testament*, 90–91, emphasis added).

[76] He adds, "Paul in Romans 15:27, [expressed] that the Gentile churches had a certain material obligation to the church in Jerusalem, to be given in gratitude for the spiritual gift that it had given them..." (Ibid., 91)

[77] N.T. Wright writes, "The letter [Galatians] is about unity: the fact that in the Messiah, particularly through his death, the one God has done what he promised Abraham all along. He has given him a single family in which believing Jews and believing Gentiles form one body. What Paul says about the cross in Galatians is all aimed toward this end: because of the cross, all believers are on the same footing" (Wright, *The Day the Revolution Began*, 234).

their own agenda at the expense of others, declare their way as the only way, and run roughshod over the hard and careful work of others, we can suspect it is inauthentic Christianity.

Forcing Gentiles to obey Jewish law as part of their commitment to following Christ frustrates the purpose for which Christ came in the first place, which is to deliver us from evil and restore our true humanity in relationship with the Triune God of grace. Such requirements set Jewish agendas above God's agenda of reaching all of humanity. For that reason alone, focusing on faith in Christ apart from the law became a necessary process in restoring our relationship with God.

There is no doubt that the Spirit was at work in the life and ministry of Paul, and this is seen in the trajectory of the early Christian community as they brought the good news beyond the borders of Judea where it began.

What are the boundary lines that God is challenging in your context? How have you responded to them? Are you pushing your own agenda at the expense of others, wanting your own way regardless of what others may think? Are you carefully considering what the Spirit is doing through the present challenge and leaving your heart open to understand what He wants? Are there authentic expressions of faith in those on the other side of the issue? Have you understood where they're coming from? How are you handling the dissenters and those who are trying to sabotage what the Spirit is wanting to accomplish?

You can be sure that the way in which you care for those you're involved with, respecting your community while trying to move forward to new possibilities, is evidence of the authenticity in the challenge before you.

There is a maturity that comes from the good news of Christ, and that maturity helps us to focus our attention on loving God and others. A sign of this maturity is not letting the hierarchies we create cloud the fact that everyone plays a part in God's community. Paul points out that the Apostles in Jerusalem—Peter, James, and John—were the pillars of the early Christian community. Regardless, he didn't let their status affect how he carefully dealt with them. As an Apostle, and fellow brother in Christ, he dealt with them on an equal plain.

He reminds the Galatians that no one individual is bigger than the good news itself. The Jerusalem Apostles were conveying God's grace in the same way his own missionary team was. The same God was involved in both endeavours, and so Paul didn't show partiality or favouritism.

Is there something the Spirit is doing in your context right now that doesn't fit your trusted paradigm of how He moves?

What the Spirit is doing right now in the culture around us challenges our own notions of how people both come to and stay in Christ. If the structures of faith we hold on to, like the candles and flashlight, frustrate those whom the Spirit is bringing to Christ, we need to re-examine what we hold to and evaluate whether we've made the good news too much about what we do, and not enough about what Christ does through the Spirit in the lives of those around us.

As we move into the next section of the letter, Paul will demonstrate that there are rare occasions when confrontations are needed, to prevent us from raising walls that stifle the work of Christ, creating a community that doesn't represent Him or His good news. Confrontation can be important to prevent others from being led astray and away from Christ. Seeing this in action gives evidence to the authenticity of our embrace of Christ.

Chapter Five:

FREEDOM TO SPEAK THE TRUTH

Galatians 2:11–21

But when Peter came to Antioch, I confronted him in person because he was at fault. Before a visit by some from James' community, he ate with Gentiles. But when the visitors arrived, he withdrew and excluded himself [from eating with the Gentiles] fearing those who were of the law-keeping group.[78] The rest of the Jews [in the Antioch community] took on the same hypocritical behaviour; so that even Barnabas was caught up in the peer pressure. But when I saw that they weren't reflecting behaviour consistent with the good news, I said to Peter, in the presence of everyone, "If you being a Jew, live your life like a Gentile and not a Jew, what right do you have to pressure Gentiles to be Judaized? We, having been brought up godly, and not pagan,[79] still know that an individual is not put right[80] [with God] by keeping the law but rather through faith in Christ Jesus, for even we believed in Christ Jesus in order that we might be put right by the faith of Christ and not by law-keeping. No human being will be put right by the law."

But if, as we seek to be put right in Christ, we discover that we are sinners, does that make Christ a servant of sin? Never! For if I establish again the things that I left behind, then I am the law breaker. For through law, I died to law so that I can live with God. With Christ, I was crucified. It's not me that lives any longer, but Christ living in me. I

---

[78] Paul refers to them as ἐκ περιτομῆς, translated as "of the circumcision." I chose to keep the translation consistent with law-keeping. Circumcision was the one physical sign Jews could use to determine whether others were law-keepers. The point is that they were focused on the law.

[79] The literal translation of this phrase is *"We, being Jews by nature, and not Gentile sinners."* I translated the phrase to read *"having been brought up godly, and not pagan,"* to show that Paul is making a statement of equality. He's saying, "Even though we've been brought up in the Jewish laws and customs, and not as Gentile sinners, we know that we still aren't any better or have any advantage over Gentiles when it comes to our standing with God."

[80] I chose to use Craig Keener's translation of δικαιόω, since I believe that this is as accurate as we can get to the original meaning of the word. As will be elaborated on later, righteousness is established by relational connection, not a change in substance, which "being made righteous" alludes to. Rather, "being put right" with God is what Christ does as He restores relationship with us and with the Father.

now live in my present humanity by faith in the Son of God, who loved me, and gave Himself for me. I'm not rejecting God's grace [because I live dependent on Christ]. If the law could have put me right with God, then Christ died for nothing!

TRUTH ABOUT WHAT DIVIDES A COMMUNITY

In Paul's encounter with Peter, we see evidence of the distorted gospel and its impact. The event took place in Syrian Antioch, in a community made up of predominantly Gentile Christians and Greek-speaking Jewish Christians.[81] It was the first place where followers of Christ were identified as "Christian" or "Messiah-people."[82]

This early Gentile community was the first Christian outpost outside Judea. Jews and Gentiles worshipped here together, exemplifying what it looked like to practically live out the good news Paul had been defending all along in this letter.

The "one new humanity" of Ephesians was being lived out among these people.[83] They gave testimony to the true good news of having been delivered from evil. Equality characterized their environment, where peace and love reigned and their efforts were concentrated on sending out missionaries to other territories. The goal of the mission was for Gentiles and Jews to come to know Jesus and the transformation of their fallen humanity into a new humanity.

Peter found his way to the city after having been incarcerated in Judea due to being a follower of Christ and especially a leader of the new movement.[84] Antioch was to be a safe place for him until the tension died down between Jewish authorities and the Jewish Christian community in Judea.

---

[81] Hebrew-speaking Jewish Christians were found mainly in Judea where their language, customs, and religious centre was located. The Jews scattered throughout the rest of the Roman Empire were mainly Greek-speaking. So clear was this division that Greek-speaking Jews had their own Greek-speaking synagogues in Judea for when they visited during Passover. We see this evidenced in Luke, who mentions that Saul/Paul belonged to the Synagogue of the Freemen, a Greek-speaking Jewish synagogue (Acts 6:9).

[82] N.T. Wright states, in a passage on Galatians 2:11–14, "Antioch, near the north-eastern corner of the Mediterranean, about 300 miles away from Jerusalem, was one of the great centres of early Christianity: according to Acts 11:26, this was the first place where the followers of Jesus were called 'Christians', 'Messiah-people'" (Wright, *Paul for Everyone*, 21).

[83] Lombardi, *A New Humanity*, 43–52.

[84] Scot McKnight writes, "It is not completely clear when Peter 'came to Antioch,' but Acts 12:17 is as much evidence as we have. Luke tells us there that after Peter's miraculous deliverance from prison, he 'left for another place.' He knew he had to vacate Jerusalem temporarily because of the persecution (cf. 12:18–19)" (McKnight, *The NIV Application Commentary: Galatians* [Grand Rapids, MI: Zondervan, 1995], 1980). Jewish authorities in Judea were putting the heat on Jerusalem Christians and Peter sought refuge in Antioch to wait until things died down.

This Apostle had his own conversion experience in Acts 10. When on a roof top in Joppa, God gave him a vision that challenged his separatist Jewish sensibilities. In that vision, Peter learned that God's desire was for the Gentiles to join Christ's community and become followers of Jesus.[85]

In Antioch, Peter interacted with believers by eating with Gentiles, demonstrating a most intimate relationship with them. Sharing meals was akin to being family, and Peter had no issue with sitting at a table with Gentiles. He was demonstrating what it looks like to practically live out the good news of Christ, exemplifying the "good works" that come from being in relationship with God and living in the new humanity.

This is the behaviour Paul describes as the fruit of living in relationship with the Triune God and His creation. It demonstrates the knowledge that we are created as masterpieces, and that we might do the good works that God desired for us long ago (Ephesians 2:10). These works are very different than the works of the law which Paul talks about in Galatians.[86] The Galatians' source was the love of the Father, and they were governed by His love through Christ and experienced in the freedom of the Spirit.

The problem arose when certain individuals from the Jewish Christian community in Jerusalem visited Antioch.[87] These visitors were probably connected to the ones who were smuggled into the meeting of Paul, Barnabas, and the Apostles in Jerusalem. They were of the law-keeping kind, distorting the good news by adding the Jewish requirements to Jewish and Gentile Christian practice.

Paul specifically mentions that Peter was "at fault."[88] This strongly points out the divisiveness of Peter's behaviour in refusing to eat at a table with Gentiles. Paul says that Peter's actions didn't demonstrate equality with the Gentiles.

---

[85] The vision Peter had that day was of all the forbidden foods being lowered from the heavens and the voice of God saying to him, "Take and eat." The message to Peter was that Gentiles can be embraced by Jews without contamination or penalty (Acts 10:9–29).

[86] Gordon D. Fee writes, "It is a simple matter of fact that Paul regularly urges his churches to 'do good works.' But here Paul is dealing not with 'good works' but specifically with doing 'works of the law' meaning keeping certain requirements of the law as a means of gaining, or being in, right standing with God" (Fee, *Pentecostal Commentary Series*, 84). Fee acknowledges that Paul will speak of these "good works" in Galatians 6, giving examples of what they look like in terms of the degree of love and compassion we are called to have for one another.

[87] Paul identifies them as "certain men from James." Given the narrative in Galatians 2, and that of Acts 15, James was in full agreement with Paul's mission to the Gentiles and not forcing them to follow Jewish laws as followers of Christ. These men may have come from James's community, but they didn't share the same convictions as Paul's message or mission.

[88] The perfect passive form κατεγνωσμένος indicates the use of the dramatic perfect tense, where the past action of Peter with the Antioch believers now condemns him in the present. The passive indicates that Peter's past action of segregation from the Gentiles is now coming back to accuse him (Longnecker, *Word Biblical Commentary, Volume 41: Galatians*, 72).

It came down to the difference of inclusion versus exclusion. The inclusive actions of eating with the Gentiles confirmed the good news of deliverance from evil and equality among people living in the new humanity. Peter's exclusive behaviour reinforced his past actions of separatism and nationalism, giving priority to Jewish laws and customs over Gentile relationships. This betrayed what Peter had learned from the vision in Acts 10, and also his agreement at the Jerusalem council where he had joined the other Apostles in approving Paul's mission to the Gentiles and the good news of Christ that Paul and Barnabas had shared.[89]

Paul calls Peter's behaviour as "hypocritical." The term has roots in the Greek theatre, where actors wore masks to portray certain characters. It later entered common usage to denote someone who pretends to be someone else.[90]

Peter wasn't acting according to his core beliefs; he responded out of fear for what the visitors might think. Feeling pressure to show his allegiance to his countrymen, Peter behaved like the imposters Paul had been combating in the Galatian letter.

Peter's demonstration of sticking to Jewish laws of custom created division in the community of Antioch. The other Jews, and even Barnabas, the one characterized by his character of support and encouragement, bowed to the peer pressure and followed in the same hypocrisy.

This is what happens when distorted good news enters a community. Rather than promoting unity, it encourages division and segregation, behaviours which are inconsistent with the person of Jesus and His work of bringing humanity together. The character of the Father, who Paul described as someone who does not show partiality, is undermined when we present a Father who would promote such divisive activity.[91] It gives a foothold to evil, breaking down a community and setting people against one another.

Such a condition couldn't go on any longer and Paul used his authority as a fellow Apostle to confront Peter and end the charade.

As an aside, what would prompt Peter to turn like he did?

This uncharacteristic behaviour is a symptom of the tension that existed in the Christian community of the early first century. As Gentile converts were

---

[89] Craig Keener writes, "Kephas was party to the Jerusalem agreement that recognized gentiles as the primary sphere of Paul's ministry rather than Peter's (2:7, 9). Jerusalem was not to add requirements to faith in Christ for gentiles" (Keener, *Galatians: A Commentary*, 138).

[90] W. Gunther writes, "The use of the verb—is close to the meaning to play a role, act as if, pretend:— Gal. 2:13—Peter did not remain true to his commission; he was playing a double game, trimming his sails to the wind. Clear knowledge of the right course of action is assumed; but it is the actual situation that gives the decisive judgment on his behaviour, and thus Peter became a hypocrite" (Gunter, "Lie, Hypocrite," *New International Dictionary of New Testament Theology, Volume Two*, 469).

[91] Compare this with Galatians 2:6 and Ephesians 6:9. The Father does not show favouritism.

added to Christ's community, it challenged the followers of Jesus who remained Jewish in their following of laws and traditions. Paul, and others, challenged this need to follow Jewish laws and traditions by not requiring them for Gentiles. The basis of this was Paul's own conversion experience and what the Spirit was doing through their preaching of the good news to Gentiles.[92]

It would be wrong to say that Paul was combating Judaism; he was combating the notion that the way to Christ included observance of the law.[93] Later he argues for the fact that this was God's intention from the beginning through His promise to Abraham and the giving of the law.

It became a delicate matter of helping Jewish Christians understand that Gentile Christians don't need to be Jewish to follow Christ. Gentile conversion was a sign from God that the law was not a requirement.

Being a Jewish Christian in Judea was a careful balancing act between identifying with the Christian community but also staying connected to one's fellow non-Christian Jews through allegiance to Jewish customs. The followers of Christ, in the Jewish community, were viewed by their non-Christian Jewish counterparts as cultic and misguided.[94]

Realizing Paul's own pre-conversion response to these early Jewish Christians should bring to mind the perceived threat that these Christians posed to the Jews, who held high nationalistic and religious ideals.[95] The Jewish community

---

[92] This can be seen in how the Jerusalem contingent at the Jerusalem council in Acts 15 identified the legitimacy of Paul's Gentile mission. The Spirit was coming upon Gentiles before they had become Jews or declared allegiance to the law. See Peter's words at the Jerusalem council in Acts 15:8.

[93] E.P. Sanders writes, "The argument of Galatians—is against Christian missionaries [the imposters], not against Judaism, and it is against the view that Gentiles must accept the law as a condition of or as a basic requirement for membership" (Sanders, *Paul, the Law, and the Jewish People*, 288). Sanders has highly influenced Pauline studies toward the perspective that Paul was not posturing against Judaism in his focus on faith in Christ. Judaism had in its beliefs a process of salvation for Jews and atonement for their idolatry and waywardness. The correction for Paul was to understand that focus of faith is not on Torah-keeping but on trusting Jesus. This is the fundamental difference that caused the Christian community to emerge as its own religion altogether.

[94] For these non-Christian Jews, Jesus of Nazareth was a failed Messiah, an imposter. Any notion of his resurrection and ascension were viewed as fantasies constructed by their Christian Jewish counterparts to keep alive their allegiance to this failed Messiah.

[95] According to G.W.E Nickelsburg, "His autobiographical accounts in Gl 1:12–17 and Phlp 3:2–11 juxtapose his own Torah piety and his persecution of the church, and this strongly suggests a connection between the two. Paul's persecution of Christians was connected with their attitudes about the Torah.—Acts 7–9 describes a similar juxtaposition; this persecution is triggered in connection with Stephen's claim that Temple and Torah are no longer viable" (Nickelsburg, "Jews and Christians in the First Century: The Struggle Over Identity," *Neotestamentica*, 1993, 380). It is significant that he mentions Stephen, since Saul had been present to hold the coats of those who stoned him to death. Temple and Torah were sacred symbols that reinforced Jewish identity. To challenge them was to challenge the entire nation of Israel.

in Judea had experienced a long persecution of their own over the centuries by ruling powers who had challenged their legitimacy.

These powers had subjugated the Jews to various degrees to comply with their own ways. In the first century, the Jewish community had managed to achieve some degree of identity and autonomy while under Roman rule.[96] The way to distinguish themselves from the Romans was to hold on to their religious national identity. All the markers that identified them as Jews—Sabbath-keeping, circumcision, food laws, temple worship, etc.—were practiced openly and rigidly policed.[97]

The reason for such hypervigilance was to preserve the Jewish way of life as well as the hope that God would return to vindicate them and free them from their oppressors.[98] Anyone who challenged these markers of their identity, including their own co-nationals, were dealt with to the full extent of their scrutiny and criticism.[99]

The Jewish Christians emerged as posing enough of a threat that it created ongoing tension in Judea. Peter, living in Jerusalem, would have known all too well what that tension felt like. He had just spent time in jail because of it.

Before we throw Peter under the bus, though, we need to understand the delicate balancing act of embracing Gentiles into Christ's community and living in harmony with the Jews. In Jerusalem, Jewish Christians avoided backlash by attending the temple and observing the laws, customs, and traditions of the day. This reduced suspicion from their non-Christian counterparts.

Peter's behaviour in Antioch, under the scrutinizing eye of the visitors from Jerusalem, would have triggered the placating actions he later used in Jerusalem.

---

[96] Eckhard J. Schnabel points out that Julius Caesar had approved the Jews to live according to their ancestral laws, and the subsequent emperors, such as Augustus, ratified this. The Jews held the Roman leaders accountable to this dictate. Schnabel gives ample evidence that Jews across the Empire fought for the right to observe their way of life and religious practices without persecution or sanction by municipal authorities (Schnabel, "Jewish Opposition to Christians in Asia Minor in the First Century, *Bulletin for Biblical Research*, series 18, volume 2, 2008, 244–245).

[97] See Luke 6, where Pharisees of the same type as Saul of Tarsus followed Jesus and His disciples to catch them breaking the Sabbath. This is evidence of a high degree of self-monitoring among the Jewish people.

[98] N.T. Wright says that "in the intertestamental period, *'Wisdom' was identified with Torah.* Those who possessed and tried to keep Torah were therefore the true humanity: it was they who would be exalted to the place where humanity belonged, under the creator and over the creation" (Wright, *The New Testament and the People of God* [Minneapolis, MN: Fortress Press, 1992], 265, emphasis added).

[99] Craig Keener wrote, "The strictest of Judeans considered those who compromised Judean customs to be as damnable as gentiles themselves" (Keener, *Galatians: A Commentary*, 145).

Paul would have been very aware of this,[100] but he was of a different opinion in terms of the way Peter handled it.

Paul's view was that Peter, being in Gentile territory, should hold to behaviour that reflected the good news they were preaching to the Gentiles.[101] Jerusalem Christians needed to be sensitive to the Gentile context just as they expected the Gentiles to be sensitive to the Judean context.[102]

The law used to identify oneself as a follower of Christ deterred others from following Christ, especially those of Gentile background. It deterred by excluding them unless they followed the Jewish law. This was not the good news.

Through His sacrifice, Christ modelled that Gentile and Jew were equal. Jesus found them to be equally separated from the Father, making it possible for them to be equally reconciled to the Father.[103]

By trying to appease their Jewish co-nationals by observing the law, Jewish Christians alienated Gentiles and prevented them from coming to Christ. For those Gentiles who wanted to respond to Christ, the unfair requirement of observing the law was thrust on them by Jewish Christians. This tore at the goal of unity in the Christian community.

Peter unfortunately felt the pressure from his Jewish co-nationals and succumbed to that pressure by alienating Gentile believers.

Paul will speak to unity later in Galatians when he encourages his readers to not focus on the markers of law-keeping, but rather focus on faith that expresses itself in love (Galatians 5:6).

---

[100] Paul's visit to Jerusalem in Acts 21 shows that he was being compliant to James's suggestion that he show himself as a Jew at the temple by paying for the Nazarite vows of four young men. This was to combat the rumour that Paul was jeopardizing the Jewish faith in the outer territories of the Empire (Acts 21:21). Paul was bringing famine relief from Gentile churches to Jerusalem as an act of solidarity and unity of the Gentile Christian communities with the Jewish Christian community in Judea.

[101] These Gentile communities saw themselves as separate from the Jewish communities, not an extension of them. Eckhard J. Schnabel points out that the conversion of Jews to followers of Jesus would deplete the membership in synagogues and create a concern of diminishing numbers among the committed Jewish nationals (Schnabel, "Jewish Opposition to Christians in Asia Minor in the First Century, *Bulletin for Biblical Research*, 263).

[102] Craig Keener writes that "Peter, who knew that there was nothing inherently wrong with this gentile sort of lifestyle, was compelling gentiles to adopt a Jewish lifestyle. This compulsion violates the agreement that allowed both groups to follow their own culture (2:9; Acts. 15:29; 21:21, 25), an agreement that Paul believed he still followed" (Keener, *Galatians: A Commentary*, 171).

[103] *"For God has imprisoned everyone in disobedience so he could have mercy on everyone"* (Romans 11:32, NLT).

TRUTH ABOUT WHAT DELIVERS US FROM EVIL

There is nothing as evil in a community as holding others to expectations that one doesn't expect of oneself. Paul, infuriated by Peter's hypocritical actions, called Peter out in front of Christ's community in Antioch. His actions resulted in the "pressuring"[104] of the believers to go along with the divisive behaviour Peter exhibited.

While trying to be careful not to offend the visitors, Peter offended Paul and the Gentile believers at Antioch. His actions worked toward "judaizing"[105] the Gentiles, something that the visitors were attempting to do all over Asia Minor.

This was not representative of the good news, nor of the person of Christ. In fact, it represented the ongoing historical division among nations, people set against people, exhibiting hostility, hatred, and prejudice, symptoms of the present evil age.

The distorted good news perpetuated evil. This is the subtlety of how evil works. It takes what is good, the law, and takes advantage of it to make it death to us (Romans 7:22–23).

Paul then points out that he and Peter had no advantage as Jews over Gentiles in the matter of one's standing before God. One's background can't change the reality that righteousness doesn't come from law-keeping, but rather by faith. Righteousness isn't what a person becomes by their own effort; it's the product of a restored relationship with God through Christ. This has been true from the beginning of the biblical witness.

The first time that the term "righteousness" appears in the Bible is when the writer of Genesis 15: 6 comments, *"He [Abraham] trusted Yahweh, and He [Yahweh] counted it to him as righteousness"* (my translation).[106] The term has a relational foundation, as it's a byproduct of being in relationship with God.

In fact, the Hebrews, with their many titles for God, said that the Lord *"is our righteousness"* (Jeremiah 23:6, NLT).[107] This is a messianic reference where

---

[104] Walter Bauer tells us that the first order of meaning for the Greek word ἀναγκάζω is "necessity, pressure of any kind, outer or inner, brought about by the nature of things, a divine dispensation, some hoped-for advantage, custom or duty, etc." (Bauer, *A Greek English Lexicon of the New Testament and Other Early Christian Literature* [Chicago, IL: University of Chicago, 1979], 52). The hoped-for advantage of Peter in the presence of those from Jerusalem put pressure on the Antioch believers.

[105] The word ἰουδαΐζειν, literally translated in its infinitive form, is "to live like Jews do." I chose the word *judaize* since the goal of the imposters from Jerusalem was to make the Gentile believers comply with Jewish customs and become Jewish—in essence, to be judaized.

[106] According to James D. G. Dunn, "the issue addressed by Paul is how someone is 'justified.' His key text is Gen. xv.6 (Gal. iii.6; Rom. iv.3), which he clearly understands to say that Abraham was justified by his faith. Gal. ii.16 is most obviously heard as sounding the first note on that theme" (Dunn, *Black's New Testament Commentary*, 139).

[107] There is no focus on individual righteousness that puts the nation of Israel in relationship with God besides the righteousness expressed by the Messiah.

the Lord promises to send a new king to Israel, bearing this title. This king will renew the people's covenant with God and re-establish them as God's people. This demonstrates that, in the Jewish Scriptures, righteousness is not something to be earned by law-keeping but rather a product of what God does for humanity, putting us into right relationship with Him.[108]

Paul's conversion opened his eyes to the risen Jesus, who had fulfilled this prophecy of Jeremiah. Paul then reminds Peter that believers, both Jew and Gentile, are drawn into a relationship with God by putting their trust in Christ. One could speculate that this subject came up between Peter and Paul when Paul visited the first time, based on his biographical sketch at the end of Galatians 1.[109]

For the sake of clarity, the essence of this is best considered by adopting what, in this author's estimation, seems to be the most logical conclusion. This section of Galatians is historical and theological, accounting for a human being's atonement and deliverance. Jews trace their identity back to Abraham, a Gentile who heard the voice of God and converted from idolatry and a culture that sought to establish its own power.[110] God promised that all nations would be blessed through Abraham. This is parallel to the Adamic promise from Genesis 1, evidence that God was redeeming the idolatry and waywardness of the pre-patriarchal history.[111] Abraham responded to the promise by trusting God for an heir to carry on a lineage of his relationship with God.

At this point in the biblical narrative, the focus of relationship for humanity was on what God would do. If the nation that emerged from Abraham remained in covenant relationship with Him, then through them He would draw the

---

[108] T.F. Torrance writes, "That he is our righteousness, is the gospel message, so that its being freely offered to us for our righteousness is the glad tidings of the gospel. That is why repentance is not ascetic love of feeling guilty but the life of joyful self-denial in which we find our righteousness and truth *not in ourselves but in Christ alone*" (Torrance, *Atonement: The Person and Work of Christ* [Downers Grove, IL: IVP Academic, 2009], 108, emphasis added).

[109] Two Apostles in dialogue, meeting for the first time, could no doubt have covered a wide spectrum of content over the course of fifteen days. I think of what my colleagues at Master's College and I talk about in the span of just a couple of hours! A lot of ground must have been covered in that first meeting.

[110] For example, consider the lineage of Cain that createed the violent culture of Lamech in Genesis 4:17–25.

[111] Chee-Chiew Lee tells us, "The divine initiative to make Abraham into a great nation and to make his name (שׁם) great (Gen. 12:2) stands in stark contrast to the humanly initiated attempt by the nations, which was thwarted by God, to make a name (שׁם) for themselves (Gen. 11:4)" (Lee, *The Blessing of Abraham, the Spirit, and Justification in Galatians* [Eugene, OR: Pickwick Publications, 2013], 64). Compare this with what we read from N.T. Wright: "Abraham emerges within the structure of Genesis as the answer to the plight of all humankind" (Wright, *The New Testament and the People of God*, 262).

nations to Himself.[112] If it didn't, God would accomplish His purpose of recovering humanity regardless.

Gentile God-fearers who joined Jews in their synagogue worship proved that Jews still understood God's purpose of drawing other nations into relationship with Him. Their anticipation of the Messiah's appearance in the first century reiterated their expectation concerning what God would do for Israel and the nations.

Over the course of Hebrew history, the nation deviated from their God-given calling in Abraham. The Torah became a single definitive marker that set them apart from their pagan neighbours. Observing the laws in the Torah that were challenged by their neighbours—such as Sabbath-keeping, food laws, and circumcision—became the evidence that a person was Jewish.

Through exile after exile, occupation after foreign occupation, challenge after challenge, the Jewish psyche developed a law-focused religion. Many expressions of this existed in the world of the first century. From Zealots to Essenes to would-be Messiahs, people held up their Jewish practices against the pagans, holding them with great commitment.[113]

When Paul called out Peter in Galatians 2:16, he referenced the understanding that God made Israel righteous because its people trusted God's promises and actions. By doing this, he reminded the Galatians of the true Jewish understanding of what it meant to be in relationship with God, in terms of the narrative found in the Torah. He pointed out that Jesus was the fulfillment of that promise to Abraham.[114]

The distorted gospel instead focused on law-keeping along with faith in Christ. These imposters represented the Jewish preoccupation with law, inherited from centuries of exile. They added law to where it didn't belong.[115]

---

[112] Thomas Cahill reiterates the focus of Israel as the people to whom God reveals Himself and through whom others would come to Him as the real and true God: "If God—the Real God, the One God—was to speak to human beings and if there was any possibility of their hearing him, it could happen only in a place stripped of all cultural reference points, where even nature (which was so imbued with contrary, god-inhabited forces) seemed absent. Only amid inhuman rock and dust could this fallible collection of human beings imagine becoming human in a new way. Only under a sun without pity, on a mountain devoid of life, could the living God break through the cultural filters that normally protect us from him" (Cahill, *The Gift of the Jews* [New York, NY: Doubleday, 1998], 161).

[113] N.T. Wright, *The Challenge of Jesus*, 37.

[114] We'll discuss this further when we get to Galatians 3.

[115] They used the law as a tool of protection so that they were in control over their own culture. Jesus pronounced warnings over those who hid behind their manmade barriers of protection. Jacques Ellul writes, "Woe to the Pharisees who put their confidence in their personal holiness, in their strict observance of tradition. Woe to the scribes and doctors of the law who put their confidence in a perfect knowledge of the law and in their science of sacred things.—what characterizes these woes—is that they are all aimed at one attitude of man. In every case, man may be observed putting his confidence elsewhere than in God. In every case, man tries to make himself the center of his

The Jews of the time believed that their faith was, and should remain, a strictly Jewish thing, and therefore they felt that Gentiles must become Jewish for God to continue what He was accomplishing through Jesus the Messiah.

The reality of Paul's and Barnabas' mission is that God was showing them otherwise. The Holy Spirit came on Gentiles as they embraced Jesus as Messiah, expanding their understanding of how God was going to save Gentiles through Israel.

God's promise to Abraham would be accomplished through the work of Christ, and the emergence of Christian communities all over the Empire was a sign that God was progressing in His Abrahamic promise and that law observance didn't play a part in the transformation of Gentiles. The good news was bigger than the nation of Israel. In fact, it is of cosmic proportions.

Paul emphasizes to Peter and those listening that *"no human being will be put right by following the law"* (Galatians 2:16, my translation). The law doesn't have the power to deliver fallen humanity from sin, nor the ability to keep people faithful. But Christ has delivered fallen humanity from evil, and the pleasure of the Father is to recover Jews and Gentiles through His overall plan to wipe out evil and redeem His creation.

The only way to keep relationship with God in the present evil age is to trust in the faithfulness of Christ, who is delivering us from evil and leading us into the age to come by giving us His Spirit.

This is the continuation of Jewish eschatology, with a focus on Jesus the Messiah. The metaphor of righteousness is then not a declaration of "acquittal," but rather an expression to explain how Jesus has pardoned us and put us right with the Father. What this does for us, as followers of Christ, is give us access to the Father through Christ and by the Spirit.[116]

Paul explains this free access in Ephesians 2:

---

life, to put his reason for existing in something he possesses, and which he uses to protect himself against God" (Ellul, *The Meaning of the City* [Grand Rapids, MI: Eerdmans, 1993], 116–117).

[116] Fee points out that righteousness is but one metaphor describing both the condition and process of salvation of humanity on God's part. In his estimation, it's wrong for scholars to declare that "justification by faith" is the primary metaphor. We need to properly understand the context in which Paul uses it. There are other metaphors: "if enslaved by sin—then the metaphor is redemption, if enmity with God—then the metaphor is reconciliation, if under God's wrath—the metaphor is propitiation." He points out that Paul never mixes these metaphors, where "slave is reconciled" or "one under God's wrath" is redeemed. When Paul uses one metaphor, he sticks with it to make the point in a particular passage. Fee reacts to the translation of δικαιόω as meaning "to justify," since this Latin word expresses acquittal, assuming that the guilty party has done nothing wrong. Only innocent people are acquitted. Fee prefers to define this word as "being put right" or "righteousized," demonstrating both pardon by Christ and restoring of relationship with the Father (Gordon D. Fee, *Pentecostal Commentary Series*, 83).

...he announced the good news of peace to those who were far away [Gentiles] and to those who are near [Jews]. Now through Jesus we both have access by one Spirit to the Father. You are no longer strangers and foreigners belonging nowhere, but citizens of God's community built on the foundation of the Apostles and Prophets; its cornerstone is Jesus Christ himself, in whom the whole community is joined together, growing into God's holy dwelling place. You are being built into this community where God dwells by His Spirit.
(Ephesians 2:17–21, my translation)

In this passage, Paul articulates the nature of the new people of God. They're made up of both Gentile and Jew who have direct access to the Father. This access comes not through their law-keeping but through Christ and by the Spirit. It is a free access built upon the message of both Apostles and prophets, or the witness of Jesus and Old Testament witness of God. The result is the establishment of a new temple. Paul uses the term *"holy dwelling place."* In this new temple, there is no sacrifice or rigid law-keeping, but rather a community defined by the Spirit and in relationship with the Father and Son.

Peter's behaviour put all this at risk, deceiving others into dividing themselves into categories of worth fuelled by privilege and segregation. None of this was promoted by the witness of God in the Torah or the witness of Christ through His life, death, resurrection, and ascension. It was distorted through the insecurities of the Jewish nation that chose to hold to a flashlight and set of candles to preserve their identity.

This was enough for Paul to confront Peter and stop the damage being done.

As shepherds of Christ's communities in our present day, we must intervene when our communities create division. In fighting to keep the freedom Christ has given us, we must find the courage to confront those who set out to model a distorted theology that destroys community. No one individual is bigger than the good news!

Paul cashed in all his relational capital with Peter that ominous day when he pointed out Peter's hypocrisy. Surely he didn't do it lightly but was compelled by the true nature of the good news of Christ. His obvious goal was to stop the divisive behaviour by Peter and remind Christ's community that we are all called to freedom that exemplifies the true nature of the Father, Son, and Spirit. Such a community shows to the world the true humanity the Father has always desired for them, regardless of their background.

TRUTH ABOUT LAW-KEEPING

There is a clash of perspectives in what Paul addresses next with Peter. Galatians 2:17 reads, *"But if, as we seek to be made right in Christ, we discover that we are sinners, does that make Christ a servant of sin? Never! For if I establish again the things that I left behind, then I am the law breaker"* (my translation).

The phrase *"that we are sinners"* is best interpreted as how those imposters assess a faith-focused relationship with Christ. In their minds, if the law is ignored, the one who focuses only on faith contravenes the law and is deemed sinful. In this verse, Paul takes on the voice of his opponents, rather than his own perspective.[117] Consistent with the imposters is the criticism that if one ignores the law and focuses solely on faith, they insinuate that Christ Himself is sinning, the implication being that Christ is ignoring the law as well.[118] Paul draws this out as the natural conclusion of the imposters' criticism of the good news he preached.

Paul's rebuttal is a clear and strong declaration that this is reflective of the distorted good news. It's far from where the good news lands on the issue of law-breaking. Abandoning law-keeping and embracing Christ through faith is at the heart of the good news. Adding law-keeping as a requirement causes one to break, or transgress, the good news, reverting to a structure that Paul observed prior to conversion, where the law was worn as a badge of nationalism.

Rebuilding what was destroyed is the actual act of law-breaking. In this sentence, Paul uses the word παραβάτην[119] to indicate that the imposters are the law-breakers. They are contravening God's covenant action of forgiveness through Christ that marks one as righteous and restores them to relationship.

N.T. Wright exclaims that this is a foundational change of identity:

> Who then are we? We are the Messiah's people, with his life now at work in us. And, since the central thing about him is his loving

---

[117] Ronald Y.K. Fung, *The New International Commentary on the New Testament*, 119.

[118] *"But suppose we seek to be made right with God through faith in Christ and then we are found guilty because we have abandoned the law. Would that mean Christ has led us into sin?"* (Galatians 2:17, NLT)

[119] This word comes from the Greek verb παραβαίνω. The noun form used by Paul in this sentence, παράβασις, "is associated with more general concepts rather than with concrete individual commandments—it derives its basic meaning in the LXX to neglect God, to break the covenant" (W. Gunther, "Sin," *New International Dictionary of New Testament Theology, Volume Three*, 584). Gunter points out that Paul uses this word to convey that "the law is no longer central in the Christian faith. It has been displaced from its function as a way of salvation by *pistis*, faith, which is made possible through the coming, the death and the resurrection of Jesus Christ. Hence the concept chiefly appears in Paul where he is involved in argument with the Jewish theology of law" (Ibid.)

faithfulness, the central thing about us, the only thing in fact that defines us, is our own loving faithfulness, the glad response of faith to the God who has sent his son to die for us. This is the very heart of Christian identity.[120]

The fabricated conviction of observing the law to stay in relationship with God is a deviation that goes against God Himself. Paul emphasizes that if law-breaking is a concern, going against this foundational faith-focused relationship with God is the true sense of being a lawbreaker.

According to author Scot McKnight, "The regulations of the Jews are fine (cf. Rom. 7:12), [but] the guidelines for the Christian are to be found in following Christ and living by the Spirit."[121] Breaking faith with Christ by rejecting the pathway He has laid out for righteousness is to reject Christ's way as the culmination of covenant with God the Father.

All this should warn us that if we add anything to Christian practice that hints at our actions giving us an advantage over others, we're moving back to the old identity of law-keeping to remain in community. Our advantage, which belongs to everyone, is that Christ has drawn us close. His actions demonstrate His faithfulness and draw us back to community with the Trinity.

This is the essence of righteousness. Our view should be that of complete and total trust in Christ for all that we are and will become in our restored relationship with the Father. This is the kind of freedom that gives us a place of connection with God whereby the Spirit helps us stay connected and focused on faith in Christ. When we embrace this new identity, we give up proud, defensive, fearful, divisive, judgmental, and prejudiced behaviour. In turn, we assume the behaviours of love, acceptance, forgiveness, and grace that speak of who God truly is and gives others a glimpse of what life in Christ has to offer (Galatians 5:16–22).

In Galatians 2:19–20, Paul explains how he now functions in relationship to Christ. It became possible to focus on Christ by dying to the law altogether. By this, Paul means death to having to live focused on law-keeping as a marker

---

[120] N.T. Wright, *Paul for Everyone*, 26, emphasis added.

[121] Scot McKnight writes further that "the Jewish Christian—forfeits the opportunity of ever turning to the law as the ground of one's acceptance with God or the basis of one's morality and the guide for life" (McKnight, *The NIV Application Commentary*, 2187). If Jewish Christians want to continue with the law, it would only be effective in terms of their outward demonstration of allegiance to their country and co-nationals. Staying connected to their relationship with Christ through law-keeping isn't possible since that connection comes from Christ alone.

of our relationship with God. His old life made law-keeping the focus so he was unable to truly live in relationship with the Father.[122]

The crucifixion of Jesus was an event whereby Christ took on the fallen humanity of Paul, along with all of humanity, freeing him from condemnation through the law and enabling him to live by Christ living in him. This idea of Christ living *in* him is the desire of the Father, Son, and Spirit to be in relationship. It's mentioned by the Apostle John, in Jesus's words to His disciples: *"Since I live, you also will live. When I am raised to life again, you will know that I am in my Father, and you are in me, and I am in you"* (John 14:19–20, NLT). This giving of Himself opened the door for the life of the Trinity to abide in Paul.

Paul now lives in his human flesh, by faith, not by law-keeping. Faith keeps him focused on Christ and Christ's faithfulness ensures that he stays connected. Rather than being motivated by the fear of being left out (the old identity of law-keeping) he lives motivated by knowing that he is loved (the sacrifice of Jesus that opens the door to relationship with the Father).[123]

This is the focus of the point Paul makes in the letter. If a person has any hope of being in relationship with Christ, they must die to their old self so they can live toward their new self, which finds its source in the life of Christ through intimate relationship with the Trinity.[124] This shift in identity makes it possible for fallen humanity to have hope in moving toward the new humanity Christ has given.

---

[122] James D.G. Dunn writes, "And that encounter [with Christ] so completely turned upside down his understanding of the law and the covenant promises, that the law ceased from that time to exercise the same hold over him; that which had been his constant stimulus to action now failed to find any response in him; he became dead to what had previously been his primary motivating force" (Dunn, *Black's New Testament Commentary*, 143).

[123] This is the prospective aspect of Christ's work that continually brings more of the life of Christ to us so we can move toward who the Father wills us to become. Righteousness has this prospective aspect. Scholars, pastors, students, and members of Christ's community need to be careful not to rest completely on the retrospective aspects of righteousness (that which Christ saved us from). There is a purpose and goal to the retrospective aspects of righteousness, and that is the prospective realities that are to come as we live in relationship with the Father and the Son, through the help of the Spirit. J. Macleod Campbell writes that "the atonement is to be regarded as that by which God has bridged over the gulf which separated between what sin had made us, and what it was the desire of the divine love that we should become" (Campbell, *The Nature of the Atonement*, 127).

[124] Paul encourages the readers of his Ephesian letter to make this very important shift: *"What you learned was to put away your old way of living, which only made you worse because of the insatiable appetite for empty things, and to be renewed in the Spirit of your mind. Put on your new humanity that has been created for righteous relationship and holy living"* (Ephesians 4:22–24, my translation; see Lombardi, *A New Humanity*, 83).

The believer is in a process of transition. Sin is still possible in this new identity, but the connection of relationship with Christ through faith gives us access to the Spirit, who helps us press forward to our transformation as new humanity.[125]

The love of the Son is felt by Paul through what was seen in his autobiographical section in Galatians 1–2. The Son revealed Himself to Paul, transforming his life and setting him on the path of preaching the good news. The love is so divine and complete that Paul desires to live in it. It bears no comparison to the life of dependence on the law.

There was no desire at all for him to return to the angry, hateful man he had been, going out of his way to force others to live in slavery to the law. He would not throw out the grace of God by continuing to focus on law-keeping.[126]

This total dependence on Christ as the source of life is the focal point of Paul's response to the good news. It has clear implications of giving oneself over to God, considering the incredible sacrifice of love that the Father, through Christ, has given humanity.

There is a parallel statement in his letter to Romans 12:1:

---

[125] Several scholars translate σάρξ to mean simply "the body." Their focus is to identify how Paul will go on living given his new relationship with Christ living in him. One should not miss as well that Christ living in him is Christ aligning Himself with Paul's fallen humanity, so that the gift of new humanity can gradually take shape. If it was a complete transformation, so that Paul was living in a state of completion, then he wouldn't later write that *"if another believer is overcome by some sin, you who are godly should gently and humbly help that person back onto the right path. And be careful not to fall into the same temptation yourself"* (Galatians 6:1, NLT). Since Paul uses this word sixteen times in the Galatian letter, it is difficult to separate it from the fallen quality which he attributes to it in the other passages. Most likely, he speaks of how σάρξ, the person who puts faith in Christ, will eventually become new humanity, otherwise they will self-destruct. A.C. Thistleton writes, "On the one hand, Paul can say that the believer no longer lives in the flesh (Rom. 7:5; 8:8f.; Gal. 5:24). But on the other hand, as a believer, Paul still lives in the flesh" (Thistleton, "Flesh," *New International Dictionary of New Testament Theology, Volume One*, 676).

[126] The verb ἀθετῶ is a derivative of τίθημι, meaning "to set aside," with the prefix α giving the action of setting aside a negative connotation (Harold K. Moulton, ed., *The Analytical Greek Lexicon Revised* [Grand Rapids, MI: Zondervan, 1977], 8). In this sense, Paul uses the verb to denote the negative act of "rejecting" grace as the result of being a law-keeper. The negative particle οὐκ that precedes the verb indicates that Paul will not deal with God's grace so flippantly, especially after what he experienced with Christ. He says in his letter to Titus what they once were without the grace of Christ: *"For we were also once foolish, disobedient, deceived, serving various lusts and pleasures, living in malice and envy, hateful, and hating one another"* (Titus 3:3, my translation). He encourages Titus to now, in Christ, *"speak evil of no one, not to be contentious, to be gentle, showing all humility toward all men"* (Titus 3:2, my translation).

And so, dear brothers and sisters, I plead with you to give your bodies to God because of all he has done for you. Let them be a living and holy sacrifice—the kind he will find acceptable. This is truly the way to worship him. (NLT)[127]

Rather than focusing on the Torah and its observance as an act of sacrifice, Paul says that it's the whole person God desires, not the actions we perform. Our whole person in the hands of God benefits from the work of Christ and has the capacity to become the new humanity that the Father has desired for us at creation. It is the most logical thing to do.[128]

Law-keeping will never achieve this. At best, it will placate the Jewish Christian's non-Christian counterpart and satisfy the prevailing view that kept one part of Israel. But it has no ability to offer the kind of transformation that comes through Christ's work for us.

Paul makes the nature of righteousness evident in the last sentence of this section. In Galatians 2:21, Paul uses the word *dikaiosune,* which has the connotation of "being made right" or "in right standing." The verb form, *dikaioo,* denotes "to justify" or "to be righted."[129]

God's acts of mercy and grace keep the people in covenant, which is consistent with the Old Testament view of God's righteousness benefiting the people of Israel. In this sense, according to author Colin Brown, it was "not a matter of actions conforming to a given set of absolute legal standards, but of behaviour which is in keeping with the two-way relationship between God and humanity."[130]

God's righteousness was displayed by His forgiveness of Israel's idolatry and waywardness. Israel remained in covenant by keeping God's commands

---

[127] In Romans 12:1, Paul uses the Greek σώματα for "body." This is the more generic term for the physical body, but for Paul the use of this form refers specifically to human existence. Even in the sense of spirit, for Paul it is a bodily, somatic existence. This passage shows how Paul identifies the σῶμα: "not merely as an outer form but the whole person" (S. Wibbing, "Body, Member, Limb," *New International Dictionary of New Testament Theology, Volume One,* 234).

[128] Paul's use of λογικὴν expresses the act of giving oneself to God as the "reasonable" thing to do, given the knowledge of Christ's work of love for us. The NIV translates this word in Romans 12:1 as "reasonable." The NLT further interprets it to reflect the type of spiritual worship that makes sense for a God who gives us His life in return.

[129] Colin Brown writes, "Paul thus makes the most frequent use of this whole word-group and gives it its widest range of meanings. Of all NT writers, he it is who establishes the closest connexion with the OT, when speaking of God's righteousness and God's justification of sinners, God's righteousness is essentially his covenant dealings with his people, who are thereby constituted a new humanity, a new—Israel comprising both Jews and Gentiles" (Brown, "Righteousness, Justification," *New International Dictionary of New Testament Theology, Volume Three,* 363).

[130] Ibid., 355.

and remaining close to God in relationship.[131] Later rabbinic thought identified righteousness completely with Torah-keeping, a shift away from God and toward human achievement, placing the onus on the individual to stay in covenant.[132] Paul makes it clear that such a focus will never accomplish righteousness. *Dikaiosune* is an exclusive act of God toward humanity through the life of Christ, not an act of humanity that keeps one in relationship with God.

The fallout of law-keeping is that it doesn't accomplish righteousness at all; it fulfills the role God gave the law, which is to make humanity aware of its sin and subsequent need of God (Galatians 3:19ff). Law-keeping doesn't result in the surrender of one's fallen humanity to God. Without surrender, one cannot be transformed into the new humanity for which we are destined. No actions are required on our part to conform to God's law, but rather we are to offer ourselves to God in Christ so that by His Spirit He can work in us to be truly human.[133]

By following the law, Christians infer that Christ didn't need to come and die. The resurrection is declared null and void. God's grace is not real for such people, as they prefer to take matters into their own hands and secure their own righteousness. In doing so, they secure their own condemnation.

This is the point Paul has made so far. Law-keeping doesn't ward off evil by keeping one in covenant with God under His covering. In fact, it promotes evil by keeping evil ever in front of people.

I hope it's becoming clear to you that to legalize your faith, to apply rules and regulations to earn your relationship with God, is to ensure that distance is created between you and God. Controlling the process of our continued membership in Christ's community is an act of rebellion against Christ Himself.[134] It creates a

---

[131] This was the purpose of God giving way to the sacrificial system: to provide Israel with a way of continuing in relationship in light of their waywardness.

[132] Brown, *New International Dictionary of New Testament Theology, Volume Three*, 358.

[133] As T.F. Torrance writes, "The great problem here is that the law does not really deal with the root of sin, but on the contrary helps to maintain sin in being before the law. From the sinner's angle, it suits them well that God should deal with them in terms of law, because law is planted between them and God and keeps God at a distance from them. That is why the dialectic of sin always yields the legal outlook, for under the pressure of God the sinner falls back upon formal observance of the law in which as much of the responsibility is thrown upon the law for the rightness or wrongness of action as upon the human person. *It is thus that the sinner can yield obedience formally to the law without actually surrendering the citadel of the soul, without committing themselves in really responsible action. Likewise, the dialectic of sin produces an impersonal and abstract outlook, for sin refracts the immediacy of truth and exchanges the spirit for the deadness of the letter, exchanges God for an ideal*" (Torrance, *Atonement*, 113, emphasis added).

[134] John Stott tells us, "For both the grace of God and the death of Christ become redundant, if we are masters of our own destiny and can save ourselves" (Stott, *The Bible Speaks Today: The Message of Galatians* [Downers Grove, IL: InterVarsity Press, 1968], 66).

divisive environment. It is Christ who causes us to belong, regardless of what we do to keep ourselves in community. Fabricated righteousness is a distraction and deterrent to true life in Christ.

As I think of Paul's words in these two chapters, I think of my own walk with Christ and whether I have created any false constructs that seem to keep me in relationship with Christ while they in fact put up a wall. Like Peter, in my desire not to offend others, am I promoting a false sense of righteousness? Or do I cling daily to the work of Christ and let His Spirit work in me to transform me?

I pray that I will never be so foolish as to think I can achieve relationship with the Triune God of grace on my own. May we let Christ live in us so that His life becomes the source of our daily living. May we realize the freedom that comes from simply giving ourselves to Christ and letting His life refresh and restore us.

It is Christ who has given Himself over to rescuing us from our bondage to evil. That rescue is solely performed by God in Christ, and we have nothing to do except surrender to His saving work. In this work, He causes us to taste of the age which is to come,[135] an age which is the same for both Jew and Gentile, bringing freedom for us to live in a world void of evil, where God is present with us all. Staying in relationship with Him then is to let Him continue the work of our transformation through the Spirit working in us. The end goal will be our full transformation to our new humanity.

As we move into the next chapter, Paul will work through the covenant history of God's relationship with Abraham to confirm the foundation of Israel's salvation story, which is Jesus fulfilling the world's deliverance. We will also see how the law fits into this promise. Paul will show us how the Spirit has been present all along, through the work of Christ, to bring us continually into relationship with the Father. This is our true deliverance.

---

[135] N.T. Wright writes that "the important thing was to live within and celebrate the new world, not go rushing back to the old one where sin and death still held sway and where Jews and Gentiles ate at separate tables" (Wright, *The Day the Revolution Began*, 243). Compare this with what we read from Gordon D. Fee: "Christ, by his death 'for us,' has brought an end to Torah, opening up a way of life that is based on faith alone; but that life is not merely 'positional' righteousness, it is the real thing predicated on Christ by his Spirit living out God's own life in us. The rest of the letter spells it out in detail" (Fee, *God's Empowering Presence*, 377).

Chapter Six

WHAT STEALS OUR FREEDOM

Galatians 3:1–6

Stupid[136] Galatians, who brought this ill-fortune on you who saw clearly in our presentation to you that Jesus Christ was crucified? One thing I want to know from you: did you receive the Spirit by law-keeping, or by hearing the [good news] of faith? Are you stupid enough to think that having started with the Spirit, you can now finish it off on your own? Did you experience all this for nothing, if in fact it was for nothing? Does the one [Christ] who gives you the Spirit and works mighty deeds among you do it through law-keeping or through hearing [good news] of faith? Abraham trusted God, and it was credited to him as righteousness. Those who trust [the good news of faith] are the children of Abraham.

THE ATTRACTION OF A DECEPTIVE ARGUMENT

In this passage, Paul appeals to the Galatians based on their experience of the Spirit at their conversion. Paul's preaching of Jesus crucified resulted in the Galatian hearers receiving the Spirit.

This empowerment had transformed them in a way that was real and tangible. There had been a distinctive change in their outlook on the world and one another. They had completely embraced Christ and entered relationship with the Father, Son, and Spirit, putting their trust in Christ through the message

---

[136] The word Paul uses here is the root word for intelligence, νοέω, with the negative prefix ἀνόητος, indicating "unintelligence" (Moulton, *The Analytical Greek Lexicon Revised*, 31). The opposite of intelligence is stupidity. It's a strong and crass word but represents the emotion Paul felt about how the Galatian believers embraced the deception of the imposters in following the law as an obligation of their faith in Christ. Longnecker points out that Paul's tone is "biting and aggressive" (Longnecker, *Word Biblical Commentary, Volume 41: Galatians*, 99). Ronald Y.K. Fung says, "With obvious emotion (indicated by the word 'O': AV, RV, RSV) Paul chastises his readers as 'stupid Galatians.' Anoetoi denotes either an insufficient or mistaken use of mental powers or a deficiency in understanding itself" (Fung, *The New International Commentary on the New Testament*, 129). N.T. Wright adds that the word should be translated as "mindless" or "witless" (Wright, *Paul for Everyone*, 28). Finally, *La Sacra Bibblia Antico e Nuovo Testamento: La Nuova Diodati* (Brindisi, Italy: La Buona Novella, 1991) translates the word as "insensati" or "senseless." In all cases, it was a significant lack of judgment.

they'd heard and opening their hearts to receive the Holy Spirit whom Jesus had promised His followers. They had felt the Spirit's help as they began to live in relationship with Christ and perceived the unity that the Spirit brought to their community, where Jew and Gentile worshipped the Lord Jesus together.

How had they gone from such a transformation to living their life in Christ by law-keeping? Paul received word that they'd made a complete about-face, becoming keepers of the Torah and adhering to Jewish laws and customs, abandoning what they had experienced at their conversion.

It is not certain what the imposters did to convince the Galatians to shift over to law-keeping. There may have been some very persuasive individuals in this group of false missionaries. Could there have been some pressure tactics? Probably. Was there some massaging of Paul's message to make it sound like Paul was in line with what they were teaching? Most likely, since badmouthing Paul wouldn't have garnered the compliance they sought from the Galatians.

The deception of the imposters made the Galatians think that their teachings were part of Paul's good news, and it fooled the Galatians into thinking that Paul agreed with this. Perhaps they believed that Paul had missed a major piece of what was required as a follower of the Messiah. This argument would have been made by referencing Scripture[137] and the covenantal obligations of Israel, with a focus on the stipulations of circumcision in the Abrahamic covenant and the keeping of the law in the Mosaic covenant. By pressuring the Jews who were among them with scriptural evidence, and those Jews convincing the Gentiles in the Galatian community of their approval of the imposters' teaching, a radical shift occurred in their view of the good news.

Realizing that a community can be so easily deceived through convincing arguments, we should understand that we in the present could suffer the same fate. There seems to be a fine line between the intelligence of the good news of Christ and the stupidity of law-keeping that puts control in our hands rather than the Lord Jesus Christ.

The use of Scripture to support such a line of thinking can come across as biblical and authentic while at the same time being deceptive and distracting from the truth of the good news. The subtle advances of evil to undermine faith know no limit. Paul reminds Christ's community that the battle is *"not against*

---

[137] Gordon D. Fee writes, "Scripture played a crucial role in the agitator's [imposters] attempt to persuade the Galatians of the rightness of their case, and therefore that Paul's own use of Scripture is an attempt to outflank them, as it were, by showing that Scripture actually supports the inclusion of Gentiles by faith alone, apart from doing any aspect of the Law" (Fee, *Pentecostal Commentary Series*, 99).

fellow humans, but against heads, powers, and world rulers of our dark days and against the spiritual forces of evil in the heavens" (Ephesians 6:12, my translation).

Those people need to be rescued, like the imposters in Galatia; their minds and hearts have been drawn away by evil.

The powers at work through the distorted good news took advantage of the insecurity of the Jewish nation and caused them to believe that their law-keeping would protect them from evil, all the while perpetuating an internal evil they would perpetrate on others. The allure of the half-truth is enough to create a distortion of the truth.[138]

Like Paul with the Galatians, we need to address such distortions of the truth. The core of the good news is found in the story of Jesus giving Himself over to undo the evil that has been done to us and deliver us from the present evil age. Responding to all that seeks to undermine this good news is the role of Christ's community as it comes up against challenges from outside forces that seek to destroy both its focus and mission. Anyone or anything that opens the door to evil in Christ's community is a distortion that hinders the community's ability to share the good news with others.

The imposters no doubt made the Galatians believe they had missed a crucial piece of the puzzle. The sign of the Spirit should have been evidenced in their law-keeping. After all, the prophets had said that God would give the Spirit so the people could obey the law.[139] Being Jewish, they would have felt that Paul had ignored the Abrahamic and Mosaic stipulations on the law, which included circumcision, the observance of food laws, and Sabbath-keeping. Their critique would have centred on Paul being too general and focusing too much on Gentile conversion rather than Israel's covenantal fulfillment.

Paul responds to this critique by reminding the Galatians that the promise to Abraham is the clue to explaining what they had experienced upon hearing the news of Christ crucified. The Spirit coming on them resolved their disobedience. The resolution was in them being restored by God, not by keeping commands.

---

[138] In C.S. Lewis's *The Screwtape Letters*, the senior devil coaches the junior devil: "The real trouble about the set your patient is living in is that it is merely Christian. They all have individual interests, of course, but the bond remains mere Christianity. What we want, if men become Christians at all, is to keep them in the state of mind I call 'Christianity And'. You know—Christianity and the Crisis, Christianity and the New Psychology, Christianity and the New Order, Christianity and Faith Healing—If they must be Christians let them at least be Christians with a difference" (Lewis, *The Screwtape Letters: Letters from a Senior to a Junior Devil* [Glasgow, UK: Collins, 1987], 126).

[139] Craig Keener writes, "By contrast, Paul's opponents probably envisioned biblical prophecy differently: the Spirit should enable God's people to keep the law, as in Ezek. 11:19–20; 36:26–27. Paul might agree, but he envisioned the law in a very different way, by a very different, specifically Christocentric hermeneutic (cf. Gal. 5:14, 16–18, 22–23; 6:1–2)" (Keener, *Galatians: A Commentary*, 21).

This difference of opinion shows that Paul looked on the law not as command-keeping but rather a narrative providing guidance into what the Father planned for humanity.

The Spirit's coming fulfilled Old Testament prophetic promises telling us that the Gentiles would turn from their wickedness and be put right with God. This work of the "seed" of Abraham would fulfill both the Abrahamic promise for his descendants to bless the nations and Mosaic covenant promising a relationship with Israel.[140] That relationship would be sustained in the life of both Jew and Gentile as a continuing work of Christ by the Spirit, not by keeping the law.[141]

This will be elaborated in further detail when we get to Chapter Seven.

---

[140] See specifically what Chee-Chiew Lee writes: "As the Mosaic covenant was broken time and again, in the history of Israel, by their disobedience and failure to keep the covenantal stipulations, the prophets not only pronounced Yahweh's judgment in terms of the execution of the covenantal curses (e.g., Jer 11:1–17; Ezek. 20:1–38; Zech. 7:8–14; cf. Lev. 26:14–39; Deut. 28:15–68), but they also announced that Yahweh would restore his covenantal relationship with Israel after the judgment in terms of a new and everlasting covenant (e.g., Jer. 31:31–34; 32:36–44; Ezek. 37:26). Yahweh's Spirit, whose bestowal is described by the metaphors of 'outpouring' (Isa. 32:15; 44:3; Ezek. 39:29; Joel 2:28–29 [MT 3:1–2] and 'putting within' (Ezek. 36:27; 37:14), is the means by which the covenantal blessings are restored to Israel (cf. Lev. 26:1–13, 40–45' Deut. 28:1–14; 30:1–10). This vivifying Spirit: (1) restores life and prosperity to the people and their land (Isa. 32:15;44:3; Ezek. 37:14); (2) signifies the restoration of the divine-human covenantal relationship (Isa. 44:1–5; Ezek. 39:29); and (3) empowers the people to obey Yahweh (Ezek. 36:27), so that the covenantal blessings may be perpetuated, and the covenantal curses subverted permanently. This new and everlasting covenant not only restores the Mosaic covenant, but also ultimately fulfills the Abrahamic covenant (cf. Lev.26:40–42; Deut. 4:29–31)" (Lee, *The Blessings of Abraham, the Spirit and Justification in Galatians*, 134). Because of this reality in the Hebrew story, Lee emphasizes that "there will be a people from among the nations who will 'join themselves to Yahweh' by keeping covenant, and they shall thereby also become the people of Yahweh (Isa. 56:3–7; Zech. 2:11; cf. Isa. 19:18–24). These nations shall gather at the throne of Yahweh to worship him and walk in his ways (Isa. 2:2–3; 66:18–24; Jer. 3:16; 4:2; Zech. 8:20–23)" (Ibid.).

[141] Richard B. Hays says, "Paul's reading of the story of Abraham seeks to 'uphold the Law' by showing that the gospel of righteousness through faith is prefigured in the Law, that is, in the Genesis narrative. Obviously, such a construal of the Law is possible only in light of a profound hermeneutical shift. This shift has at least two important dimensions. First, Paul shifts from a reading of the law as *commandment* to a reading of the Law as *narrative of promise*—Second, the promise expressed in Scripture's narrative is a word addressed immediately to the church of Paul's own time. Paul repeatedly assumes that the word of Scripture is addressed directly to himself and his readers…" (Hays, *The Conversion of the Imagination: Paul as Interpreter of Israel's Scripture* [Grand Rapids, MI: Eerdmans, 2005], 96–97, emphasis added). Gregory A. Boyd adds, "Paul is well aware that disciples cannot live this cruciform life and share in Christ's suffering by their own power. It is only by means of the Spirit of the crucified and risen Lord working in us that this is possible (Gal. 2:19–20; Phil. 3:10; 1 Tim. 1:8). Indeed, Paul declares that the same 'incomparably great power' that raised 'Christ from the dead and seated him at [God's] right hand in heavenly realms' is now available 'for us who believe.' (Eph. 1:19–20)" (Boyd, *Crucifixion of the Warrior God, Volume One*, 198–199).

Paul points out in this section that refocusing one's faith on Torah-keeping betrays everything the people had experienced so far. It also betrays the scriptural evidence in the Hebrew story.

He concludes that evil has fallen on the Galatians, clouding their experience in the Spirit and turning their focus to law-keeping. It was like someone had cast a spell on them.[142] Paul saw the evil behind these imposters and perceived that Satan would have been glad to keep this movement contained.[143]

If the imposters came from the same attitude as the one Saul of Tarsus had, then no doubt they came to the Galatians with the agenda of making them Jewish and preventing this antinomian spread of the good news of Christ.

Their selfish intent robbed the Galatians of the freedom they had experienced in the Spirit. Such freedom is maintained by trusting in Christ and the work of the Spirit, not in confirming the Spirit's presence by Torah-keeping.

Undoubtedly, evil was working through the efforts of these imposters, just as the Spirit was working through the Apostles' missionary endeavours to bring the message of Christ crucified to the Gentile world.[144]

THE GOOD NEWS OF FAITH

Paul reminds the Galatians of the vivid picture he and his missionary team painted for them of Christ's crucifixion. The phrase "Jesus Christ crucified" was understood by the early Christian community to represent all that Jesus had done for them in His incarnation, life, death, resurrection, and ascension. It wasn't a singular focus on the cross as much as a reference to how much Jesus had accomplished for them.[145]

---

[142] The term ἐβάσκανεν, from the root βασκαίνω, describes the ancient superstition of giving one the evil eye: "to bewitch someone with the evil eye" (Frederick W. Danker, Walter Bauer, and William F. Arndt, *A Greek-English Lexicon of the New Testament and Other Early Christian Literature* [Chicago, IL: University of Chicago Press, 1979], 137). Also, Craig Keener describes the practice of magic in the culture of the first century, specifically pointing out evidence that the evil eye was used among Jews as well. He implies that these Jewish imposters may have invoked an "evil eye" on the Galatians to get them to abandon Paul's teaching (Keener, *Galatians: A Commentary*, 11–14).

[143] James D.G. Dunn tells us, "Paul may indeed be suggesting that the Galatian about-face could only be put down to 'demonic power'" (Dunn, *Black's New Testament Commentary*, 151).

[144] Acts 15:28 references the agreement between the Apostles at the Jerusalem council: *"It was good to the Holy Spirit, and to us, to put no greater pressure on you than is essential…"* (my translation) The Holy Spirit's involvement in leading Christ's community to expand beyond the Jewish community is clearly mentioned by Luke.

[145] Scot McKnight writes that "many times, Paul uses 'shorthand' by simply saying 'gospel' or 'my gospel' or the 'gospel of salvation' *or even 'Christ crucified.* But he always means this gospel—the gospel of the full, saving Story of Jesus resolving the Story of Israel, the one we found in shorthand in 1 Corinthians 15, and which then is fully expounded in the Gospels themselves…" (McKnight, *The King Jesus Gospel: The Original Good News Revisited* [Grand Rapids, MI: Zondervan, 2011], 61, emphasis added)

In Galatians 3:1, the phrase references not only the details of the actual crucifixion of Jesus[146] but the implications of that crucifixion on the curse of the law.

Paul's burden was to help the Galatians see the full story of God's work through Christ, not the smaller story of Israel's relationship with God and relationship to the law according to the distorted good news of the imposters.

Paul points out that just as Abraham's experience of faith, which resulted in restored relationship with God, occurred prior to the giving of the law, the Galatians' experience of the Spirit occurred before they were ever made conscious of the law.[147]

The result of their hearing the good news was that they received the Holy Spirit. How the Galatians received the Spirit isn't mentioned. More important to Paul is the fact that it was central to the Galatian experience at conversion.[148] It wasn't connected at all to law-keeping since that was not part of the good news they had received, nor would they have thought that it had any connection whatsoever. The imposters were the ones who had brought law into the picture of Christ being crucified.

Paul's rhetorical questions present the obvious conclusion that come from the Galatians themselves. They hadn't received any teaching on the law when they heard the good news from Paul. Having experienced what it was like to live by the Spirit as a follower of Christ, how could they then haven taken over and finished off the work of Christ on their own?

This of course is what focusing on law-keeping behaviour does to a follower of Christ; it forces a complete turn from being held and supported by Christ to

---

[146] According to David Wenham, "In his letter to the Galatians—it is probable that Paul is referring to how he and others explained the Christian good news to the Galatians" (Wenham, *Did St. Paul Get Jesus Right? The Gospel According to Paul* [Oxford, UK: Lion Hudson Place, 2010], 45). Wenham especially points out Paul's consistency with the Gospel narratives. The actual stories of Jesus would have been conveyed at the beginning of Paul's encounter with a new city and group of people, but in his letters he focused more on theologizing about their significance in relation to Christian practice and living. See also: Ibid., 54.

[147] Gordon D. Fee, *Pentecostal Commentary Series*, 102.

[148] James D.G. Dunn tells us, "Their experience of the Spirit was something to which Paul, and they could refer directly. What that experience amounted to—whether, for example, they spoke in tongues as evidence of Spirit reception (as in Acts. 10:44–48)—we cannot say. [That] the transformative power of the Spirit was the divine response to faith, to faith alone, means that for Paul the gift of the Spirit had the equivalent role from the divine side in the event of becoming Christian as faith has on the human side. And not just in becoming Christian, but in being Christian—as Paul makes clear in the rest of the letter" (Dunn, "The Christian Life from the Perspective of Paul's Letter to the Galatians," *The Christian Life from the Perspective of Paul's Letter to the Galatians*, 11).

holding and supporting oneself. It causes a follower to pick up their candles and flashlight.

Paul then encourages them to compare what they had experienced through the Spirit and evaluate whether it was valuable. Was it for nothing that the Spirit had come to them? Was there no benefit to what they'd experienced?

One wonders what the Galatians truly felt as they heard these words of Paul read aloud to them. Their obvious response would have been to question how they had come to faith and what they had experienced when they embraced the good news. Although there is no detail as to what their experience was, the account of Luke in Acts tells us that their receiving of the Spirit had been accompanied by inner transformation and mighty deeds of healing and restoration.[149]

Paul next asks the Galatians what motivated Christ in the work He had done among them. Was it law-keeping or His faithfulness to the mission of the Father to restore Israel and the Gentiles in His plan of recovery for humanity?[150] Again, the obvious answer would have been Christ's faithfulness. Jesus did not give the Spirit and work mighty deeds among the people by keeping the law. Christ died to this curse of law-keeping.

The reality of Paul's own experience is that he died to the law (Galatians 2:19). This is evidence of Paul's Christological view of Jesus's vicarious work of putting to death the subjugating influence of the law, freeing both Jew and Gentile from law-keeping altogether. Sin, being attached to fallen human flesh, incurs the curse of the law upon every human being. Putting this fallen flesh to death, as Christ did, breaks the power of sin that takes advantage of law and makes it death to us. Jesus took on the penalty of the law, disarming sin and the negative effects of the law.[151]

Paul uses his own experience to point out that he died to the law so that he might live for Christ. It was in Christ that Paul died, and it is "in Christ" that Paul continued to live.

---

[149] In Pisidian Antioch, Luke says that Gentiles were filled with "joy" and the Spirit upon hearing the good news, Acts 13:52. In Iconium, Luke says that *"the Lord proved their [Paul and Barnabas] message was true by giving them power to do miraculous signs and wonders"* (Acts 14:3, NLT). In Lystra, Paul prayed over a crippled man, and he was healed and could walk again (Acts 14:10).

[150] Surely Paul had related many of the gospel stories we can easily read from our own Bibles. One should remember that the Gospels were not in circulation among the Christian community in the first century. They relied on the teaching of the Apostles for the narrative of Jesus's time on earth.

[151] Paul elaborates on this concept in detail in Romans 7, where he describes to the Roman believers what it's like to live a life under the law instead of faith in Christ. Gregory Boyd highlights the type of warfare Christ uses, which conquers the tide of evil upon the human race. He uses the analogy of aikido warfare, which takes the force of the opponent and uses it against them (Gregory Boyd, "God's Aikido Way of Defeating Evil," *Renew.* April 1, 2013 (https://reknew.org/2013/04/gods-aikido-way-of-defeating-evil)].

The evidence of living "in Christ" is the marker of the Spirit, not the marker of law-keeping. The Spirit and work of Christ have to accomplish this transformation, because the law has been taken advantage of by sin, nullifying the ability of the law to obtain what Christ has achieved for us.

This was evident in the conversion experience of the Galatians. As an Apostle and pastor, Paul was trying to stop the distorted good news of the imposters from robbing the Galatians of their Christ-given freedom. He didn't want them to go back to the bondage of focusing on the law to stay in relationship with God.

Who would truly want that anyway? There was no freedom in keeping the law in the cultural way those of the Jewish nation in Paul's day required of one another. Law-keeping certainly didn't reflect the freedom that had come to the Gentiles when the Spirit came on them upon hearing the news of Christ crucified. It was a fabrication on the part of first-century Jews, their attempt to battle the storm of evil with two candles and a flashlight of their own making.

Paul continues in this chapter to show them how small and restricted was their historical memory of God's plan. His hope in this endeavour was to bring the Galatians back to their senses and help them see the big picture of the true scriptural narrative being fulfilled by Christ.

ABRAHAM AND RIGHTEOUSNESS

Paul ends this section by reminding the Galatians, both Jew and Gentile, that just as they had received the promise of God by hearing about Jesus and responding by putting their trust in Him, Abraham had also heard the voice of Yahweh and put his trust in Him. The result of this was that Abraham had been "put right" with God, just like the Galatians had been put right with the Father by trusting in Jesus Christ. For Abraham, this event preceded God's calling on him to circumcise all the males in his tribe.

At a lecture at Regent College in Vancouver in 1994, James B. Torrance affirmed his teaching on atonement: "The indicatives of grace always come before the imperatives of law."

The law is what God gave Israel to show them His expectation that they would be His people. But the law came after He had shown them what kind of God He is: a God who ransoms His people from oppression of evil and puts them in a place of freedom where they can live in relationship with Him.

In Abraham's encounter with God, he didn't find a law-based God but rather a God who loves humanity. God repeatedly instilled in Abraham that He wasn't like the gods of other nations; He had given Himself to humanity out of love.

The Father, Son, and Spirit, through the action of the cross, have demonstrated their deep love for humanity. It is the Triune God's deep desire to rescue men and women from evil and draw them back into fellowship.

As Paul points out, this rescue plan was put in place before humanity was created.

> *He chose us in Christ before the foundation of the world was put in place, to be holy and blameless in His sight. He lovingly planned beforehand our adoption through Jesus Christ in keeping with His own pleasure found in the fame of his glorious grace which He freely gives us from His loving relationship.* (Ephesians 1:4–5, my translation)

Paul identifies the reality of the Trinity's love for creation and humanity before they were brought into existence. The Trinity preempted the fall of humanity by setting in motion the plan of redemption through Christ even before their act of creation. Their foreknowledge moved them to come to humanity's rescue.

In this sense, God is truly Father of the human race. Everything else that comes into play through the story of humanity, including the giving of the law, must first and foremost be filtered through the love of the Triune God of grace.

It is the voice of the Father that Abraham heard, and he responded by trusting that this God, apart from all other gods, had his best interest at heart.

Today, the voice of the Father has resounded in our hearts through the life of Christ, especially in His sacrifice on the cross, to show all humanity that He has our best interest in mind. He rescues us and restores us as sons.

Interpreting God's character through the law-keeping focus of the imposters is to distort who He is. He cannot be defined through law, which is a secondary guide that points to Him as protector and redeemer. The law reminds humanity of its brokenness and need for God, but it cannot restore humanity (Galatians 2:16, 3:22, 5:6).

The law also doesn't have power to draw us into relationship with Father, Son, and Spirit, because it rests in our fallen hands. And although the law carries some light, like a set of candles and flashlight, it's not what you use as an ultimate source of light. It is temporary and weak at best. The true source of light, Jesus Christ, provides a constant connection for humanity to God as the Trinity sustains humanity, calling on it to trust.

The question is, who will you trust? Yourself? The law in your own hands? This sets us at a disadvantage, since our righteousness comes to depend on our own abilities. We don't have the ability to connect ourselves in relationship with God and keep evil at bay. Our fallenness has left us in this impotent state. We need God to remain in relationship, free from evil.

In the next passage, Paul will show the Galatians how misguided it is to make law the foundation of relationship with God. Such a structure betrays the way God desires relationship. He will use the example of Abraham's story of faith to highlight the basis of having an ongoing relationship with God. It is not circumcision that keeps one in relationship but rather putting one's trust in God and remaining in that trust as the relationship develops and matures.

Chapter Seven

THE PROMISE OF FREEDOM

Galatians 3:7–18

Those who trust [the good news of faith] are the children of Abraham. The Scriptures anticipated that by faith, God would put right the Gentiles, having shared this good news to Abraham that through him all the Gentiles will be blessed. That means that those who are of faith are blessed along with faithful Abraham. All those who are under law-keeping are cursed. It's documented that, "All who don't consistently keep all that is written in the law are cursed." Clearly no one is put right before God by the law, because "The righteous through faith will live."[152] The law is not of faith but rather [requires] that the one who keeps it will live by it. Christ ransomed us from the curse of the law, by becoming a curse for us. It's also documented that, "Cursed are all who hang up on wood," so that the blessing of Abraham may come to the Gentiles through Jesus Christ, and that we might receive the promise of the Spirit through faith.

Family members, when we speak of a human will, we know that when its confirmed, no one can change it or cancel it. The promises flowed to Abraham and his seed. It doesn't read, "To seeds," referring to many [such as the nation of Israel] but to one seed, which is Christ. That means that a covenant confirmed beforehand by God, cannot be made invalid by the law that came four hundred and thirty years later, destroying the promise. If the inheritance [of Abraham's blessing] comes through the law, then there is no more promise, but God graciously gave it to Abraham as a promise.

FAITH IN CHRIST AS FOCUS OF CHRISTIAN LIVING

Paul now moves into addressing the core argument presented to the Galatians by the imposters, that there was a two-pronged requirement in

---

[152] I chose to translate this phrase in the order Paul places the words since it opens the possibility to consider that Paul referenced both an objective, genitive reading—indicating the faithfulness of God as the keeper of the individual from the divine side—as well as a subjective, genitive reading—indicating the faith of the individual keeping them connected from the human side.

the Abrahamic story of both faith in God (Genesis 15:6) and circumcision (Genesis 17).

This two-sided emphasis on Abraham's covenant relationship with God was a predominant focus in Jewish writings.[153] These writers argued that Gentiles should expect that, by putting their faith in Christ, they must by necessity also follow the requirement of circumcision and law-keeping.

Paul's response is that the focus of the Abraham story, when it comes to both Jews and Gentiles, is our relationship with God based on faith. This came before the requirement of the law. The promise of blessing for the Gentiles was given by God to Abraham in Genesis 12:3 and was confirmed in Genesis 15:6 when Abraham was declared to be in relationship with God through placing his trust in Him. God then ratified His promise to Abraham by asking Abraham to bring animals for sacrifice and God burning the animals as a sign of His promise.[154]

Paul indicates to the Galatians that this is the best representation in the Hebrew story of what Christ did for them. By putting their faith in Christ, Christ offers them relationship with the Father through His sacrifice. Jesus sacrificing His life for their sake continues the pattern of God making provision for humanity to be in relationship with Him. Adding stipulations of law, like circumcision, is to take matters into one's own hand. The result is that one stops trusting in God.[155]

The imperatives of the law will always work toward leading humanity to God's gracious redemption and reconciliation. It does this by being relentless in its requirement on those who depend on it, and by not being associated

---

[153] Scot McKnight writes, "Jewish writers saw two features of his [Abraham] life: (1) he was considered righteous because he remained faithful through the test of God, and (2) Abraham's faith of Genesis 15:6 was intimately tied to his submission to circumcision in 17:4–14. Thus, believing and keeping the covenant stipulation of circumcision were to be done together; believing without being circumcised was contrary to Abraham" (McKnight, *The NIV Application Commentary*, 2884).

[154] The regular form of sacrifice was that the individual brought an animal to God and sacrificed it on an altar by burning the quartered pieces of the animal to send up an aroma that pleased God. But in this instance, God burned the quartered pieces to confirm His promise. This would have been foreign to Abraham. God showed Abraham that He was different from the other gods, who demanded sacrifice. This God gave of Himself for the sake of Abraham and humanity.

[155] N.T. Wright writes, "If Genesis 15 speaks of faith as the sign of covenant membership, Genesis 12, the opening of Abraham's story, promises that God will bless all the nations through him. Put the two together, and what do we have? In a short, tight-packed form, we have Paul's whole argument: when people believe the gospel of Jesus, they are already Abraham's true children. Not only is there no need to abandon faith as the badge of membership and try to ensure it some other way; to do so, like climbing off the back of the tight-rope walker [story of Blondin crossing the Niagara River on tight rope], is to court disaster" (Wright, *Paul for Everyone*, 31).

whatsoever in fulfilling the reception of the Spirit among both Jews and Gentiles. The law is a dead end.[156]

By being an end in itself, the law doesn't fulfill the ultimate goal of the Trinity restoring relationship with humanity. It leads one to condemnation. It is the faithfulness of Christ and trusting in that faithfulness that brings the promise of the Spirit to fulfillment.

The Spirit's presence in the Gentile community showed that God had been consistent in how He had related to humanity throughout history. By making provision through Christ for humanity to be in relationship with the Trinity, the presence of God by virtue of the Spirit's presence among the Gentiles confirmed that the focus of the good news is faith and not law-keeping.

As Abraham existed by faith in a relationship of trust with God, so by faith did the Galatians exist in relationship with the Spirit through trusting the message they had heard of Jesus the Messiah. The faith focus of the Abraham story demonstrates consistency in what the Galatians experienced, not the law part of the Abraham story that focused on circumcision. Abraham's story gets caught up into the Christ story.[157]

The Jesus story continued the promise God had made to Abraham concerning the nations. Law-keeping, as a focus of maintaining relationship with God, did not factor. In fact, in the beatitudes Jesus pointed out to the listeners in attendance that *"unless your righteousness is better than the righteousness of the teachers of religious law and the Pharisees, you will never enter the Kingdom of Heaven!"* (Matthew 5:20, NLT)

As Jesus went around teaching, people's faith led them to receive their salvation. The key to entering the kingdom, which is synonymous with being part of God's people, was to put one's trust in God. The kingdom doesn't come

---

[156] Scholars like E.P. Sanders say that Paul didn't condemn law-keeping but rather law-keeping for Gentiles so that they could be part of the new people of God who followed Christ. Although law-keeping may have had a benefit, it was of no use to anyone, Jew or Gentile, in terms of their right standing with God. Yes, the law is good, as Paul says in Romans 7, but the law in the hands of fallen humanity is destructive and divisive. As N.T. Wright puts it, it stands in the way of God creating one new family and redefining election around the Messiah (Wright, *Paul and the Faithfulness of God,* 860ff).

[157] Richard B Hays says, "The Abraham story is for Paul taken up into the Christ story, and the Christ-story is understood, with the hindsight of narrative logic, as the fit sequel to the Abraham story. Looking back upon the Abraham story from the world established by Christ-story, Paul perceives the proleptic character of Abraham as the recipient of a promise which was inherently unfulfillable in Abraham's own lifetime, a promise destined for fulfillment only in his seed" (Hays, *The Faith of Jesus Christ: An Investigation of the Narrative Substructure of Galatians 3:1–4:11* [Chico, CA: Scholars Press, 1983], 226).

to law-keeping religious leaders.[158] Law-focused righteousness results in keeping one from doing good on the Sabbath, putting rules and regulations ahead of people.

This became clear for Paul in his encounter with Jesus, who pointed out that such an action would be contrary to his mission of restoring people to relationship and the promise of the indwelling Spirit. This is the same behaviour that prevented both Jews and Gentiles from being brought close to the promise.

Jews, like Paul prior to his conversion, missed the point of what God had promised. Gentiles missed the promise because Jews were blinded to it with their law-centeredness. This law-keeping focus would have to die for the Gentiles to become people of God, and for their Jewish Christian brothers and sisters to receive the promise. According to Craig Keener, this made Paul's dismissal of the law, "maintained at great cost despite centuries of hostility… appear akin to betrayal of one's own people."[159]

The imposters were promoting an ongoing Jewish focus that nullified the benefit of the promise the Triune God desired for all humanity. Holding on to the Jewish focus on law-keeping robbed Christ's sacrifice of its benefit. They viewed the Abraham story by filtering it through a focus on commands, which led to this nationalistic and culturally protective behaviour. Paul later writes that Christ is "of no benefit" to those who lean on the law this way.[160]

Abraham was neither a law-keeper nor did he receive the law in such a way as to maintain relationship with God. It was faith that Abraham focused on for his relationship with God. Paul addresses him as *faithful* Abraham, not *law-focused* Abraham (Galatians 3:9).

Being a child of Abraham is to be a person of faith, one who puts their trust in Christ. It has nothing to do with blood lineage. Being a member of the Hebrew people doesn't automatically make one a child of Abraham, as Paul

---

[158] Consider what Jesus said to the woman whose many sins were forgiven in the event at Simon the Pharisee's home in Luke 7:50: *"Your faith has saved you; go in peace"* (NLT). Also consider the gracious acts of the Samaritan toward the injured Hebrew who was sidestepped by a priest and temple assistant because of the law's rules against defilement. In Luke 10:37, Jesus encouraged His listeners to *"go and do the same"* as the Samaritan in being gracious to others. Finally, think of the blind beggar who called out to Jesus and was healed of his blindness. Jesus says in Luke 18:35–42, *"All right, receive your sight! Your faith has healed you."* Here, Jesus affirmed that it wasn't law-keeping but trust that brought about the beggar's healing.

[159] Craig Keener, *Galatians: A Commentary*, 75.

[160] *"Be clear that I Paul tell you, if you accept circumcision, Christ will be of no benefit to you"* (Galatians 5:2, my translation).

defines in this letter. Although Abraham was the father of the Hebrew nation, and circumcision marked the nation,[161] this doesn't factor into the economy of faith. The currency spent in relation to Christ is that of faith, not law-keeping.

In this sense, we who have put our trust in Christ are children of Abraham. As a child of the father of faith, we put our trust in the faithfulness of Jesus so He can restore us to the Father. We focus that trust on the Triune God of grace who has adopted us into His family. Any move on our part to instead focus on behaviour creates a roadblock[162] for us and others. By focusing on the law, we make room for sin to take advantage of the law's curse and bring condemnation (Romans 7:13). The result is that we block the promise of the Spirit. Focusing on faith gives sin no room and allows the life of Christ to set us free. This freedom then opens the door to experiencing the indwelling Spirit and be drawn into the very life of the Father and Son.

Like the Jewish people using the law as evidence of their relationship with God, we can create behaviours and patterns that become identity markers that distract us and others from our true connection with God. We can minimize the benefit of our Saviour's sacrifice by placing requirements on others that prevent them from drawing near to Christ and being restored to the Father.

Shades of "anathema" resound again from Galatians 1. The horror of placing roadblocks in the way of getting near to God and embracing Christ should send a shiver across the Christian community.[163]

We need to examine what we hold as requirements of living out the Christian life and weigh them in terms of their merit in supporting the faith-focused good news Paul writes of in Galatians.

---

[161] Gordon D. Fee tells us, "Although Paul does not make a point of it here, it should be noted that this covenant [circumcision ratification in Genesis 17] had specially to do with the land, not with Abraham's relationship with God per se" (Fee, *Pentecostal Commentary Series*, 115). In the Old Testament, God's land assignments were something He dealt with personally with other nations, including Israel (Luciano Lombardi, "Land and Judgment: Toward a Clearer Understanding of God's Wrath on Other Nations in the Old Testament," *McMaster Journal of Theology and Ministry*, volume 8, 2007, 82–96).

[162] N.T. Wright refers to it as a traffic jam, writing, "Paul has just said that Abraham is to have a world-wide covenant family, characterized by *pistis* (3.6–9). That is what he says the covenant of God has achieved through the Messiah's death…" (Wright, *Paul and the Faithfulness of God*, 863) The eschatological destination of God's plan is one family made up of Jew and Gentile, ordered by Christ, chosen by the Father, and empowered by the Spirit.

[163] Paul's blindness after his encounter with Jesus in Acts 9 was both physical and theological. His focus on the law had blinded him to the reality of life in Christ and the freedom which the Father desired for him. We too are blind if we create obstacles that prevent us from embracing the full life of freedom in Christ that the Father has willed for us.

The candles and flashlights we have imported into our faith are flesh-focused utensils that serve no benefit. They render what Christ gave us useless, making room for sin to use the law against us.

Such is the danger of straying from a faith-focused life. Faith is the one and only move on our part that brings us into the freedom Christ has given us. Such freedom allows us to live empowered by the Spirit. Our Spirit-led lives then bring life to our world.

This all speaks of the kingdom that is to come, giving others a glimpse of their true humanity. Our human-made requirements take away that freedom and stifle any chance of living the free life the Father has intended for us since creation.

THE LAW CARRIES A CURSE FOR THOSE WHO FOLLOW IT

A life that depends on following the law is a cursed life. That's how Paul describes those who focus on law-keeping as the condition that keeps them in relationship with God.

If by the law Paul is referencing the Torah, then to understand this concept of a curse it 'is necessary to return to the story of the fall in Genesis. The one stipulation God put on Adam and Eve was to not eat of the fruit of the tree of the knowledge of good and evil. This was a law given to protect them. God's warning was that breaking this law would lead to death.

The story then tells how Adam and Eve broke this law. The cause of their fall was the serpent in the Garden who deceived them into altering their view of God, introducing doubt in their minds about the truth of God's warning.

The result was not immediate death, but rather the loss of their close relationship with God. This is noted by their exclusion from the Garden and their ideal existence. Adam and Eve entered a distorted state where everything in life presented a struggle, from giving birth to farming the land. They also struggled to stay connected to God even amid His continued connection with them. Their descendants promoted divisive and destructive behaviours that created strife among the emerging human race.[164]

God set in motion a rescue plan to restore humanity to its true form. The plan included calling Abraham and restoring His promise of blessing to all people through the relationship He fostered with the patriarch. This promise is one of redemption from the near collapse of the human race.

---

[164] This is what Paul means by living "in the flesh," referring to life before and outside of Christ as well as living in the present evil age (Gordon D. Fee, *Pentecostal Commentary Series*, 108).

This pattern of creation, uncreation, and re-creation is seen repeatedly through-out the biblical narrative.[165] In this pattern is the continual threat of death and ex-clusion, yet also the response of God to alleviate such threats by His gracious acts.

The curse of death and exclusion appears as well in the laws that were given at Sinai, particularly as defined in Leviticus and Deuteronomy.[166] In these two books of the Torah, and in the Genesis account of the fall, it seems clear that the ultimate penalty for breaking the law is death. Symptomatic of such a curse is exclusion from the covenant of blessing, which we read about in Deuteronomy 30–31.[167]

What this means for Paul is that law-keeping puts one in danger of suffering the curse of exclusion, rather than causing one to be included. The curse comes on Jew and Gentile alike.

The imposters were seeking to continue the requirement of Gentiles to be nationalized into Judaism in order to be included among God's people. We learn from Paul that this excluded Jews and Gentiles from receiving the promise. Paul points out that "denationalizing" God's people makes room for all to be accepted by faith, which is the core of the good news of Christ.[168]

Looking to the promise as what will bring Jew and Gentile together is consistent with the biblical narrative. This view of Paul's didn't sit right with Jewish Christians who sought to continue protecting their national identity and way of life. Yet Paul was not vying for the dismantling of Jewish identity; he wanted to expand it to the larger context represented by God's promises to Abraham and the fulfillment of those promises with the coming of Christ.[169] In this larger context, a truer picture of the law's place in the plan of God is made

---

[165] Chee-Chiew Lee tells us, "The recurring cycles …indicate the intensification of sin, but each cycle is always accompanied by the extension of God's grace" (Lee, *The Blessing of Abraham, the Spirit, and Justification in Galatians*, 63).

[166] All the sanctions in Leviticus 18 have attached to them the penalty of death in Leviticus 20. In Deuteronomy 21:23, mentioned by Paul in Galatians 3:13, the curse is represented in someone who's been put to death by capital punishment. In Deuteronomy 30, a list of blessings and curses are cited in reference to whether Israel will follow God and God's decrees (blessings) or be idolatrous and behave like the other nations whose practices are destructive (curses). In Deuteronomy 31, Moses shares God's prediction that Israel will follow foreign gods and be cursed, being destroyed in the process.

[167] N.T. Wright sees this as exile, living as distant from God like the Gentile nations (Wright, *Paul for Everyone*, 31).

[168] Scot McKnight, *The NIV Application Commentary*, 2947.

[169] N.T. Wright tells us that "ethnic Israel is not left in the ditch, nor simply shunted to one side. What Israel needed, according to prophets like Jeremiah, Ezekiel, Joel, and others (each of whom Paul refers to regularly in his writings), was for the covenant to be renewed at last: for God to pour out his spirit on Israel and enable it to believe, and so, set upright again, to join the stream of traffic flowing down the road to God's promised inheritance" (Wright, *Paul for Everyone*, 34).

clear by Paul. He doesn't jettison the law but rather gives the law its proper place in salvation history.

There is some debate regarding what triggers the curse of exclusion and death, represented in Paul's specific statements in this passage in Galatians. The following options are present.

Option one. The curse can be the requirement to keep the law in its entirety, maintaining every single stipulation outlined in it. When translating Deuteronomy 27:26, Paul uses the word "all" twice: *"cursed are all who do not keep all the things written in the book of the law, to do those things"* (my translation).[170] It looks like Paul has gone as far to say that the curse is present in keeping everything contained in the law.[171]

Option two. The curse represents the requirement to keep the law outright. The constant focus of one's immersion in law-keeping causes one to be under the threat of its curse. This relates more to the burden of law-keeping altogether, since one always lives in it. The Hebrew text Paul quotes from Deuteronomy 27:26 reads, "Cursed is he who doesn't confirm the words of the law to do them."[172] Paul intends this same sentiment regarding his use of the Septuagint in the Galatian letter.[173]

Option three. The curse underlies the focus on law-keeping. Failing to keep the law and remain in community results in one's exclusion from covenant relationship.[174]

Some scholars debate option one, given that the law by implication provides ways of restitution and forgiveness through its prescription of offering sacrifices to restore relationship with God when one has broken law and thus broken covenant. With the opportunity to atone for sins, even if one breaks the law, they continue keeping it and living within it by exercising the offer. These scholars feel that this is cause for Paul to say in his Philippian letter that as far as keeper of the law, he was faultless.[175]

---

[170] Paul quotes from the Septuagint version (William Hendriksen, *New Testament Commentary*, 126). The thinking as to why Paul does this is given some credence by Ronald Y.K. Fung: "Paul further generalizes the original denunciation of 'the man who does not uphold the words of this law by carrying them out' (NIV in Dt. 27:26) into a curse on 'every one who does not abide by all things written in the book of the law, and do them' (RSV in Gal. 3:10): whereas 'this law' refers to the twelve curses pronounced from Mount Ebal (the 'Schechemite dodecalogue'; Dt. 27:15–26), 'the law' is in Paul's mind a reference to 'the written Torah (cf. Dt. 31:26; Jos. 1:8) in all its details" (Fung, *The New International Commentary on the New Testament*, 141).

[171] Boice, Hendriksen, Fung, and Keener specifically lean toward this view of the curse.

[172] Ibid.

[173] Fee and Longnecker are of this opinion.

[174] McKnight, Sanders, and Dunn share this opinion.

[175] James D.G. Dunn, *Black's New Testament Commentary*, 171.

Even in light of this critique, law-keeping in its sense of completion—whether in not breaking it at all or being sure to enact restitution through atonement when one does—lies outside the atonement that comes through Christ.[176]

Those who adhere to option two focus more on an either/or scenario. If a person is all-in regarding the law, they are excluded from faith in Christ. If a person is all-in regarding faith in Christ, law has no bearing whatsoever.[177]

The idea here is that a mix of law-keeping and faith in Christ undermines one's ongoing relationship with Christ and dependence on the Spirit.[178]

Option three focuses on the specific psyche of Jews in Paul's period, along with assuming that Judaism is a way to God. But Judaism lies outside the relationship Paul establishes for Gentiles through the good news of Christ. Focusing on inclusion in God's people through identity law-keeping[179] results in excluding believers from faith in Christ, and subsequently from a covenant relationship with God.

The best conclusion to this issue of the curse comes from Craig Keener:

At the very least—those under law remain under threat of a curse due to nonfulfillment.—Whether Paul regarded perfect obedience or not—he warns readers not to place themselves in a position of finding out. Gal. 5:3.[180]

Regardless of whether the curse is a result of not keeping the law in its entirety, operating in law and not by faith, or using identity law-keeping to remain in covenant with God, the penalty is exclusion and ultimately death. This is not a stroke against the law's validity but rather a recognition of its not

---

[176] Craig Keener writes that "although provision is present in the law for atonement, Paul sees atonement in Christ… and law was not intended to 'put right' the human race" (Keener, *Galatians: A Commentary*, 56).

[177] Richard Longnecker puts the emphasis on this part of the passage. Paul has consistently used this sense of "being under" the law, both directly and indirectly. He uses it ten times in Galatians, so the focus is on the phrase "all who are under" (Longnecker, *Word Biblical Commentary, Volume 41: Galatians*, 116).

[178] Gordon D. Fee says, "The 'logic' is thus certain and forceful, and Paul's point is clear: You Galatians cannot have it both ways; it is an either/or situation. One either comes to life, and continues to live, on the basis of faith, or one is condemned to living by the law and that alone, and that quite excludes living by faith" (Fee, *Pentecostal Commentary Series*, 121). In this, Fee points out that it is not "inability" but rather "necessity" that is the issue in terms of law-keeping.

[179] According to James D.G. Dunn, "And 'works of the law', as we have seen, is Paul's code for those requirements of the law in particular which brought to sharpest focus Israel's claim to be distinctive from others as God's covenant people…" (Dunn, *Black's New Testament Commentary*, 172)

[180] Keener, *Galatians: A Commentary*, 55.

being the focus or tool by which the Triune God fulfills the promise of the Spirit.

The law's focus is on the behaviour of those who live under it. All three options mentioned above open the door to sin. Sin is a controlling influence that takes advantage of the law and its curse, condemning us.

The reality is that no one can be put in a righteous relationship like the one Abraham had with God through keeping the law. The capacity for it is nonexistent. Even the prophets affirm that the way to live in relationship with God is to live by faith.

Paul quotes the prophet Habakkuk to remind Israel that they must trust God, even though the circumstances of their day don't make sense. Trusting that God knows and that His plan will prevail is their reaction to ambiguity and confusion. The prophet questioned why God didn't prevent the wicked from advancing over Israel. Why would He let the wicked wipe them out? (Habakkuk 1:12)

Habakkuk submitted a complaint to God and waited at the "watch tower" for God's reply. The reply came by an impending vision that hadn't fully arrived and that the prophet, and Israel, would need to wait on. While they waited, God responded that *the righteous will live by his faith* (my translation). The forthcoming vision would put everything in perspective.

Although Paul's reason to cite Habakkuk is to show the consistency of a faith-focused relationship with God, the prophet's intent in questioning God forms an underlying parallel to the Galatian situation.

Peter C. Craigie outlines the prophet Habakkuk's state of mind:

He [Habakkuk] has a view of how he thinks God ought to act, but God's intimation of coming action is not in harmony with his presuppositions. Habakkuk has discovered, in other words, that the divine response to his initial questions has raised more difficulty than it has solved. And so now the new problems must be resolved, yet the approach of the prophet must be delicate. He does not want to imply that God's "theology" is unsound! And yet, if he is honest with himself, Habakkuk has to admit that what God has said seems to be out of harmony with all that he knows of God.[181]

Paul picks up on the confusion of the Galatians and the imposters and reminds his readers, by Habakkuk 2:4, that God doesn't work according to our

---

[181] Peter C. Craigie, *The Daily Bible Study Series: Twelve Prophets: Volume 2 Micah, Nahum, Habakkuk, Zephaniah, Haggai, Zechariah, and Malachi* (Philadelphia, PA: Westminster Press, 1985), 89.

expectations of Him. Like the prophet, who expected God to behave one way only to experience Him behaving another, Paul points out to the Galatians that the outpouring of the Spirit on the Gentiles, although unexpected, is how God has chosen to continue His relationship with humanity. The law doesn't give people the right standing with God that the imposters might expect; only the faithfulness of Christ can maintain one's connection with God.

Along with building his argument around maintaining a relationship with God based on the story of Abraham and being put right with God by faith, Paul shows how other Old Testament writers confirm faith as the source of one's right standing with God.

For Habakkuk, the law didn't help him in his relationship with God during Israel's moments of crisis. As Habakkuk waited for an answer from God to his complaint, the law was not his recommended focus; instead it was staying faithful and keeping in covenant with God.

In this sense, the law is not an accurate interpreter of God's character, nor a full representation of what He requires and how He will act. Jesus as mediator is a much more accurate communication to humanity of who God is.[182]

Given this hermeneutical perspective, what we see in the Triune God is our rescue from enslavement and subjection to the curse of the law. The word Paul uses in Galatians 3:13 is ἐξαγοράζω, which translates as "redeem" or "ransom." The idea comes from the marketplace, or the slave market.[183] The character of the Father, exemplified in the work of the Son's death, shows us that the Triune God desires to free us from enslavement.[184]

The human race was at a standstill regarding its relationship with God. Jews had focused on law-keeping and observance as their way of maintaining relationship with God and Gentiles were blocked from ever hearing of the promise of Abraham because of the Jewish nation's obsession with the law. Both were condemned, regardless of how close or distant they were from the law.

---

[182] Gregory A. Boyd states, "Scripture should be regarded as the 'secondary text' that mediates, and points us toward, the 'base text,' which is the mediator Jesus Christ.—As the one who fully embodied God, Jesus 'becomes a key hermeneutical principle in dealing with the biblical text... it is only when we read Scripture in light of this 'living commentary' that we can begin to see how the OT's depictions of Yahweh as a violent ancient Near Eastern (ANE) warrior deity bear witness to God's non-violent, self-sacrificial, enemy-loving nature that was most perfectly revealed in the crucified Christ" (Boyd, *Crucifixion of the Warrior God, Volume One*, 61, 67).

[183] See D.H. Field's note in *The New International Dictionary of New Testament Theology, Volume One*, 268. The concept is to free an individual from his or her enslavement to an owner.

[184] Robert H. Gundry translates Galatians 3:13a as *"bought us from under the Law's curse"* (Gundry, *Commentary on Galatians* [Grand Rapids, MI: Baker Academic, 2010], 45). Freedom from enslavement is key to receiving the Spirit.

The law was a roadblock to understanding how God would draw the nations to Himself through His promise to Abraham.

It is helpful to refer to Paul's writing to the Corinthians, in the second letter, which sheds light on this matter. Writing predominantly to Gentile believers, as with the Galatians, Paul identifies the limitations of the law in 2 Corinthians 3. He identifies two covenants: the old covenant, which focuses on the letter of the law, and the new covenant, which Paul describes as *"the Spirit that gives life"* (my translation).[185] The old covenant cast a veil over the reading of the law. Paul emphasizes in 2 Corinthians 3:14 that the same veil remains—until Christ is revealed.[186]

For similar reasons, Paul points out that the way to relationship with Christ and the Spirit is apart from the law. The law serves a different function, which Paul will emphasize later in Galatians 3:19–23.

There is no way that one can experience the Spirit through the law. The Spirit comes to us through Christ. The law leaves us in a condemned state, with God taking over to accomplish for humanity what humanity could not accomplish on its own.[187]

PROMISE VS. CONTRACT

Back to Galatians, Jew and Gentile have been enslaved by the law, but the Son came to die to free humanity from this slavery. He bore the curse on Himself,

---

[185] In 2 Corinthians 3:6, Paul uses the word γράμμα to identify the law. This is a reference to the Torah, which is written down, as opposed to the Spirit, which is experienced through an encounter with Christ, something the Torah points to but is veiled to those who focus on it. There is a parallel here to the mountain of blessing and cursing in Deuteronomy 11. At this point, God predicts, through Moses, Israel's falling on the side of curse. God also predicts in Deuteronomy 30, through Moses, that blessing will be restored to Israel. Rather than the law being the vehicle to blessing, it is God who will "change the heart" so that the people can return to a relationship of love with the Father, Son, and Spirit. The result of this is freedom from exile (Deuteronomy 30:1–10).

[186] *"But to this day, when Moses is read, a veil lies on their heart"* (2 Corinthians 3:16, my translation). We see here a third reference to the Torah, or more specifically to Moses who delivered the Torah to Israel. Paul uses the analogy of Israel not being able to gaze on Moses's face as being equivalent to Israel's inability to see Christ for who He is through the Torah. The giving of the Spirit by Christ frees Jew and Gentile from the veil of the law. 2 Corinthians 3:17 adds, *"Now the Lord is the Spirit. Where the Spirit of the Lord is, there is freedom"* (my translation).

[187] N.T. Wright tells us, "[Paul] does not say 'the law cursed Jesus, but the resurrection showed the law to be in the wrong.' His argument depends on the validity of the law's curse, and on the propriety of Jesus, as Messiah, bearing it on Israel's behalf. It is therefore impossible to argue from the present passage, as is often done, that Paul rejected Torah because he saw it had been shown to be in the wrong. According to this passage, Torah was correct to pronounce the curse. It merely did not have the last word. Exactly as foreseen in Deuteronomy 30, there was blessing on the other side of the curse, restoration the other side of exile" (Wright, *Climax of the Covenant*, 152).

with all its guilt and shame, so that by offering His life He could free humanity from its enslavement to the law.[188]

His life is the currency with which the Triune God purchased our freedom. This purchase has made possible the blessing of Abraham to both Jew and Gentile. It also gives the one purchased access to the Spirit through the faithfulness of Jesus.

The string of verses from Galatians 3:13–17 indicates that the promise of Abraham, which came prior to the law, is what God desires to fulfill for the human race. This covenant of God leads the Father, Son, and Spirit to restore humanity back to its true identity.

Paul then describes the nature of this promise, how it supersedes the giving of the law and is the prime focus for how God establishes connection and relationship with the human race.

The promise was made by God to Abraham in the form of a will, or covenant. The term Paul uses for covenant, διαθήκη, refers to a "one-sided action" where a binding and irreversible commitment is made.[189] As J. Guhrt writes, "If a human will cannot be annulled, how much less can God's covenant with Israel (3:17), through which it has incomparable privileges…"[190] This commitment on God's part becomes the promise of the Triune God to solidify their relationship with humanity.

This loaded promise, upon which all creation depends, was not put in the hands of Abraham's descendants. In the account of the binding of Isaac in Genesis 22, God makes it clear to Abraham that Isaac's sacrifice wouldn't be enough to solidify a relationship with Him. God then declares an oath to Abraham to provide a sacrifice for Abraham and Isaac.

---

[188] Paul references the law in the Torah—specifically, Deuteronomy 21:23—to give legitimacy to the fact that Jesus absorbed a curse of the law through the way He died. Being hung on a tree in the form of crucifixion would have satisfied the law in this case. In this, the law became death to Jesus. On the other hand, the resurrection became life for all those who identify with Christ in His curse and death.

[189] J. Gurht points out that the Greek word *diatheke* is predominantly used for a one-sided action, whereas *syntheke* is used for a binding contract between two people. There is Old Testament evidence showing us that covenants between two human parties cannot be annulled (Gurht, "Covenant, Guarantee, Mediator," *New International Dictionary of New Testament Theology, Volume One*, 365–370). Another writer, Scott W. Hahn, writes, "Of particular relevance to Paul's point in Gal. 3:15 is the narrative of the covenant between the Israelites and the Gibeonites in Joshua 9 (and the epilogue of the story in 2 Sam 21:1–14) which illustrates the binding nature of a human covenant" (Hahn, "Covenant, Oath and Aqedah: Διαθήκη in Galatians 3:15–18." *The Catholic Biblical Quarterly*, Volume 67, 2005, 84).

[190] J. Guhrt, "Covenant, Guarantee, Mediator," *New International Dictionary of New Testament Theology, Volume One*, 370.

Since Paul uses this Genesis passage as the backdrop to his point in Galatians 3:13–17, it's important to determine which "seed" he is referring to.[191] The seed isn't plural (*spermasin*) but singular (*spermati*). Paul is saying that the promise spoken to Abraham was the same promise of the coming of Christ. In no way is this promise dependent on Israel being faithful to the law, just as the promise wasn't dependent on Abraham sacrificing his own seed, represented by Isaac. The seed will be one the Father sends, His own Son, to release the blessing of Abraham onto his progeny—and through his progeny to the nations.

The promise was not a binding contract where God expected a certain response from Israel, with Israel being obliged to respond accordingly or miss out on the benefit the contract offered. The promise to Abraham was that the seed would appear through the nation of Israel, in whom the Father would send, through whom the freedom of humankind was contingent. This one seed (*spermati*) would benefit all the seed (*spermasin*) of Abraham.

Paul affirms that this promise is what drives the Trinity in its work of redemption. The Judaizers focused on the Mosaic law as the fulfillment of the blessing of Abraham, feeling that it would be a contradiction to offer it to the Gentiles, since God's binding covenant was unilaterally established with Abraham.

The promise preceded the giving of the law on Mount Sinai by 430 years, and the law did not undo the promise. The law doesn't exist in a contractual relationship with the promise or the seed. The law would have had to be part of the terms of the promise, but that is not the case. If the law had that role in the promise, humanity would through it have inherited the promise.

There is no evidence in God's dealings with Abraham and Israel that the law had any part in God's promise to Abraham. The imposters hung on to God's request of Abraham to circumcise the males in his family, but that doesn't tie the promise to the Mosaic law. The promise in the Abrahamic narrative supersedes the commands of God regarding circumcision. Faith and trust were the basis of

---

[191] Scott W. Hahn writes, "Paul's argument is also a *reductio ad absurdum*: he shows that his opponent's position leads to an unacceptable conclusion. The Judaizers argue that obedience to the Mosaic Law is necessary for the Abrahamic blessing to reach the Gentiles, that is, for them to become children of God and children of Abraham. In Paul's view, this concept would be tantamount to placing the Mosaic Law as a condition for the fulfillment of God's covenant with Abraham to bless the nations through his 'seed' (Gen 22:16–18). Since at the Adeqah, God put himself under a unilaterally binding oath to fulfill his covenant with Abraham, this would be nonsense. To suppose that God added conditions (the Mosaic Law) to the Abrahamic covenant, long after it had been unilaterally sworn by God, would imply that God acted illegally, reneging on a commitment in a way not tolerated even with human covenants. This would be an utterly unacceptable conclusion…" (Hahn, "Covenant, Oath and Aqedah: Διαθήκη in Galatians 3:15–18," 95).

the relationship God established with Abraham, the foundation of which was not law but the gracious character of the Father.[192]

It is integral to understand that law and law-keeping will never carry an advantage in terms of our relationship with Christ. There is no pre-existing contract between us and God that will allow our behaviour to influence His grace and love toward us.

The Triune God delivered a promise to Abraham—an old, imperfect pagan man—of cosmic proportions that stood above all other commands given both in the past and in the coming future. The fulfillment of that promise lay in the hands of the Trinity and was to be later fulfilled through the work of the Father, Son, and Spirit, independent of any human action. It was a unilateral covenant and could not be invalidated by any other command, decree, or system of rule and law.

As a pastor, the question begs to be asked, "Then why do so many believers battle with legalistic tendencies as they work out their relationship with God and his community?"

Part of the problem is that we don't fully understand what Jesus came to accomplish. This stems from believers neglecting to understand the New Testament as its writers interpret the Old Testament Scriptures to explain their encounters with Jesus and what they witnessed during His time on the earth.

As N.T. Wright mentions continually, Jesus didn't come to make bad people good, but to make dead people live.[193] Condemned through sin, which takes advantage of the law and makes it death to us, Christ came and delivered us (Galatians 1:4) by taking on our fallen humanity and undoing what evil had done to us. This is the essence of the good news experienced by Paul and borne in the witness and testimony of the other New Testament writers.

We in turn respond by giving our lives to Christ, entering the relationship that the Trinity has offered to us. As we are drawn into relationship with Father,

---

[192] Paul doesn't simply use the idea of "give," but rather of "grace" as the action in which the promise was given (Gordon D. Fee, *Pentecostal Commentary Series*, 128). James D.G. Dunn adds, "However, justified was the response that divine commands (including circumcision) were bound up with the promise more or less from the first, Paul's insistence on the priority of divine grace (cf. again Rom. 11.6) effectively relativizes everything else, including not least a rules and regulations (what we today would call a 'bureaucratic') mind-set" (Dunn, *Black's New Testament Commentary*, 187). And Richard Longnecker states, "Paul insists that law and promise must be kept separate, for they operate on entirely different planes. To bring them together as equals, in fact, is to destroy all that God has graciously established by promise. So, on the question of acceptance before God, Paul is radically opposed to any mingling of God's promise and grace with the Mosaic law" (Longnecker, *Word Biblical Commentary, Volume 41: Galatians*, 134).

[193] There is no specific reference for this quote, but I have heard N.T. Wright mention this on many occasions.

Son, and Spirit, we live in the benefit of the new humanity Christ has given us. We do that through the presence of the Spirit, empowering us to live out our new humanity in the present fallen world. Rather than focusing on what we can do to acquire a good standing with God, we should live in the benefit of relationship we have with the Trinity.[194]

The response is to live in freedom. Who wouldn't want freedom? Who wouldn't want to live in a loving relationship with the Creator of the Universe? Who would second-guess the eternal cosmic benefit of life in Christ lived by the Spirit in relationship with the Father? Who would shun the love of a family who embraces you with complete acceptance?

Every time we pick up our candles and flashlight, we second-guess the benefits that come through Christ fulfilling the Father's promise in our lives. Every time we hinge our relationship with God on our positive behaviour, and require others to do the same, we forgo the benefit of living in our new humanity. Every time we're tempted to take pride in our religious performance, we drive away the Spirit and prevent Him from helping us live free from condemnation and the curse of the law. Leaning on the law prevents us from enjoying the inheritance of the freedom that comes from the Father, Son, and Spirit.

This is what makes the Apostle's words so pointed and specific when he wrote against the imposters and their negative impact on the Galatian believers. We should take his words to heart and examine our focus, rooting out any temptation in us to live within the confines of the law as opposed to the freedom of relationship with the Trinity. Every time we encounter law, it should remind us of our freedom in Christ, no matter how convincing the arguments are from those imposters who teach law-keeping plus grace.

---

[194] This is made evident by John Mcleod Campbell: "The atonement retrospectively finds us in the condition we are in through God's grace and prospectively raises us to a new condition" (Campbell, *The Nature of the Atonement*, 50). Believing that one's behaviour can acquire justification from God focuses on the retrospective aspect of salvation that has been taken care of by Christ through the work of the Trinity. Our focus should instead be on the prospective benefits of living in this law-free state. This is how we stumble and get in the way of what God wants to accomplish in us. Paul will in Galatians 5 discuss living in the freedom of what the atonement of Christ has acquired for us.

Chapter Eight

FREEDOM FROM THE LAW

Galatians 3:19–29

What then is the purpose of the law? It came alongside because of transgressions, until the seed would come to whom the promise was given. It was ordered through angels by the hand of a mediator. The mediator is not the one [who gives the law], but God is the one. Does the law work against the promises of God? Never! If a law was given that had the power to make one live, then it would be certain that righteousness is connected to the law. But [the law in] the Scriptures confined all things under sin, in order that the promise of the faithfulness of Jesus Christ might be given to those who put their trust in Him. Before faith came [through the good news of Christ] we were under the watchful eye of the law, kept there till faith was revealed.

Now that faith has come, we don't need the watchful eye of the law. You are all sons of God, through faith in Christ Jesus. For those of you who were baptized in Christ have put on Christ. There is neither Jew or Greek, slave or free, male, or female; you are one in Christ Jesus. If you belong to Christ, then you are Abraham's seed and an inheritor of the promise.

WHAT IS THE ROLE OF THE LAW?

Having presented the imposters' view of the law as contrary to the promise of God, Paul now attempts to identify what the purpose of the law is in God's redemptive plan.

Paul opens by explaining that the law occupies an assistive role in God's goal of redeeming humanity and the world from evil. The language Paul uses is that of an "addition."[195] The law plays a supportive role; it is not the main entity in the story of salvation. In that supportive role, it has a specific task that contributes to the Trinity's overall goal.

---

[195] The Greek word used here is προσετέθη, from the root προστίθημι (Harold K. Moulton, *The Analytical Greek Lexicon Revised*, 348). Paul uses the first order meaning of the root word, which is "add, put to—of things that are added to something already present" (Walter Bauer, *A Greek English Lexicon of the New Testament and Other Early Christian Literature*, 719). The passive mood used here refers to God's action of putting the law in place to function as He intended.

The reason for its addition, writes Paul, is because of transgressions. What Paul means by this requires some explanation. Three passages in particular from Romans expand on what Paul means in Galatians 3:19.

In Romans 3, Paul makes a point of emphasizing to the Roman believers that "doing law" doesn't rectify the distance that exists between humanity and God. The law doesn't draw one close to God but rather, in Paul's words, *"through the law comes the knowledge of sin"* (Romans 3:20, my translation). The law brings with it the understanding of what sin is. In this sense, the law makes the reader aware of God's requirements and the consequences that come by not abiding by those requirements.

Later in Romans 4, Paul points out that the work of the law is to enact punishment for those who don't abide by the commands and requirements set out in the law (Romans 4:15).[196] In Romans 7, he talks about the vicious cycle of living under the law, emphasizing that he would never have known what sin was if the law hadn't pointed it out.

Paul gives us the example of covetousness (Romans 7:7). Although his choice of example is apparently random, it's interesting to note that he chooses this one while addressing a Christian community that's divided by their sense of superiority over each other in their commitment to Christ. Might there have been a covetous sense of ownership of the law among Jewish believers in Rome and their using it to present themselves as superior to the Gentile believers among them? This subject is for another time in another book.

In Galatians 3:19, keeping in mind the Romans passages, Paul is referring to the purpose of the law, which is to give definition to and awareness of sin. He uses the word *parabaino*, as opposed to *hamartia*, which has the general meaning of failing to stay on a certain path or direction; the meaning of *hamartia* has the more specific meaning of missing the mark related to one's own ignorance and deficiency.[197]

---

[196] The word for punishment, ὀργήν, can also be translated as wrath. The idea here is that the law brings with it the anger of authority that has put the law in place, the result of which is punishment for malevolent behaviour. In this sense, an act of judgment is inferred by the use of the word in conjunction with law (Bauer, *A Greek English Lexicon of the New Testament and Other Early Christian Literature*, 579). The intent was that the punishment would draw one toward God to seek restitution through the various ways in which restitution could be made through the law. See Psalm 32 for an example. In Romans 4, Paul points out that this function of the law has nothing whatsoever to do with the promise that comes through Abraham. This is like the argument Paul makes in Galatians 3. The law brings condemnation, whereas grace is given by God as a gift outside the works of the law.

[197] W. Gunther, "Sin," *New International Dictionary of New Testament Theology, Volume Three*, 577, 583.

Paul's use of this word may be related to the timeframe he is identifying in Galatians 3:19, referring to the period that began when the promise was given to Abraham and ended when Christ came to fulfill that promise. The law functioned during this period to make humanity aware of its waywardness from God. It also was given to aid Israel and the nations in their awareness that only God can rectify their distorted living and wayward trajectory.

There is evidence in rabbinic writings that rabbis were anticipating the coming of the Messiah who would free them from the burden of the law. Such a burden was constant and continual, never letting up on the requirement to adhere to the law and the penalty related to not adhering. This led to a hedging of the law with further laws, thus preventing individuals from breaking the more severe laws. The rabbis were kept busy with constant interpretation and application.[198]

The world needed someone to rescue it from this stalemate with the law. That rescue would come through the seed of Abraham, spoken of by Paul in Galatians 3, who would bring freedom from the law and subsequent freedom for all humanity to enjoy unfettered connection to the Trinity.[199]

Paul reinforces the law's secondary purpose by stating how it came into existence. It was given by God but mediated to humanity. It seems clear from Paul's logic that the mediator is Moses. The law was given to him through angels, demonstrating that the law is twice removed from God.

On the other hand, the promise to Abraham was given to him directly by God, giving it the greater significance in the order of God's plan for humanity. This promise takes higher precedence than the law. How then can the law have the upper hand over the promise? The promise came from the one God, whereas the law came to Israel third-hand: "God—the angels—Moses the mediator—the people."[200]

Contrary to the critique of the imposters, who said that Paul desired to eliminate the law altogether, Paul points out that the law cooperates with the

---

[198] Risto Santala writes, "The hedge around the Law with its traditions and ordinances of men has now been torn down. The Ten Commandments are of course still valid as the irrevocable 'words of the Covenant.' The Christian's protective 'hedge' is Christ himself, and so Paul in his letters uses over 160 times the phrase 'to be in Christ'" (Santala, *The Messiah in the Old Testament in the Light of Rabbinical Writings* [Jerusalem, Israel: Keren Ahvah Meshlhit, 1992], 84).

[199] N.T. Wright points out that the idea of "one" comes from a God who desires to consolidate humanity into one "faithful family." The law specifically sets Jews apart from Gentiles and doesn't present a pathway to unity for the human race in terms of its relationship with God. Further to this, if the imposters' claims were true, then the inequality in the Roman church would have been willed by God, which is absurd (Wright, *Paul for Everyone*, 36).

[200] This description of the law was no doubt used to combat whatever explanation the imposters gave for giving the law a greater presence than the promise (John Stott, *The Bible Speaks Today*, 90).

promise. If the terms had been turned around and the law could bring life and unity to the entire human race, then the law would carry the day in terms of importance and focus. The point is not that Paul preferred the promise over the law, but rather that the law accomplishes a very specific part of God's overall plan. Rather than make people alive, the law brings death.

In Galatians 3:22, Paul mentions that the scriptures containing the law reinforce the reality that all life is imprisoned to a fallen existence.[201] Paul here uses the word *hamartia*, tying this statement to the original one back in Galatians 1:4. Scripture clearly defines the work of the law in the life of humanity. It pins humanity in a corner from which it cannot escape without rescue.

The faithfulness of Jesus to the promise given to Abraham brings rescue and life to all who put their trust in Him. His appearance marks the end of slavery to sin and the law.

Prior to His coming, the law acted like a guardian of sorts. The word Paul uses here is παιδαγωγός, which translates roughly into an individual who cares for the children of a household, or a pedagogue.[202] In Paul's day, slaves were entrusted with the care and protection of children in a wealthy home. This was distinct from the role of a teacher. In fact, the pedagogue would take the children to their teacher for their day's lessons.[203]

This person functioned as an extension of the parents, keeping watch over the children and their formation into adulthood.[204] They cared for the moral development of children and administered punishment and correction.[205]

A pedagogue would only serve in that role temporarily. They guided children after they had no need of nursing and watched over them until they matured into

---

[201] The Old Testament, including the Torah, identifies the helplessness of the fallen human race, in such passages as Psalm 14:1–3 and Jeremiah 17:9, not to mention narratives that demonstrate the failure of humanity, like Judges 19:29, Isaiah 55:8, and Ezekiel 36:22ff.

[202] We read, from D. Furst, "Whether Paul was thinking of the slave to whom boys were entrusted... and who beat them, or whether he was thinking in more positive terms, can no longer be determined. But in any case, he means the person who keeps the boys in order" (Furst, "Teach, Instruct, Tradition, Education, Discipline," *New International Dictionary of New Testament Theology, Volume Three*, 779). The translation above chooses to make its points by referencing the function of the pedagogue's "watchful eyes."

[203] Longnecker tells us, "He [the pedagogue] was distinguished from the διδασκαλός for he gave no formal instruction but administered the directives of the father in a custodial manner, though, of course, indirectly he taught by the supervision he gave and the discipline he administered" (Longnecker, *Word Biblical Commentary, Volume 41: Galatians*, 148).

[204] Michael J. Smith says that "often the pedagogue became a surrogate father to his charge" (Smith, "The Role of the Pedagogue in Galatians" (Smith, "The Role of the Pedagogue in Galatians," *Bibliotheca Sacra*, volume 163, April–June 2006, 203).

[205] Ibid., pg. 201.

adulthood. At that time, the pedagogue's work was done and they would go on to supervise other children, either in the same family or for other families.[206]

Paul draws on this analogy to convey the temporary role of the law as it watched over Israel, protecting it from the waywardness and lawlessness of other nations. It also watched over any sympathizing Gentiles who became a part of the Hebrew community.

Israel and its cohabitants were held in custody, as Paul describes, not under their own will but rather under the will of He who had authority over them. The law kept watch over Israel's morality, identifying punishment and restitution for its waywardness and working toward the nation's maturity in its expression and behaviour toward other nations.[207]

Besides that, the law had no other function. It didn't have the capacity to give freedom to Israel or those who lived in community with Israel. Its function was strictly supervisory.

NO MORE NEED FOR THE LAW

The duration of this period under the law ended at the appearance of Christ. The pedagogue's supervisory role was completed. The child had come of age, able to respond on its own to the faithfulness of its parents and take on adulthood in its fullness with no need for supervision. The individual was free to live in a loving relationship that formed deep connection and fidelity.[208]

This analogy, as Paul will talk about later in the letter, allows the Galatians to function with the same love towards others as the Father shared with them through their provision and care under the law. They came of age to enter into allegiances, one being their allegiance with Christ, from which they benefitted from a relationship with the Father, Son, and Spirit.[209]

This relationship establishes the deepest faithfulness available to humanity through which the faithful learn the character of Jesus in His love for humanity

---

[206] Ibid., pg. 207.

[207] James D.G. Dunn writes, "Israel was like a child growing up in an evil world (i.4): the law gave it the protection it needed from idolatry and the lower moral standards prevalent in the Gentile world; the law thus involved a degree of restriction for Israel and separation from the rest of the world; but it was a temporary role, since the child would grow up, and when that happened there would be no need of the custodial slave and the restrictive rules which separated the growing youth from the rest of the world could be removed…" (Dunn, *Black's New Testament Commentary*, 199).

[208] Craig Keener, *Galatians: A Commentary*, 168.

[209] Matthew W. Bates tells us, "What is essential for salvation? Public declaration that Jesus is Lord is at the bedrock, because this designates mental agreement with the gospel and the desire to live a life of personal fidelity to Jesus as the sovereign ruler of heaven and earth" (Bates, *Salvation by Allegiance Alone*, 98).

and creation. To be a child of God is then to trust in Jesus as the Messiah, not to be identified ethnically by a set of laws that keep a community separated from the rest of the world. This is what it means to be a child of Abraham—a descendent of faith who trusts in the faithfulness of God as He fulfills His promise to humanity. Galatians 3:26 couches this fulfillment in terms of sonship, which is available to all, meaning Jew and Gentile.[210] Paul will describe this new status of sonship in more detail in Galatians 4.

From a pastoral point of view, reverting to law-keeping is to forgo maturity in relationship with the Trinity and trade it for a formal structure of rules and regulations which govern all aspects of behaviour. Law-keeping keeps a community at a distance from God rather than in a close relationship of allegiance. It is a move back to immaturity, forgoing one's own adulthood and gift of new humanity.

Sadly, this moves one to go where God isn't willing to go in terms of relationship. It denies the power of the cross, the resurrection, and the ascension and asks for a set of rules to be placed over the people.

As a pastor, I have dealt with my share of immaturity among congregants. I have also worked through my own immaturity. Childish and immature behaviour reveals how people at times prefer to deal with issues at the law level rather than working from the loving expression of a Christ-like character.

When it was my own issue, the corrective was to renew and re-establish a deep relational connection with the Triune God of grace. When it was someone else's issue, someone who insisted on working through the letter of the law rather than the liberty of the Spirit, I attempted to guide them back to the loving character of the Trinity. I chose to respond with the deep love of Christ and draw on the Spirit's help to eliminate hatred, division, and the perpetuation of evil. I can't say that I've won everyone over in these situations, but I can attest to the fact that it put the conversation on a much higher, relational level that reminds us of the way of grace and peace.

Paul clearly tells the Galatians that the watchful eye of the law is no longer needed among those who have been baptized in Christ. When someone is baptised, they have put on Christ in such a way as to take on His character in a deeply loving and empowering relationship that becomes their source in life.

---

[210] Craig Keener adds that "in 3:26–29, preaching directly to the predominantly Gentile audience. Just as 'all' peoples are under sin (3:22), so are 'all' of the Galatian believers now God's children (3:26)… In the Greek text of 3:26, the inclusion of gentiles is more conspicuously emphatic— 'all' (panten, pantes) appears first in the sentence, underlining its priority" (Keener, *Galatians: A Commentary*, 168, 170).

The old way of the law and its supervision is left behind in the water, and the new humanity is put on with one's vision set on a journey of formation into the character of Jesus.[211]

The analogy Paul uses for this transformation is clothing.[212] The root of the word has a basic sense of being "dressed," whether by oneself or someone else. The middle voice of the form Paul uses in Galatians 3:27 indicates a bit of both.

All categories that created divisions in the world of the Roman Empire were secondary to the greater identity of being a child or son of God. This identity created a community of equality and unity. Paul characterized the community as being *"one in Christ Jesus"* (Galatians 3:28, NLT).

Christ's work is the same in each person, with no distinction or favouritism. The favoured distinctions of first-century Roman culture didn't convey any advantage over Christ's work. Jews didn't get more of the work of Christ than Gentiles. The same is true for males and females, those who were enslaved and those who were free. All experienced equally the work of Christ and had full access to the fulfillment of God's promise to Abraham. All entered into their new humanity and into the full privileges of sonship.

There is a temptation today to look at Galatians 3:28 and use it to rationalize the dismantling of gender identities, encouraging the fluidity of identity over binary descriptors. Paul in no way addresses this modern issue. He didn't tear down the markers of identity in his culture. Rather, he identified another category above those markers, one established by the Trinity in which everyone is authentically equal.

Galatians 3:29 reinforces this view. Here, Paul repeats that having a relationship with Christ is what gives one access to the promise of God—not gender, social status, or ethnic identity. The law reinforced these divisions, and in so doing prevented the Gentiles from having access to the promise.

The promise restored equality to all people through the work of Christ, bringing redemption and granting everyone an unfettered relationship with God. This is what the Trinity intended from the beginning: a dynamic reality in which unique individuals bring their presence to bear on the harmony of

---

[211] Ephesians 4:24 says, *"Put on your new humanity that has been created for righteous relationship and holy living"* (my translation). In my previous book, I write, "The new humanity they are to 'put on' is in full and open relationship to the Father, Son and Spirit and is therefore characterized as holy living—that is, living in the love and grace and fellowship that constitute the holiness of God" (Lombardi, *A New Humanity*, 85).

[212] The word Ἐνεδύσασθε indicates that the action is neither active nor passive, but a bit of both—a putting on from our end and a being clothed on Christ's end.

relationship, reflecting the relationship that the Father, Son, and Spirit have in each other.[213]

It is prudent to mention how important it is for God's community to establish a deep love of the diversity that exists within humanity. Diversity should be celebrated and exercised in the freedom of expression and liberty of the Spirit.

In the complementary behaviour of mutual submission, mentioned in Paul's letter to the Ephesians, everyone lives to help each other thrive and fulfill their God-given freedom and potential. No limitations or divisions are created to frustrate anyone. The community lives to honour and lift each other up, knowing how rich it is to experience relationship with one another. Second-tier categories are used to acknowledge each other's uniqueness. Love and freedom foster and build unity. Such a community mirrors the very life of the Trinity in their relationship with each other and with creation.

As pastors and members of our communities, it is key to acknowledge the blessing of God's promise and embrace it as a way to thrive. Anything that threatens to break this down must be dealt with in the same loving expression that brings us the freedom to live out the promise of God.

In Galatians 6, Paul will write about how we respond to each other when we fail in our behaviour, as well as the importance of lifting each other up when we have fallen and pointing each other toward the fullness of our humanity in Christ.

Paul points out in Galatians 3:29 that all people who belong to Christ are the seed of Abraham and stand to inherit the promise of blessing. The evidence that this was available to all people was that the Gentiles had experienced the Spirit because of their trust in the faithfulness of Jesus. This phenomenon opened the possibility for humanity to move towards rescue and restoration through the work of the Trinity.

---

[213] Colin E. Gunton asserts, in response to Genesis 1:26–27, "Noteworthy is the emphatic repetition of the word 'image', and also, once again, the polemical intent of the writer. For other cultures, it was—indeed still is, as those who remember the dismantling in recent years of statues of former communist rulers will know—the king who was the image of God, and his—his statue—reinforced in lands under his sway the message that he was God's representative on earth. For Israel, it was man, as male and female together, to which the status can be ascribed. All people are made in the image of God; indeed, as the gloss in the first cited verse suggests, are like God.—If there is a sacramental reality, something in the creation uniquely or especially fitted to mirror the divine, it is the human race" (Gunton, *The Christian Faith: An Introduction to Christian Doctrine* [Oxford, UK: Blackwell Publishers, 2002], 40–41). We also read, from Robin Parry, "Many contemporary theologians see the community of the Trinity as a model for God's community of the church. In God one finds mutual love between persons-in-relationship who recognize the equality and also value the difference of 'the others.' Although human relationships can never reach the unity of being one finds in God, they can be a dim analogy" (Parry, *Worshipping the Trinity: Coming Back to the Heart of Worship* [Exeter, UK: Paternoster, 2005], 56).

In Galatians 4, Paul will commandeer the term sonship away from its gender identification and use it to describe this higher category of relationship that humanity has with the Father, Son, and Spirit.[214] He will also introduce the concept of adoption in terms of humanity restoring its relationship with the Trinity as they live in Christ and by the Spirit.

---

[214] Scott McKnight writes, "As Paul describes those who are 'sons,' we should not pick up 'manly' or 'male' traits. Rather, in Paul's letters 'son' is especially related to both Jews and Gentiles (Rom. 9:26) who have been set free from the law (Gal. 4:1–7), who now live by faith in Christ (3:7, 26) and in the Spirit of God's glorious freedom (cf. Rom. 8:14), and who await God's final redemption (Rom. 8:19). The last thing on Paul's mind when he used the term son was 'manliness'" (McKnight, *The NIV Application Commentary*, 3791).

Chapter Nine

INHERITING FREEDOM

Galatians 4:1–20

But as long as the inheritor is a child, there is no difference between their position and that of a slave. They are under guardians and managers until the inheritance date set by their father. In the same way, we also were like children enslaved to the systems put in place by the world.[215] But when the time to inherit came,[216] God sent his Son born among humanity and subject to the Law so that he might ransom those under the Law and trigger[217] our adoption as Sons. And because you are now Sons, the Spirit of God's Son indwells our heart and calls out, Poppa![218] [Because Christ has come][219] you are no longer a slave but a Son and by implication an inheritor through God.

---

[215] Στοιχεῖα τοῦ κόσμου is the phrase Paul uses here, which literally translates to "elemental principles of the world." I chose to translate it as "systems," as the common meaning of στοιχεῖα is "to leading a closely regulated life, living according to definite rules" (H. Esser, "Laws, Customs, Elements," *New International Dictionary of New Testament Theology, Volume Two*, 452). When matched with τοῦ κόσμου, this phrase refers to the rules of the surrounding world. Esser notes that this phrase in Galatians 4 refers to "the Torah with its statutes and the world of false gods…" (Ibid.) Paul uses the phrase in a negative sense, so that it "covers all the things in which man places his trust apart from the living God revealed in Christ" (Ibid., 453). This includes how men and women go about observing the Torah, alluding to a construct of their own making.

[216] Paul uses the word πλήρωμα to indicate "fullness." I chose to translate it as "time of inheritance," to stay consistent with Paul's analogy of inheritance for the coming of age of the human race through the appearance of Christ.

[217] The phrase Paul uses here is ἵνα τήν… ἀπολάβωμεν, which translates to "that we might receive." I have chosen to use the word "trigger," to keep the continuity with the sense of timing that is so important to the point Paul is making.

[218] I chose to translate ἀββα as "Poppa." I borrow the term from Paul Young's book *The Shack*, based on his compelling story of how the character of Mack encounters the Trinity at the shack where his daughter was murdered. The first person Mack met is a Jamaican woman named Poppa. Young takes liberties to let the Father, who is not of human essence, take on a persona of his choosing. In so doing, Young creates an intimate portrait of the closeness of Poppa to Mack as his child, considering all that he has been through (Young, *The Shack* [Newbury Park, CA: Windblown Media, 2007]).

[219] This addition is made to keep consistent with the time reference in Paul's argument.

[Even though Christ had come][220] at the time, not knowing God, you were enslaved to idols.[221] But now that you know God, or I should say that God knows you,[222] why do you turn back again to weak and empty systems? Do you want to be in slavery all over again? You're back to your meticulous tracking of the calendar.[223] I fear for you that I have possibly been working for you to no benefit.

Be like me as I am like [what I saw in][224] you. You caused me no harm knowing that the first time I preached to you I was weak in body. And being tempted [to turn me away] because of my condition, you didn't think less of me nor reject me, but you received me as a messenger of God, even as Christ Jesus. And what was your blessing? What I witnessed in you was that if you were able, you would have donated[225] your eyes and given them to me. Have I now become your adversary by sharing the truth with you? [The imposters] are motivated to sell you cheap goods, wishing to shut you out [from the truth] so that you promote what their selling.[226] It's always good to be excited about what is valuable, you don't need me there to do it. My children, I'm feeling the twinge of birth pains again until Christ is formed in you. I wish to be present together with you now and change my tone because I'm at a loss about you.

---

[220] Ibid. The reason here is the same.

[221] Paul's phrase here, μὴ οὖσιν θεοῖς, is translated as "by nature no gods." This is Paul's way of saying that they were in bondage to idols. As Paul mentions in 1 Corinthians 8:4, *"Well, we all know that an idol is not really a god and that there is only one God"* (NLT). What lies behind the idol is by nature not of God's quality or essence.

[222] Paul is saying that God's knowledge of the people, and what He does to restore them to relationship, is more important than the Galatians' knowledge of Him (N.T. Wright, *Paul for Everyone*, 49).

[223] Paul's reference to *"days, months, seasons and years"* is most likely a reference to the Galatians' return to arguing over days in the calendar for certain celebrations, whether Jewish or pagan (Longnecker, *Word Biblical Commentary, Volume 41: Galatians*, 182–183).

[224] This addition helps to make the translation work with the context. Paul is going to remind the Galatians of how they behaved before the imposters' tainted their thinking and poisoned them with their law-keeping gospel.

[225] Paul uses a stronger word here which translates as "plucked." I went with "donate," to be a bit more idiomatic regarding our present language.

[226] I struggled with Paul's use of ζηλοῦσιν, which is a challenging verb to translate into English. The meaning—*"they are zealoting you"*—is difficult to convey in English. I decided to use the theme of "selling," since the imposters were zealous about converting the Galatians to their way, essentially selling their version of the gospel.

COMING OF AGE

Paul continues, in this section, to outline the sense of timing regarding the shift from the law to the fulfillment of the promise of God to Abraham. The coming of Christ marks such a shift.[227]

He moves both Jews and Gentiles away from guardianship under the law to freedom in relationship to the Trinity. Using the analogy of human inheritance as it applies to the life of a child, he describes how supervision under the law was always meant to be temporary. In that transitory state, one is like a child under guardianship.

The guardian's role has an expiry date. Their authority is both limited and entrusted to them only to the extent that the father of the household has charged them. The guardian doesn't determine the nature and timing of the inheritance, but rather the father, who has willed the inheritance in a specific manner. It is the father who makes a unilateral decision as to who and what will trigger the transition of the child to the position of inheritor.[228]

Paul is specific with this analogy, pointing out to the Galatians that the imposters' sense of superiority in their law-focused gospel didn't give them an advantage over others but instead kept them enslaved. The presentation of their "no-gospel" diminished their humanity, holding it at bay and preventing one from growing into freedom.

Ongoing guardianship keeps the inheritance locked up. Lesser systems prevail when managers simply provide basic supervision. The safety they create can only bide time. By keeping the law at the forefront, the inheritance will never arrive.

There is an aspect of growth in this analogy, where children are continually taken to its instructors to increase in their knowledge of the ways of the world. They learn of what is coming, something the law accomplished in telling the story of Abraham and pointing to the coming of the Messiah.[229] They wait, trusting that their father has determined what is best for them.

---

[227] Scot McKnight writes, "Paul applies this analogy to make a point about Israel's history—namely the 'childhood period' is the period of the law and the 'inheritance period' is the time inaugurated by Jesus Christ. Full rights (i.e., freedom from the law) do not come until after Christ's work is done. The time of the law is a time of slavery; the time of Christ is a time of freedom" (McKnight, *NIV Application Commentary*, 3902).

[228] I hope you do not gloss over this point. The law is not God. It is temporary and can be revised at any point. Jesus demonstrated this in the beatitudes when He delivered the "I say unto you..." statements that rewrote the law with which the Jews were familiar. The law is not the final word; the character of the Triune God and their action in our world is the deciding factor.

[229] The Torah, referred to as the law, is not reduced to a set of dos and don'ts. It is much more dynamic than this. The law expresses what God intends for Israel and the nations. In this sense, it is valuable because it creates a context by which we can anticipate the coming of the Messiah and the fulfillment of God's promise to Abraham.

Yet nothing can quite prepare them for the appearance of Christ, as we learn how unique and authentic the coming of Jesus is through the writers of the New Testament.[230]

The phrase *"when the time to inherit came"* indicates that the Messiah, who is the Son of God, comes apart from the law. His appearance becomes the transition from childhood to adulthood for the entire human race—and the time is determined exclusively from the perspective of the Father's will and the agreement of the persons of the Trinity.

Humanity had been biding its time under the law's watchful eye until this momentous occasion. The Son of God was born into fallen humanity[231]—"under the law," as Paul emphasizes—so that He could do the work of ransoming the human race. This was the will of the Father,[232] accomplished through the Spirit's help.[233]

The coming of the Son was the work of the Trinity in breaking the bond of evil that held humanity in slavery. The Trinity worked in cooperation to free humanity through the Father's sending, the Son's arrival and incarnation, and the Spirit's empowerment.

John D. Zizioulas speaks of it as the Son entering history and the Spirit coming from beyond history, freeing the Son from the bondage of fallen humanity's existence.[234]

---

[230] Although the law speaks of the Messiah's coming, it does not fully reveal His identity and the scope of His person and work—until humanity experiences His appearance and involvement in creation. Although I don't track with all the details in *Inspiration and Incarnation,* by Peter Enns, his point regarding a "cristotelic" focus of the Old Testament does make room for the Old Testament to be in movement toward the appearance of Jesus but not "all knowing" as to what that appearance entails. Such fullness can only come for us after we encounter Jesus and go back and read a second time the writers of the Old Testament regarding the revelation of Jesus (Enns, *Inspiration and Incarnation, Second Edition* [Grand Rapids, MI: Baker Academic, 2015], 143).

[231] This refers back to Galatians 1:4: *"…who gave himself over to our fallen human existence so he could rescue us out of the present evil age"* (my translation).

[232] *"This is the Father's desire proven by His eternal fame and renown"* (Galatians 1:5, my translation).

[233] It is the Spirit that empowers Jesus in our fallen humanity to break the bond of sin and the legal condemnation of the law that brings death. Colin E. Gunton speaks of the necessity of Jesus depending on the Spirit for our sake. According to Gunton, it is for our sake that the Spirit enables Jesus as He lives within our fallen flesh, because His achievement in resisting temptation by the Spirit enables us also to resist temptation—enabled by the Spirit. Jesus is functioning as you and me in our fallen human flesh and in that function relies totally on the Spirit for His perfection (Gunton, *Christ and Creation* [Waynesboro, GA: Wipf and Stock, 2005], 56–59).

[234] John D. Zizioulas writes, "Now if *becoming* history is the particularity of the Son in the economy [location of the Trinity's work—world and humanity], what is the contribution of the Spirit? Well, precisely the opposite: it is to liberate the Son and the economy from the bondage of history. If the Son dies on the cross, thus succumbing to the bondage of the historical existence, it is the Spirit that raises him from the dead. [Rom. 8:11] The Spirit is the *beyond* history, and when he

This is important to consider, as Paul says that the coming of the Son triggered our adoption as sons of God. This status of sonship comes with the inheritance of the Spirit, with the Spirit drawing us into the same intimacy with the Father that Jesus possesses as the Son both from eternity and during His life on the earth.[235]

The mention of the Spirit in this dialogue on inheritance ties in with the experience the Galatians had upon hearing the good news from Paul and his missionary team. Intimacy with the Father is not achieved through observance of the law but rather through the work of Christ and the Spirit. It is a direct action on the part of the Trinity that transitions the Galatians away from the world's system—the law given through mediators and limited in its ability to transform humanity.

The law reflected the elements of the world rather than the unhindered connection we can have with the Triune God of grace whose direct involvement and work within the world brings true freedom and blessing.[236] The Galatians had experienced this intimacy with the Trinity when they experienced the Spirit and their connection to Christ.

Paul reiterates that this happened to them in Christ and by the Spirit.[237] Through this action, Gentiles and Jews become children of Abraham and sons

---

acts in history, he does so to bring into the history the last days, the eschaton. Hence the first fundamental particularity of Pneumatology is its eschatological character. The Spirit makes Christ an eschatological being, the 'last Adam'" (Zizioulas, *Being in Communion* [Crestwood, NY: St. Vladimir's Seminary Press, 2002], 130).

[235] Baxter Kruger tells us, "The sum and substance of the work of Christ is that the eternal Son of God became human and lived out his divine sonship inside our fallen Adamic existence, and in so doing not only converted fallen Adamic existence, but also forged a real and abiding relationship, a union, between God the Father and fallen humanity" (Kruger, *Jesus and the Undoing of Adam* [Jackson, MS: Perichoresis Press, 2003], 32).

[236] T.F. Torrance says, "It is penetration of the horizontal by the vertical that gives man his true place, for it relates his place to space and time to its ultimate ontological ground so that it is not submerged in the endless relativities of what is merely horizontal [and endless reiterations of Law that hash and rehash human behaviour]. Without this vertical relation to God man has no authentic place on earth, no meaning, and no purpose, but with this vertical relation to God his place is given meaning and purpose... Unless the eternal breaks into the temporal and the boundless being of God breaks into the spatial existence of man and takes up dwelling within it, the vertical dimension vanishes out of man's life and becomes quite strange to him—and man loses his place under the sun" (Torrance, *Space, Time and Incarnation* [Edinburgh, UK: T&T Clark, 1969], 75–76). The law doesn't accomplish this clarity of identity but rather presses in on the identification of brokenness and leaves humanity to repeatedly come back to this distorted vision.

[237] Gordon D. Fee writes, "Thus 4:1–7 serves as Paul's 'final conclusion.' By moving the Spirit back into the foreground, Paul brings the argument full circle" (Fee, *God's Empowering Presence*, 400).

of God through the work of Christ and the Spirit, not through the work of observing and keeping the law.[238]

The Spirit's presence indicates that the transition has happened, that Jew and Gentile no longer operate under bondage but are free in their connection to the Triune God and to one another. It was not their law-keeping that accomplished it. In fact, it was accomplished long before the imposters came, when the Galatians experienced the blessing of the seed of Abraham in the person of Jesus Christ. This was expressed in the signs and wonders that occurred and the transformation that ensued in how they loved one another and loved Paul.

The result of their conversion experience was twofold: sonship and adoption. These comprise the essence of their inheritance.

Sonship is not gender-specific. It's a title and existence available to all humans. There is no maleness in this notion of sonship; it is the fulfillment of humanity that has transitioned from its orphaned state into familial connection with the Father, Son, and Spirit. Men and women, Jew and Gentile, exist now in a state of sonship, something that is completely foreign to the law and distant from any human structure. This is the grammar of blessing, not the grammar of the written law.[239]

When Abraham took a concubine upon learning that his wife Sarah was unable to bear children, he followed the law of the day in attempting to procure a descendent. Rather than resulting in the perpetuation of his sonship, it resulted in strife and division. God then worked a miracle in Sarah for her to have a true heir (Genesis 16:1–18:15). The birth of Isaac was accomplished outside of the law through a promise made by God Himself.

It is this logic that Paul uses against the imposters to help the Galatians see that what they embraced of the imposters' theology was destructive and further alienated Jews and Gentiles from God and one another. It placed a stumbling block in the way of the Galatians' intimate relationship with the Trinity. It sent the adherent back into the child-like supervision stage, rather than the freedom of living in their full adult stage.

---

[238] Fee continues, "At one point in human history, when God's appointed time had arrived, Christ entered human history (born of a woman) within the context of God's people (born under Law), to free people from Torah observance by giving them 'adoption as sons.' But this historical objective reality becomes realized (a 'subjective reality,' in this sense only) by the work of the Spirit. It is this twofold reality, both its historical objectivity and its experienced realization, that makes his argument work, since it is their experienced life of the Spirit who actualizes the 'sonship' Christ provided, which serves for Paul as the certain evidence that he is right, and the agitators are wrong" (Ibid., 404).

[239] I borrow this "grammar" language from J.B. Torrance's lecture, "Grace and Law in Rabbinic Judaism," given at Regent College in Vancouver in 1994.

Through adoption, we are included in the family of Father, Son, and Spirit. This is profound evidence of the deep love the Trinity has for humanity. Their desire is to gather humanity into relationship and secure the blessing of humanity abiding with them.

The use of the term adoption is considered by scholars to be drawn directly from the Roman context, where adopted children had equal rights to natural children.[240] Therefore, the attachment of adoption to sonship reinforces the equality of the Gentiles and Jews in their new familial relationship with the Trinity. What the law had separated and subjugated, at least in the mind of the imposters, the Spirit abolished.[241]

Inherent in this relationship is a deep degree of intimacy. The goal was not to immerse humanity into law observance but elevate it into deep familial connection. Paul describes this connection by the Spirit which enables the Galatians to call the Father "Poppa!" This term of endearment for a loving parent is what Paul uses to describe the intimacy that the Trinity cultivates in their relationship with humanity.[242] This is inclusion in the fullest sense. In this relationship, we have the same full rights with God as a blood relative.

This reminds me of the familial way in which Italian families such as my own welcome strangers with an intimate kiss on both cheeks and an embrace of acceptance.

---

[240] Trevor J. Burke tell us that "it is striking that Paul uses his *huiothesia* metaphor only in letters to communities directly under the rule of Roman law (Gal. 4:5; Rom. 8:15, 23; 9:4; Eph. 1:5)" (Burke, *Adopted into God's Family: Exploring a Pauline Metaphor* [Downers Grove, IL: IVP Academic, 2016], 61). He continues by saying, "Adoption was a means by which succession to power was brought about; from the late first century to the middle of the second century and later, successive Roman emperors adopted men not related to them by blood with the intention that an adoptee should succeed the emperor in the principate... When Octavia and the adopted son Nero desired to marry, special legislation had to be passed to allow Nero to marry a girl who was legally his own sister! This example illustrates the absolute nature of the adoption of Nero and that he, because of his adoption, was legally in every way considered the same as a natural born son" (Ibid., 62).

[241] Burke goes on: "This is because adoption was not only a safeguard against the demise of a family but also provided new opportunities for the adoptee that would otherwise not have existed" (Ibid., 65–66). Burke also points out that the perpetuation of the familial cult was deemed important as it related to Roman adoption law. It could be that Paul used the background of Roman adoption to indicate God's plan to perpetuate the human family according to His desire of universality and equality in relationship to Himself as Father, Son and Spirit, as opposed to the imposters' prejudice in nationalizing their faith in Christ through law-keeping and enforcing the law on Gentile sympathizers.

[242] O. Hofius points out the usage of *Abba*, "a word derived from baby-language" where children learned their first words for Daddy and Mummy, underwent an extension of meaning in the pre-Christian period so that, by the New Testament period, "the childish character of the word ('daddy') thus receded, and 'abba' acquired the warm, familiar ring which we may feel in such an expression as 'dear father'" (Hofius, "Father," *New International Dictionary of New Testament Theology, Volume One*, 614).

There is no way that a contemporary Jewish man or woman of Paul's day would have used this affectionate term. Their inherited reverence for God wouldn't have allowed them the intimacy of relationship with a loving Father that Paul characterizes in this part of the Galatian letter.[243]

Again, Paul marks out the difference in outcome between experiencing conversion through the work of Christ and the presence of the Spirit as opposed to observing the law and experiencing its continual condemnation and confinement. There is no way for someone to experience intimacy of Abba proportions by observing the law.

From a pastoral perspective, it is relatively easy to spot those who are obsessed with law-keeping versus those who have the intimate Abba relationship with the Trinity. Those obsessed with the law are crusty, hardened on the outside, and relatively angry. Their self-imposed legality robs them of the joy that comes from the freedom of intimacy and relationship with Father, Son, and Spirit.

As a pastor, I have often had to deal with the fallout of the rampage these legalistic individuals sometimes inflict on others, leaving hurt and scarred people in their path. Offering comfort to those who hurt and attempting to break through the hard veneer of those who inflict pain has been a common occurrence in my ministry. Usually, the legalist realizes that I cannot be bought with law-keeping rhetoric, so they slink back in their corner and attempt to wait me out.

Occasionally, my advance of forgiveness and embrace are met with a change of heart and a new perspective. These are unfortunately few and far between in the ongoing battle with legalistic Christians who believe that their flashlight and candles will work against evil. They never work; they always accomplish the opposite by perpetuating evil.

Those who forgo legalism and embrace the freedom of intimacy with the Father, allowing the Trinity to love them as Their children, are a joy to be with in community. For that reason, I keep teaching and preaching on Paul with the hope that the Spirit will break open the hearts of the crusty and cause them to feel the deep love that the Father and the Son have for one another.

In Galatians 4:7, Paul makes it plain: *"[Because Christ has come], you are no longer a slave but a Son and by implication an inheritor through God"* (my translation). Why would you want to go back to slavery in a home of condemnation and confinement, with your every move scrutinized and judged, when you can live in the Father's house where there is love and acceptance?

---

[243] Ibid., 615. Paul's use of "abba" confirms the role of the Father in the act of adopting humanity into the realization of full sonship.

LETTING GO OF IDOLS

Paul now addresses the Gentiles in the Galatian community, reminding them of what they were rescued from when they encountered the good news of Christ. They too were in slavery, but their slavery came in the form of allegiance to empty gods who required destructive and life-draining adherence. Paul identifies them as "no gods," although my translation refers to them as "idols."

Idols are part of the system of the world in that they drag humanity into useless and life-emptying patterns. They lead to death. Just as the law has no mercy for the observer and can only offer condemnation, idol worship subjects individuals to wayward powers of evil that work their way into people's lives.[244]

Any investigation into the pagan cults of the Roman period will uncover rites and rituals that are associated with demeaning practices, including sexual acts that dominate the worshipper and ensnare them in addictive behaviours.[245] These practices created a veil over the eyes of the Gentiles, just as the law had formed a veil over the eyes of the Jews.[246]

Law for the Jews and idolatry for the Gentiles were connected to sin and death. Paul called these systems weak and empty, enslaving both groups and robbing them of their true humanity. The imposters convinced the converted Gentiles to go back to observing special feast days and events so that it became a snare. Observing the law brought with it the same enslaving and ritualistic observances that existed in the pagan world, with veneration of idols and astrology connected to certain days and celestial entities. They traded a pagan type of calendaring for a legalistic Jewish calendaring.[247]

---

[244] *"What am I trying to say? Am I saying that food offered to idols has some significance, or that idols are real gods? No. Not at all. I am saying that these sacrifices are offered to demons, not to God. And I don't want you to participate with demons. You cannot drink from the cup of the Lord and from the cup of demons, too"* (1 Corinthians 10:19–21, my translation). This lends us to believe that although Paul didn't consider idols to be gods, he was aware that evil powers used the idol to destroy the worshipper.

[245] In my book, *A New Humanity*, I detail some of the practices of certain Roman pagan cults and their destructive results on their worshippers.

[246] *"But the people's minds were hardened, and to this day whenever the old covenant is being read, the same veil covers their minds so they cannot understand the truth. And this veil can be removed only by believing in Christ"* (2 Corinthians 3:14, NLT).

[247] Richard N. Longnecker writes, "Extensive debate has focused on what precisely Paul means by 'days… months… seasons… years.' That they all have to do with the Jewish cultic calendar in some way has seemed obvious, at least for most, from the context" (Longnecker, *Word Biblical Commentary, Volume 41: Galatians*, 182). Scholars like Craig Keener see both pagan and Jewish calendrical observances at play here: "Feelings about getting the fixed calendar correct obviously ran high on both sides. Paul's opponents apparently bought into such feelings, but Paul no longer (cf. Gal. 1:14) regarded the calendar as a matter of true consequence" (Keener, *Galatians: A Commentary*, 300).

Paul shows his desperation in this part of the letter. He shares with them his fear that all the work he and his team did was in vain. The intensity with which he entered communities and taught from the Scriptures about Christ, sharing the good news with new converts, seems to have had no impact on the Galatians, who had clearly taken a step back from their freedom in Christ and gone right back to their old ways. Just as Israel longed for the days of meat and the lash of the Egyptian taskmaster, so had the Galatians returned to the scarring servitude of evil.

There is nothing more despairing than watching those who once embraced freedom return to slavery. In this instance, it was peer pressure. Those who distorted the gospel had interfered with what God had accomplished through Paul and his missionary team, appearing holy to make the Galatians servants of evil once again. All this occurred within the believing community.

False leaders with distorted theologies are so destructive. They grieve God's Spirit and cause many to trade their freedom for what appears to be holy but is actually evil and wicked. Jesus called them sheep in wolves' clothing.[248]

I have witnessed far too often what happens to God's community when an imposter attempts to exert leadership. It seeps deeply into the community, creating a thick fog of confusion that convinces people they are doing God's work when they're following after the devil.

These imposters convince us that their flashlight and candles are the solution. They put them up for sale and mass produce them for their own profit. They take advantage of sweet and honest believers who simply want to live out the love of Christ in their community and neighbourhood.

Earlier in the letter, Paul proclaimed an "anathema" over such imposters (Galatians 1:8–9).[249] Their exclusion from God's community is necessary to protect the community from apostasy.[250]

As leaders who sincerely take up their ministry with humility and trust in Christ, we need to take a firm stand against such imposters, identifying where they have not represented Christ and carefully, with humility, turning the tide toward the Spirit's help to lead us into sonship.

The first move should always be toward restoration, but experience shows that not everyone wants to be restored or let go of their control over their captive communities. In these instances, a move of apostolic authority is important to

---

[248] *"Beware of false prophets who come disguised as harmless sheep but are really vicious wolves"* (Matthew 7:15, NLT).

[249] In my translation, the word anathema is translated as "condemned."

[250] Craig Keener describes it as "a looming threat of Paul's converts' apostasy" (Keener, *Galatians: A Commentary*, 300).

protect the body of Christ. If we are to be totally honest in this regard, we must be careful at every turn, regardless of how good our intentions, not to perpetuate the enforcement of certain behaviours that distance others from the Trinity. It's so easy to fall into the trap of believing that rule-keeping will accomplish "holier" living. We need to continually remember that "holier" living comes from our being in Christ and living by the Spirit, not from our own actions.

I tread ever so carefully to be sure not to fall into the trap of creating my own system of acceptance with God. We do best when we focus on Christ and lean on the Spirit as we lead and live in God's community, pledging our allegiance to Christ.

GO BACK TO YOUR LIFE IN THE SPIRIT

In reaching this point, Paul is near to concluding his argument regarding why the Galatians should go back to life as it was lived by the Spirit. He has argued for why following the imposters' "no gospel" is a step back into the pre-inheritance slavery they were in before.

He now describes what he experienced in his relationship with them prior to their going along with the deception of the imposters. His hope is to appeal to emotion and use his relational capital to help them move away from the "no gospel" and continue with the good news they heard from the beginning.

Paul says that what he saw in them after their encounter with Christ is what he focuses on being. Their posture and demeanour after their conversion was Spirit-dependent and Spirit-empowered, something he has always strived to be.[251]

The narrative in Galatians 1–2 describe his move away from the law toward Christ and the Spirit. This was mirrored by the Galatians' conversion and move toward Christ and the Spirit.[252] His ultimate hope in this part of the letter is that they continue, together with him, to demonstrate that same way of being in relationship with the Trinity and one another.

---

[251] Some scholars tend to put the emphasis on Paul stating here that the Galatians should imitate him. I disagree. Given the language in this section, Paul is using the argument that he is actually imitating how they were when they came to Christ and the Spirit came alive in them. I feel that Scot McKnight misses this point by focusing his entire attention on "imitating Paul" (McKnight, *NIV Application Commentary*, 4264–4310). I believe that at times our reformation roots tend to put Paul on a pedestal when Paul himself would say, "Enough about me. What about Christ and the Spirit and how they empower others!" Case in point is Ronald K. Fung, who interprets Paul's imitation through the retrospective view of grace, concluding that Paul became like them as Gentile sinners. Paul certainly focused on the prospective impact of grace in the Spirit-led behaviour the Gentiles demonstrated to him (Fung, *The New International Commentary on the New Testament*, 195).

[252] To reiterate, Paul was focused on the Galatian prospective view of their relationship with Christ.

In his first interaction with the Galatians, Paul found a people who weren't malicious and had no intention of taking advantage of him.[253] Even though he was weak in body, they were kind to him and took care of him. In fact, not only were they respectful of Paul's role as a messenger of Christ, they treated him as if he were Christ Himself. This showed their openness to the gospel. The work the Spirit performed in their hearts had moved them to respond to the good news.

The degree to which they were attentive to Paul was modelled in the way they served him during an illness that was most likely related to his eyes. No doubt he used others to write his letters, concluding them in his own handwriting to personalize them and confirm that they had originated from him. He does the same in this letter, noting the large handwriting he used to add the last few sentences of thought (Galatians 6:11).

Paul describes this eye condition as an unpleasant appearance that would have caused the most stoic of them to walk away in disgust. Instead it resulted in the Galatians caring for his needs.

Everything about how the Galatians interacted with Paul's first visit demonstrated a community that had been won over by the grace of Christ and took on the character of the Trinity in their deep expression of love and care for him.

Paul makes an attempt to appeal to this close bond, asking them, *"Have I now become your adversary by sharing the truth with you?"* (Galatians 4:16, my translation) In other words, "Don't hate me now that I love you enough to share the truth about what you are caught up in!"

The notion here is that if they accepted and embraced Paul at a time when he was at his worst, why would they reject him now? He hoped that their past bond would allow them to accept what he shared, moving them to continue in step with how he knew them to be.

To emphasize the point, Paul makes a contrast with the self-serving behaviour of the imposters, whose zeal was to win the Galatians to their side for the sake of expediency.

In my translation, I ran into difficulty translating the phrase "they are zealoting you" in Galatians 4:17. Instead I used an analogy of salesmanship. The imposters desperately wanted the Galatians to "buy" their version of the gospel to accomplish their selfish end of maintaining Jewish identity and privilege by subjugating Gentiles to Jewish ways. The imposters weren't creating a deep bond with the Galatians but rather were making a sale that allowed them to increase

---

[253] The phrase "you caused me no harm" can allude to the obvious intent by the imposters to malign Paul and use his good relationship with them for their own personal ends.

the number of people who were committed to their very Jewish and legalistic gospel. Not only that, but Paul's words indicate that their intent was to create a pyramid scheme in which the Galatians would in turn sell the same cheap goods to others.

The next sentence tells us what Paul would have preferred the Galatians do when confronted by the imposters' sales pitch. He would have liked them to counter the imposters with the truth of the good news they had received from Paul. He is pointing out that there were other options besides giving in to the imposters' teaching. They could have debated the truth of what the imposters were selling, and they could have used their exuberance for the good news to stand up for what they believed.

They hadn't needed Paul to be present to be excited about what they believed and experienced. The evidence of transformation in their lives should have been enough to make them exuberant for Christ.

Paul uses the analogy of birth pains to communicate what he had hoped was still embedded in their minds and hearts. The realization that they'd been robbed by deceptive leaders created a pain in Paul, like growing pains that occur when a community works out the truth of the gospel in the messy context of everyday life.

After all, as ministry leaders we don't work in ideal conditions. We don't have a lab-like environment where everything is carefully controlled. Rather, we share the good news in the messiness of life under the constant threat of distortion and misunderstanding. Ensuring that the truth of the good news sticks in the heart of the community is often long and arduous work.

Paul shares this hope in his Ephesian letter, as he describes what the roles of leadership in the church are to accomplish:

> [The point of this] is that we no longer be like children tossed around and led astray by every new teaching that appears from deceptive men who seek to trick others with their craftiness and seduce them with error. But by speaking the truth in love, we may be grown-up in everything in Him who is the leader: Christ! From Him all the body [is] well fitted and put together so that every piece works according to the measure of its individual part and so makes the body increase by building itself up in love. (Ephesians 4:13–16, my translation)

In Galatians 4, Paul realizes that there is still more work to be done among the Galatians to move them toward maturity in their newfound faith. This moves him to want to be with them again and reignite their bond and help them continue to grow to maturity.

He also realizes that his defensive and corrective tone throughout the letter needs to be accompanied with the gentle nurture that can only come with his presence among them. They need help getting back on track with their life in Christ and dependency on the Spirit. They need leaders to help them.

We see here the heart of Paul the pastor. He is in the business of using his leadership gifts to build up God's community. These early Christian communities needed continuous pastoral leadership that focused on helping them mature in their faith.

Leaders have the capacity to maintain a sustained level of growth and discipleship in a community. The longer they track with a community, the more their efforts bring unity and maturity among the people.

Yet Paul was also an Apostle and sought to urgently share the good news with the Gentiles across the Roman Empire. His primary calling drove him from place to place. Other leaders then settled into these new communities and continued the teaching and formation necessary for their growth.

For that to happen in Galatia, the new faith community needed mature leadership, and the way to get there was to first rid themselves of the imposters and their destructive teaching.

Chapter Ten

FREEDOM FROM SLAVERY

Galatians 4:21–31

Tell me, you who want to be under the law, don't you hear what the law says? It records the story of Abraham who had two sons, one by a slave woman and one by a free woman. The son of the slave woman was born according to human intent,[254] but the son of the free woman was born through [God's] promise. There is a deeper connection here to two covenants, one made on Mount Sinai that gives birth to slaves, represented by Hagar. She is Sinai in Arabia and answers to the authority of the present Jerusalem because she is in bondage with her children. But the Jerusalem from above is free, she is the mother of all of us. The prophet reminds us: "Sing, woman who is barren and can't give birth, burst into a loud shout, you that have not been in labour. You will have more children than women with husbands."[255]

Now we, my family members, are like Isaac; children of [God's] promise. Like in the story, the one born through human intent persecuted the one born in the Spirit, and that is happening right now [among you]. But the Scripture also says, "Throw out the slave woman and her son because the son of the slave woman will not inherit with the son of the free woman."[256]

---

[254] Κατὰ σάρκα translates literally into "according to the flesh." I chose to translate it as "human intent." Paul used the phrase to indicate that what had transpired between Abraham and Hagar, an arrangement made by Sarah to produce an heir since she had felt that she was past her childbearing years. This was evidence of her limited human reasoning. God had other plans and would cause Sarah to become pregnant and produce an heir of her own. This is how God dealt with it, which is why I add "God's" to the word promise—to make the distinction. Paul will use this distinction to make his point connected to the ongoing argument that God's promise to Abraham was fulfilled through the sending of the Son and not observance of and adherence to the Torah. The later brings slavery, not freedom.

[255] This is a quote from Isaiah 54:1. To understand the full context, it is valuable to read Isaiah 53 and hear the verse read in the context of the suffering servant passages that speak of the Messiah. The coming of God's suffering servant would cause the barren to give birth.

[256] See Genesis 21: 8–13. These were the words of Sarah when she reached her limit in tolerating Ishmael's behaviour toward her son Isaac. God confirmed these words to Abraham and assured him that Isaac would carry his lineage, but He would also cause Ishmael to father a nation because of his connection to Abraham and His promise to him.

So then, my family members, we are not children of the slave woman but of the free woman.

THE LARGER STORY

Paul, being a teacher, provides the Galatians with a lesson on the scope of the Jewish law. His goal was to provide them with a greater background on the law to help them understand the point he had begun expounding back in Galatians 3.

The law has not only a commandment focus but also a narrative that puts the commandments in context. If there is an argument over the law, it needs to encompass not only commandments—such as circumcision and other points of national expression like Sabbath-keeping—but also the story told in the books of the law. These stories carry with them essential reflections on the context within which God communicates His relationship with Israel and the other nations.

If the Galatians wanted to be people under the law, they needed to comprehend the full scope of that law from both perspectives.[257]

The imposters had been arguing at the commandment level, with an interpretation of the narrative that supported a Jewish-centric law-keeping gospel focused on keeping commandment while in relationship with Christ. Paul argued his point in relation to the larger story, with a focus on the promise-keeping gospel fulfilled in Christ, focused on God's actions in gathering Israel and the nations to Himself.[258]

---

[257] Gordon D. Fee writes, "He [Paul] now describes their condition [the Galatians] directly: they are 'those who want to be under law.' So, the challenge is, 'then let's look for a moment at what the law itself says.' This latter use of the 'law' offers clear evidence for its twofold use in first century Judaism: as the 'law' that is binding on those who wish to belong to Yahweh; and as the 'book of the law' that contains both the laws and their narrative setting. It is the narrative setting that Paul now wishes to interpret in light of Christ and the Spirit" (Fee, *Pentecostal Commentary Series*, 177).

[258] According to Richard B. Hays, "Paul reads Scripture in light of a narrative hermeneutic as a grand story of election and promise, the story of δικαιοσύνη θείου, God's covenant faithfulness reaching out to reclaim a fallen and broken humanity. That is why his use of Scripture highlights the story of Abraham (the patriarch to whom God's universal promise was made), the climactic chapters of Deuteronomy (which promise covenant renewal and restoration of the people), and above all the prophetic passages known to us as Deutero-Isaiah (which promise the revelation of God's salvation to all flesh, Jew first and then also all nations). The church is called to find its identity and mission within this epic story stretching from Adam to Abraham and Moses to Isaiah to Christ to the saints in Paul's own historical moment" (Hays, *The Conversion of the Imagination*, 147). The imposters had duped the Galatians back into the narrow story of Israel and protecting Jewish religious identity over Gentile identity so that Gentile converts would be encouraged to become Jewish in their adherence. Paul identified this as persecution, borrowing from the Abrahamic story in this section of the letter.

Paul had so far argued for what he saw as a much broader, more inclusive perspective on the biblical narrative of God in relationship with Israel and other nations. The Abrahamic story supports this perspective.

The imposters who influenced the Galatians to turn back to a law-focused gospel wanted to retain their narrow story that highlighted their relationship with God. They were comfortable asking Gentiles to conform to their Jewish story and assume a law-focused relationship with Christ. They convincingly showed that the Abrahamic story supported such a view. They chose to focus on the part of the story that was about them, rather than the all-encompassing story about God's plan to rescue and restore humanity.

Lest we get ahead of ourselves and acknowledge how obvious Paul's greater perspective is, it's important for us to look at our own view of the gospel's reach. The stories we recount about our own conduct as followers of Christ tell a great deal about how we view the crisis Paul addresses in this letter.

It has not been beyond us, as the church of the modern age, to narrow the good news of Christ to something that benefits us specifically and exclusively. It also has not been beyond us to describe in detail what the requirements of remaining in such a narrow view of gospel demand of us. It's easy to make the story about us, the church, rather than God and humanity. It is so much more tangible to identify the rules that make such a narrow gospel exclusive to us, rather than identify the actions and character that communicate the Trinity's love and sacrifice to humanity.

The moment we make the gospel about us, we practically ensure that it will be communicated in a narrow, self-serving perspective.[259] We need to ask ourselves, does our view of the gospel describe the broad biblical story of God's rescue of the human race? If we have difficulty answering such a question, we can quickly conclude that we have a far too narrow view of the gospel and God's intent toward the world.

In the Old Testament narrative, we tend to see Israel in a prominent place in the story, failing to see God's relationship with the other nations. His relationship with other nations has a consistent focus throughout the Old Testament narrative, with the same redemptive desire and quality that is present in the Israel story.[260]

---

[259] When we make the commandments more important than the story and its outcome, we have narrowed the good news and distorted it in such a way as to distract others from what God is up to in this world. The commandment is important but will always be distorted if removed from the greater biblical story at play.

[260] *"For the Sovereign Lord, who brings back the outcasts of Israel, says: I will bring others, too, besides my people Israel"* (Isaiah 56:8, NLT).

How Israel and the other nations respond is the other side of the story, and what God does is focused on Israel and these nations. In relation to this, the coming of Jesus is narrated in terms of a coming King who will unite all people and bring peace and harmony to the world.

This is what Paul is convinced of as he tackles this last point of tension regarding the interpretation of the Abrahamic story.

RECLAIMING THE CENTRAL POINT

As we enter this last section of Galatians 4, Paul takes a common story from the Old Testament, well known to his readers, and challenges the imposters' narrow view of it. He describes a much broader interpretation that supports the promise-focused gospel he is arguing for.

For Paul, God's revelation through the story of Abraham provides a richer interpretation of the scope of the Triune God's plan of redeeming the world. The imposters used the Abrahamic story to confirm their Jewish identity and God's preference of them as opposed to other nations. Paul points out that their approach is a human fabrication that intends to legitimize the view that they have a superior spiritual standing compared to the rest of fallen humanity. For there to be any hope for others, the imposters demand that Gentiles become like them in their Jewish identity.[261]

These imposters took the story of Hagar and Sarah and pointed out that Jewish identity was solidified in the birth of Isaac, who represents the chosen people of God. Ishmael, the son born to Abraham from Sarah's servant Hagar, represents Gentiles who are not of the same lineage as the descendants of Isaac. Since Hagar was not of Jewish descent,[262] Ishmael is less legitimate, like the Gentiles who come to faith in Christ.

---

[261] Scot McKnight tells us, "They [imposters] may have argued that Abraham's descendants were his 'fleshly' descendants, namely, Jews, and that the Galatians then needed to become Jews" (McKnight, *The NIV Application Commentary*, 4451). Richard N. Longnecker adds, "In explicating their position, the Judaizers undoubtedly claimed that Paul's preaching represented an 'Ishmaelian' form of truth. Their argument probably was that while Ishmael was, indeed, the first son of Abraham, it was only Isaac who was considered the true son of Abraham, with the conclusion being that only as Paul's converts are related to Isaac and so the Jewish nation, and not Ishmael the non-Jewish representative, can they legitimately be called 'sons of Abraham'" (Longnecker, *Word Biblical Commentary, Volume 41: Galatians*, 199).

[262] What's interesting about this notion is that the people of Israel existed in embryo in Abraham and his family, not yet fully developed into their Jewish identity. This harkens back to Paul reminding the Galatians in Galatians 3 that the Mosaic law didn't appear until four centuries after Abraham, arguing about whether legitimately viewing Abraham as a Jew is warranted at the point of the story in Genesis 21.

Paul takes the Hagar-Ishmael, Sarah-Isaac account and counters the impost-ers' view. He describes it as "allegorizing,"[263] pointing out that he is being drawn into this type of biblical interpretation. He works the story into a deeper mean-ing to show that God initiates the promise of Christ and the recovery of human-ity in the story of Abraham; this is opposed to the view that it is a Jewish story that enforces Jewish blood lineage and belonging.[264]

Where the imposters argued that the lineage born of "flesh"[265] is that of Isaac, Paul argues that the "flesh" connection is Ishmael. Most likely, he is referring to the intent by Abraham and Sarah to perpetuate the lineage of their family by producing a male heir through Sarah's servant Hagar, given that Sarah was old

---

[263] Allegory is a tool of interpretation that creates the freedom to deal with the reference points in a story in a way other than what was intended by the original author. Historically, this form of interpretation has garnered a negative view among conservative theologians. The point is that Paul was thrust into this by the imposters. It was not of his own choosing. Longnecker writes that "we need not see Paul as saying that allegory was built into the biblical narrative itself but that the biblical narrative is now being treated by the interpreter (whether Judaizers, or Paul, or both) in allegorical fashion" (Longnecker, *Word Biblical Commentary, Volume 41: Galatians*, 210). We also read from James D. G. Dunn, "The basic assumption of allegorical exposition is that the text has a deeper meaning or reference than appears on the surface. Such interpretation goes back to the fifth century BC (BAGD and LSJ, allegoreo), and probably entered Jewish hermeneutical practice through Alexandrian Judaism (TDNT i. 260–3)" (Dunn, *Black's New Testament Commentary*, 247).

[264] Gregory Boyd discusses the allegorical hermeneutic of the early church father Origen. He rejects Origen's belief that allegorical interpretations of Scripture were intended by the original authors, but he admires the determination of Origen in filtering all Scripture through the person of Christ as He has revealed the character of God in its fullness, along with the help of the Spirit in getting at the meaning that reveals God's true character. Boyd writes, "It is only by refusing to compromise the absoluteness and the beauty of the revelation of God in Christ while also refusing to compromise our conviction on the 'God-breathed' nature of even the ugliest and most offensive parts of Scripture that we acquire the ability to see how all Scripture points to the beauty of God's agape-love revealed on Calvary" (Boyd, *Crucifixion of the Warrior God, Volume One*, 459). This is exactly what Paul does with the Abraham story, filtering its interpretation through the coming of Christ as opposed to the historical narrowness of Israel's identity.

[265] It is likely that the imposters referenced the ancient practice of passing down lineage through natural birth, thus using the concept of "flesh," or of natural birth, attributing it to Isaac. Paul turns the idea of "flesh" on its head, being more of a desired "human intent" than a lineage that was promised by God to Abraham and Sarah. Gordon D. Fee tells us, "Returning to the language of 'flesh' that he had used earlier to contrast life in the Spirit and life under law (3:3), Paul says that 'the son of the slave woman was born according to the flesh'—which, in keeping with 3:3, the TNIV has interpreted as "by human effort,' but which elsewhere has been rendered 'sinful nature.' Thus, when Sarah and Abraham preempted God's purposes and took things into their own hands, they were acting 'in keeping with the flesh' that is, basic human fallenness, and thereby failing to put their trust wholly in God.—The irony here is that Abraham, the man of faith, himself acted in this case 'according to the flesh' and not 'by faith' in God's promise" (Fee, *Pentecostal Commentary*, 178).

in age and barren (Genesis 16:1). Paul calls their attempt to produce an heir on their own a function of their fallen humanity.

Paul continues his argument with the categories of "flesh" and "Spirit," something he has been arguing since the beginning of Galatians 3. Where "flesh" was used by the imposters as evidence of ethnic lineage and belonging to God, Paul used the term to refer to a fallen human action that produces a different outcome than the one God desires.

The birth of Isaac was not a "flesh"-inspired act, but rather a promise fulfilled by God to Abraham and Sarah. It was the arrangement Sarah made with Hagar to perpetuate Abraham's lineage, producing Ishmael, that exemplifies the act of the "flesh."

The imposters had put far too much trust in their "flesh" perspective while completely ignoring the Spirit aspect of the story. Where the imposters saw two separate groups, Jews and Gentiles, where one group was required to assume the identity of the other (Gentiles becoming like Jews), Paul saw in the Abraham story a promise to redeem both Jew and Gentile.[266]

Paul continues with the analogy to point out what the women represent in the story. Hagar is connected to Mount Sinai and the rulers of Jerusalem who perpetuate the covenant of law given on that mountain.[267] Such a covenant focuses on the actions of human intent and has perpetuated slavery. Sarah, on the other hand, represents the Jerusalem that is to come, often described in the Old Testament as Zion, which will bring freedom to both Jew and Gentile, focusing on the actions of God in redeeming humanity.[268]

---

[266] Paul emphasizes this in Ephesians 2, where both Jews and Gentiles are brought close by the coming of Christ. He breaks down hostility between the two groups and brings them into "one new humanity," establishing peace (the result of a benevolent king re-ordering a kingdom to honour all people).

[267] In my translation of Galatians 3:19–20, the reading focuses on how the fruit of what was given on Mount Sinai is mediated by the leadership of the "present Jerusalem," who hold Jews "in bondage."

[268] According to Herman H. Ridderbos, "This quotation [Isa.54:1] is taken from the prophecy of Zion's restoration and magnitude after the captivity. In this prophecy the promise is made that she that is barren and forsaken, like a woman separated from her husband and without children, will have more children than in the time when she, before the captivity, had not yet been forsaken by the Lord. This the apostle applies to the relation between the present Jerusalem and the heavenly one. The last is a mother by the grace of God, even as Zion was after the captivity. Her progeny does not depend upon natural development or exertion, but upon the divine miraculous power which grants life where it seemed impossible, and that in such abundance that it far surpasses the possibilities offered by the flesh" (Ridderbos, *The New International Commentary on the New Testament*, 179). See also N.T. Wright: "His opponents claim authority from Jerusalem; well, maybe so, but they are talking about 'the present Jerusalem', as opposed to the heavenly Jerusalem, 'the Jerusalem above', which is the real home of all believers" (Wright, *Paul for Everyone*, 59).

To make his point even clearer, he quotes from Isaiah 54:1, a passage which "immediately follows the suffering servant making God's people right with him. (Isa.52:13–53:12)."[269]

The barrenness of Sarah represents the inability of humanity to restore itself. The intervention of God in allowing Sarah to give birth is evidence that the Trinity is directly involved in leading humanity toward its intended restoration. It is this work of the Trinity that would go on to produce the Messiah who would redeem and restore the world. Paul reminded the Galatians that this was the promise the Spirit had brought them.

THE CLASH OF HUMAN EFFORT VS. THE SPIRIT'S WORK

Paul emphasizes that what the imposters proposed to the Galatians is a gospel of slavery. Their message of a flesh-based gospel, requiring full adherence to the law along with faith in Christ, promoted a controlled environment where people were subjugated to the requirements of the law and kept at a distance from the freedom that comes from the promise of Christ.

Paul points out that as children of God, the Galatians were called to the freedom of the promise. The activity of the imposters, like Ishmael, who represents the fallen human structure of the law, persecuted the children of promise.

This is a direct comment on what had been happening in the Galatian churches. The imposters were working to rob the Galatians of the freedom they had experienced in Christ, trying to confine them to rules and regulations that would keep them enslaved.

Moving to a law-focused gospel based on fallen human effort eliminated the inheritance of freedom promised by God to humanity. The only solution, from Paul's perspective, was to eliminate the law-based gospel altogether. The imposters' "no-gospel" was a stumbling block to receiving what the Trinity had always wanted to give humanity. Living in the freedom of relationship with the Father, where one's relationship with Christ is empowered by the Spirit's presence, is the Trinity's goal for both Jews and Gentiles.

It's important to note that although Paul had been attempting to repair the damage the imposters had done in the Galatian community, he didn't intend that the imposters be eliminated. He just said they should give up the law-focused

---

[269] Craig Keener writes, "The promised eschatological restoration to God has come; Jesus's followers in Galatia have entered that restoration, whereas the Jerusalemites [imposters] who reject it continue to live as in the pre-restoration judgment" (Keener, *Galatians: A Commentary*, 414).

gospel that had been received at Mount Sinai and guarded by the leadership in the present Jerusalem.[270]

Paul's intent was that both imposters and Galatians throw out the slavery to which they had returned and experience the freedom of living in their true humanity.

It's important to acknowledge in our own churches that a similar persecution continues today, breaking down the unity that comes when we all live free in relationship with Christ. It happens when one group feels the need to transpose the gospel of freedom into a law-based system that focuses on fallen human effort to stay in community and fellowship with Christ. Their dependence is placed on Christ, but in fact they brandish their own flashlight and a few candles to fashion their own acceptance into relationship with the Trinity. Such a perspective creates unrealistic parameters that deny the beauty and freedom of our new humanity.

As a pastor, I have worked hard to move congregations and believers to lay down their flashlight and candles and place their full trust in Christ and full dependence on the Spirit. It takes a lot of patience, the love of Christ, and "putting up" with individuals who continue to veer toward human effort to move into the freedom of Christ as a community. But the struggle is worthwhile when people see that there is no comparison between living a law-based gospel by human effort versus living in the freedom of the promised inheritance of our new humanity in relationship with the Trinity.

Gregory Porter, a jazz artist who was also a professional football player, and whose mother led a storefront church in Los Angeles, wrote a song titled "Be Good." The song is about a relationship he was in where his girlfriend always wanted him to be something he was not. Her expectations of him were confining, to the point that he broke up with her. She had certain rules about behaviour and appearance that Gregory found constricting. He could never measure up to them and eventually realized that she was robbing him of his free spirit and expression

---

[270] Susan G. Eastman writes that "the pattern of correspondence between the parallel opposing columns set up by Paul's allegory suggests that the metaphor of the 'slave woman' does not represent the circumcising missionaries themselves. Rather, it denotes their circumcising message and methods, which impose the Sinai covenant on Gentile Christians and enact a reliance on the nexus of the flesh and the law that has no place in the life of the Spirit-led community (5.6–21)" (Eastman, "Cast Out the Slave Woman and her Son: The Dynamics of Exclusion and Inclusion in Galatians 4:30." *Journal for the Study of the New Testament*, 28.3, 2006, 318). Eastman notes that Paul uses the aorist, active, imperative in the second person singular, ἔκβαλε, and not the second person plural. The idea here is that Paul is encouraging them to throw out the theological construct of their law-based gospel. She notes that Paul saves the imperative second person plural for "commands for the positive exhortations of Galatians 5:1 about 'standing fast', 'not submitting.' Perseverance in the freedom of the gospel, not expulsion, is Paul's command to the Galatians" (Ibid., 324).

of his true self. In the song, the girlfriend's name is "Be Good." He represents himself as a lion—large, strong, and untamed. Every time she comes around, she moves him into a cage and dances around, telling him to "be good."[271]

As I allegorize Gregory's song, I see "Be Good" as representing the law from Mount Sinai in the hands of people. It comes with all its expectations that puts us in a cage to be what we were not meant to be, nor who we truly are. We try our best to clean ourselves up, looking presentable and meeting the law's expectations, but every time she comes around, it's the same thing: we go back into the cage where she wants us.

Paul wanted the Galatians and the imposters to leave these harsh limitations behind so they could be who the Trinity had restored them to be. We need to eliminate this confining lifestyle in order to live in our new humanity and be able to enhance the world around us. Living in Christ by the Spirit should cause people and the world around us to thrive! That's the passionate plea of Paul to the Galatians.

If our behaviour as followers of Christ confines people to cages, if we use the law to keep others and ourselves in a lesser humanity, then we need to reassess our gospel and hear the urgent cry of Paul to stop focusing on our fallen human effort and trust in Christ and the empowering Spirit of God to help us thrive. After all, the Trinity's goal for us is to be children of freedom, not slavery.

The underlying lesson in Abraham's story is that we are not children held in slavery but rather children of the free woman, Sarah, whose womb was opened by God to give birth to a son of promise in Isaac. This promised birth is the anticipation of the Son who would come after him and restore Israel and the nations to their true humanity. Israel would become the vehicle through whom this Son would enter the world, redeeming it from within, gathering all humanity to Himself, and freeing it from the bondage of evil.

This is the theme Paul started the letter with back in Galatians 1:4–5. It will be the theme he concludes with in Galatians 5–6, describing what freedom in Christ looks like and the scope of the influence of such freedom on humanity.

---

[271] Gregory Porter, "Be Good (Lion's Song) Official Video," *YouTube*. March 20, 2012 (https://www.youtube.com/watch?v=9HvpIgHBSdo&ab_channel=motemamusic).

Chapter Eleven

FREEDOM IN CHRIST

Galatians 5:1–26

Stay in the freedom that Christ freed you with, don't get caught again in the shackles of slavery.[272] Be clear[273] that I Paul tell you if you accept circumcision, Christ will be of no benefit to you. I record again [my words of warning to you] that every person who [focuses on] circumcising [and law-keeping] is indebted to keeping it in its entirety. You who seek to be made right by the law are cut off[274] from Christ and have fallen away from grace. We [on the other hand], through the Spirit by faith, are eagerly waiting for the hope of righteousness, because in Christ, outward expressions of law-keeping[275] count for nothing. Only faith working through love [matters].

---

[272] The word Paul uses is Ζυγῷ, which is translated as "shackles," means a "yoke." Its origins come from the tool used to brace an animal for the purpose of it pulling a load. The word is used for both animals and slaves. H.G. Link has written, "In Gal. 5:1, Paul may well be taking up Jewish pronouncements about the yoke of the law- Paul denounces the yoke of the law as a yoke of slavery" (Link, "Yoke," *New International Dictionary of New Testament Theology, Volume Three*, 1164). The heavy burden of the law is that it must be observed in full in order to be able to maintain relationship with God—or in this case, relationship with Christ. Since the word "yoke" isn't commonly understood, I decided to use "shackles" instead.

[273] Ἴδε, the aorist active imperative of εἶδον, comes from the root ὁράω, meaning "to see" (Harold K. Moulton, *The Analytical Greek Lexicon Revised*, 117, 291). Paul wants it to be clear, based on his argument regarding the law that started back in Galatians 3:1, that anyone who puts the law front and centre to their relationship with Christ will not reap the benefit of what Christ has given to those who put their trust in Him.

[274] Καταργέω, when used with God as the subject, indicates being put out of action; this refers to destructive powers that threaten a man's spiritual well-being. But when humans are the subject, this results in "attempts, witting or unwitting, to contradict and cancel those principles and powers of divine working which bring salvation" (J.I. Packer, "Abolish, Nullify, Reject," *New International Dictionary of New Testament Theology, Volume One*, 73).

[275] Paul uses circumcision as the object that "counts for nothing." I have broadened it to be representative of anything that outwardly displays law-keeping, since this was most likely Paul's intent. Craig Keener points out that circumcision was the outward sign of law-keeping being abused by the imposters and imposed on Gentile converts. It's not so much the outward practice as the abuse of it that matters. He wrote, "Paul's concern about circumcision was only about it being imposed on gentiles as a spiritual demand… in the new creation, the old outward sign became a matter of indifference, just as complexion or nose shape would be in the choosing of athletes" (Keener, *Galatians: A Commentary*, 471).

You were running in the right direction. Who cut in on you [and kept you] from obeying the truth? This did not come from Christ who called you.[276] A little bit of distorted teaching can permeate the whole community.[277] I am convinced by the Lord that you will not follow their point of view and whoever is stirring up confusion will sustain[278] judgment. Now if I was still preaching to you, my family members, the outward adherence to the law [as has been said by the imposters], why am I still being persecuted [by them]? I would have left out the offensive parts of my preaching on the cross [if that were true].[279] I wish that those who stirred you up would cut off themselves.

You were called to freedom, my family members, only don't let your freedom be an incentive for the flesh, [rather use your freedom] to serve one another through love. For all the law is fulfilled in this one statement, "Love your neighbour as yourself." But if you bite and devour one another, be on the alert lest[280] you are destroyed by one another. On the other hand, I say walk by the Spirit and you will not fulfill such

---

[276] Paul's words can be literally translated this way: *"This convincing is not from him who called you."* I've made this sentence more explicit and eliminated the word "convincing," as I believe that idea is already implicit in what he has written so far in this chapter.

[277] Here Paul uses a baking metaphor, of leaven affecting a whole lump of dough. I have chosen to concretize the statement to make it obvious that the distorted teaching of the imposters has affected the whole faith community of the Galatians. I side with Gordon Fee when he concludes that Paul was addressing communal tension: "…quite in contrast to how this material is read by the most of us—and is presented in many of the commentaries—the concern from the beginning to end is with Christian life in community, not with the interior life of the individual Christian" (Fee, *Empowering Presence*, 425). My translation is an effort to keep this focus front and centre.

[278] The common meaning of βαστάζω is to "bear, endure, or carry." I chose to use the word "sustain," as it is consistent with the use of the word by Paul in Romans 11:18 (Harold K. Moulton, *The Analytical Greek Lexicon Revised*, 68).

[279] I have massaged this statement from Paul, who said, literally translated, *"As a result, the offense of the cross has been removed."* It is difficult to get after what Paul is saying, but when taken in context it's clear that Paul's focus on Christ—in this sentence, he references the cross as a short form for all that Christ had accomplished by His coming—is what had caused tension with the imposters. If he had left this out of his preaching, there would have been no tension. Note what N.T. Wright says: "Wherever he [Paul] goes he is attacked by those Jews who think he is letting the side down, who cannot bear his message of a crucified Messiah. As always in this letter, the cross is at the heart of Paul's gospel, and Paul knows it is always a 'scandal'—it demolishes the boast of those Jews who suppose themselves superior to the rest of humanity simply because of their ancestry" (Wright, *Paul for Everyone*, 66).

[280] The negative μη used here as a conjunction. G. Abbot-Smith wrote, "II. As a conj., 1. after verbs of fearing, caution, etc., that, lest perhaps (M, Pr., 192 f.): c. subjc. praes., He 12:15; c. subjc. aor., Mt 24:4, Mk 13:5, Lk 21:8, Ac 13:40, Ga 5:15" (Abbot-Smith, *A Manual Greek Lexicon of the New Testament* [New York, NY: Charles Scribner's Sons, 1922], 290). It follows that βλέπετε can be literally translated as "watch," but I have chosen to capture its cautious intent: "be on the alert."

desires.[281] For the desires of the flesh push against the Spirit, and the desires of the Spirit push against the flesh [and are clearly] in opposition to each other, keeping you from doing the things you want to do. If you [choose] to be led by the Spirit, you are not under [the suppression] of the law.

Now the actions of the flesh are in full view: sexual immorality, uncleanness, lewd behaviour,[282] idolatry, witchcraft, hostility, discord, jealousy, rage, fighting, dissensions, divisions, envy, drunkenness, orgies, and similar things. Like I have said before, I tell you again, those who do these things will not inherit the Kingdom of God. But the fruit of the Spirit is love, joy, peace, patience, kindness, goodness, faithfulness, humility, and self-control; there is no law that limits these things.[283] Those in Christ Jesus have crucified the flesh with its passions and cravings.

If we live by the Spirit, we will also keep in line with the Spirit. So let's not become arrogant, agitating, and begrudging one another.

ONE WAY OR THE OTHER, BUT NOT BOTH!

Paul now summarizes the argument he has built from Galatians 3 through to the end of Galatians 4: freedom in Christ is the focus of the Christian life. For this freedom to be the focus, the law must be viewed in its proper place, as a placeholder in time, only to be relied upon until Christ appeared and brought to fruition our inheritance as sons of God.

After Christ, we can now move on from the law's supervision and live free, in full relationship with Christ, by the help of the Spirit, who draws us into fellowship with the Father. This is the promise God gave to Abraham. We are now drawn to Christ and those who believe become the true sons and daughters of Abraham, children of the Father.

---

[281] Paul adds the word σαρκός here, which means "of the flesh," but I have left it out so that the verse reflects the obvious desire of the flesh to do violence to one another. The next sentence points out how the flesh combats what comes with the Spirit, the act of loving one another.

[282] Some translate ἀσέλγεια as "sensuality." I have chosen "lewd behaviour," to be more specific to its negative sexual connotation. According to David J. Sigrist, "This refers to a lack of control over oneself, often in the form of excesses of sex and/or food. It is often linked to other vices that are associated with undisciplined and wasteful living; it occurs 10 times in the NT, mostly in vice lists where it is linked with sexual sins" (Sigrist, "Sin," eds. D. Mangum, D. R. Brown, R. Klippenstein, and R. Hurst, *Lexham Theological Wordbook* [Bellingham, WA: Lexham Press, 2014]).

[283] Paul's actual words are *"against such things there is no law."* Taking this in context with how Paul described the confining and limiting aspects of the law prompted me to translate it the way I did. These relational behaviours of the Spirit enhance and promote community and have no limit.

Ethnic lineage plays no part in this, and neither does human effort in ascribing certain advantages to one group over another. Paul's desire was that the Galatians, both Jew and Gentile, remain free to live in the sonship Christ brought them.

The important point Paul makes in Galatians 5 is that it's either one way or the other, but not both. A person either chooses to live by the Spirit in Christ and live out their Christian life in love toward others or they focus on law-keeping as their outward mark as a Jewish believer, their aim being to fulfill the law in order to belong to Christ.[284]

Paul warns that anyone who decides to focus on outward law-keeping has been cut off from Christ. Their decision to be law-focused causes them to fall away from the grace of restored relationship and renewed humanity Christ brought through His incarnation, life, death, resurrection, and ascension.

In Galatians 5:4–5, Paul contrasts these differing views of what righteousness looks like. For law-keeping believers, the goal is to seek to be made right with God through the law. For those who live by the Spirit, the goal is to put their faith and trust in Christ, living in relationship with the Trinity until righteousness comes in its fullness at the end.

The group that lives by the Spirit focuses entirely on loving others as they put their trust in Christ. They know that any attempt at law-keeping is useless in the economy of grace. Righteousness, as a relational concept, is established through trust, not human effort.

In Ephesians, Paul makes it very clear that those who have been chosen in Christ are declared to be holy and blameless (Ephesians 1:4). These elements of character are achieved only when humanity gives itself over to relationship with Christ. They are a product of relationship, not law-keeping.

Paul highlights this in Romans 12, when he tells the Roman believers that the only reasonable thing to do in the face of the Trinity is to *give our lives as living sacrifices to God.*" (Romans 12:1, my translation).

The outcome of Paul's Galatian argument is that believers focus on their connection to Christ through faith, their enablement by the Spirit towards love, and expressing that love in a continual and faithful connection with others. This Christ-focused, Spirit-enabled behaviour points toward what Paul calls the hope

---

[284] John Stott explains, "The slogan of the false teachers was: 'Unless you are circumcised and keep the law, you cannot be saved' (cf. Acts 15:1, 5). They were thus declaring that faith in Christ was insufficient for salvation. Circumcision and law-obedience must be added to it. This was tantamount to saying that Moses must be allowed to finish what Christ hand begun" (Stott, *The Bible Speaks Today*, 133).

of righteousness, which comes with an eternal reality of living with the Trinity in the end (Romans 12:1).[285] Paul writes that this is what matters now that Christ has come.

The fact is that the Galatians were running in this direction. Reiterating their puzzling shift towards law-keeping, Paul asks them again who "cut in" on them and kept them from being obedient to the revealed truth of Christ and His work. This is rhetorical, since Paul had already identified the imposters. The point is that he wants the Galatians to take a hard look at who "cut in"[286] on them and evaluate them based on the argument he has made so far in the letter.[287]

Those who followed Paul in Galatia and persuaded the Galatians to adopt a law-focused gospel didn't come from Christ. These imposters came into the Galatian faith community and began sowing their distorted gospel. The seed of their teaching took hold and permeated the entire community. Paul's use of the analogy of leaven and its effect on dough makes the point that however subtle their distortion was, it gained traction and touched them all.[288]

---

[285] Gordon Fee writes, "By that same Spirit and on the basis of faith in Christ alone, we eagerly await our hope of realizing the eschatological goal, - Our present justification/righteousness based on the work of Christ and the Spirit is what will be realized—provided we continue in faith and the Spirit and do not return to slavery, which promises no eschatological reward, only death.—The latter not only fails to provide righteousness now but offers no hope for the future; life in the Spirit, includes living a life of genuine righteousness now ('faith expressing itself through the Spirit's fruit of love') and having absolute certainty about its final outcome" (Fee, *God's Empowering Presence*, 419). Fee emphasizes that ἐλπίς is "a 'content' word, expressing surety, not uncertainty" (Ibid.). Craig Keener adds to this that "the English word 'hope' does not fully communicate Paul's thought, since it might convey merely a wish; Paul's expressions of hope are secured in reality, so the term 'expectation' or 'expectancy' better conveys the idea in English" (Keener, *Galatians: A Commentary*, 469).

[286] Although Paul used καταργέ in Galatians 5:4 and ἐγκόπτω in Galatians 5:7, there is a theme of being "cut off" from the gospel. The Galatians embraced the distorted gospel, which "cut them off" from Christ; the imposters "cut in" on the Galatians. This destructive theological perspective translates into destructive communal behaviour. It isn't difficult to see the contrast of this with a gospel of faith in Christ, empowered by the Spirit, toward love which embraces humanity. That love spills over into behaviour that promotes acceptance and harmony.

[287] Richard Longnecker tells us, "The Judaizers must have assured the Galatians that in accepting supervision for their lives from the prescriptions of the Mosaic law they were not forsaking Christ or renouncing grace, but rather were completing their commitment to both. Paul, however, tells them the opposite: commitment to Christ and commitment to legal prescriptions for righteousness, whether that righteousness is understood in forensic terms (i.e., 'justification') or ethical terms (i.e., 'lifestyle' and expression), are mutually exclusive; experientially, the one destroys the other" (Longnecker, *Word Biblical Commentary, Volume 41: Galatians*, 228).

[288] Craig Keener goes on to say, "The entire batch of dough—refers to the Galatian congregations. The leaven's corrupting influence has not yet finished its work, but if left unchecked it can destroy their faith in the gospel" (Keener, *Galatians: A Commentary*, 480). In fact, Paul may be working the analogy to the point that the leaven of the imposters was taken from a past batch of dough to extend it to a new batch. This was the intent of the imposters—to keep Christianity Jewish in its identity and expression of law-keeping.

The Galatian believers were a community that lived in harmony, sharing the love of Christ with one another. The intimacy and depth of their relationship and love strengthened the community as a living organism. When something foreign entered the community, contradicting the foundation of faith expressing itself through love, it affected everyone.

I think of how distorted views of the gospel affect our present faith communities. I've seen firsthand how a deviant belief enters communities, takes hold, and creates confusion. Slowly it permeates and affects the stable harmony that was previously established. Works of the flesh begin to creep in, passed off as fruits of the Spirit.

At this point, a spiritual shepherd must respond to what has crept into the fold and deal with it head on, with the same faith expressing itself in love. This is the crucial part of the response, because there is a real temptation to get drawn into fleshly behaviour.

Paul's letters have been a guide for me in times when I've had to deal with distortions and infiltrations of the kind Paul writes about to the Galatians. Both his attitude and approach have modelled how to deal lovingly and forcefully to bring a community back to what matters: faith expressing itself through love!

Paul was convinced that the Lord would protect His people, and that through his faithfulness as their spiritual mentor Christ would persuade the Galatians of the truth Paul so faithfully shared with them. He was also convinced that those who had stirred up confusion among the Galatians would suffer judgment for their actions.

As Paul models his own trust in God to bring the Galatians back to the truth, he shows us how to trust God to hold the imposters accountable while still being the loving redeemer God revealed to us through Jesus. Only the Trinity can win over agitators like the imposters, holding them accountable while at the same time working toward their redemption. After all, Paul had been just like them at one point. He marvels over the fact that God chose him to be an Apostle, reaching the Gentiles with the good news of Christ.[289]

What would happen if the imposters were converted to a Christ-focused, Spirit-empowered gospel? What influence could they have in living out their calling in Christ?

---

[289] Acts 9 records Jesus holding Saul accountable for his persecution of "people of the Way." His subsequent blindless and then healing through the prayer of Ananias is the demonstration of forgiveness and love. Our culture today has attempted the same process through truth and reconciliation, although with varying results.

It was difficult for Paul to know that the imposters had distorted his teaching and put in his mouth words that were not his, reflecting inaccurately the gospel he had shared with the Galatians. The imposters had told the Galatians that Paul also taught outward law-keeping.

Paul informed the Galatians that this was a lie. The evidence was seen through the fact that he had been persecuted by the same law-focused Jewish Christians on his journey of church-planting across the Roman Empire.

He told the Galatians that to agree with the imposters he would have had to set aside the cross-centred gospel he had preached to both Jews and Gentiles. By mentioning his preaching on the cross, the scope of his teaching encompassed not only the narrative of the incarnation and last days of Jesus's life, but also the entirety of His mission, death, resurrection, and ascension, evidenced by what Paul writes. His mention of the cross is but a representation of the full theological perspective on the work of Christ and its impact on the world and humanity.[290]

Along with embracing law-keeping as a way of acceptance with God, the imposters had "cut in" on the Galatians and their living in the Spirit. Paul ends this thought by acknowledging a wish that in no way would be fulfilled:[291] that the imposters would cut themselves off.[292] He probably wrote this in defence of

---

[290] N.T. Wright writes, "The point throughout is that the crucifixion of the Messiah is not just an event in the past that changed the world once and for all, though it certainly is that. It is not just the 'mechanism' of salvation, though if we must use that language, we can do so without inaccuracy. The Messiah's crucifixion was not a strange, one-off deal through which God played a trick on sin and death, after which normal operations were resumed—the Messiah's crucifixion unveiled the very nature of God himself at work in generous self-giving love to overthrow all power structures by dealing with the sin that had given them their power, that same divine nature would now be at work through the ministry of the gospel not only through what was said but through the character and the circumstances of the people who were saying it" (Wright, *The Day the Revolution Began*, 251).

[291] Paul uses the word Ὄφελον, an interjection identified by Bauer as "a fixed form, functioning as a particle to introduce unattainable wishes" (Bauer, *A Greek English Lexicon of the New Testament and Other Early Christian Literature*, 599).

[292] It is difficult to ascertain how far Paul truly goes with the violence of this statement. It could refer to mutilating a body part, given that the Greek origin of ἀποκόπτω is widely used to indicate the "cutting off of limbs and body parts" (Ibid., 93). It can also serve as a reference to the pagan obsession of "cutting," represented in circumcision compared to the Cybeline cult where clergy castrated themselves in ritual observance. Timothy George has written that "the Judaizers who made so much of circumcision were really no better guides to the spiritual life than the pagan priests who castrated themselves in service to an idolatrous religion" (George, *Galatians, Volume 30* [City, State/Province: Broadman & Holman Publishers, 1994], 372). Or it could be a stylistic use of vocabulary, since Paul had used ἐγκόπτω, and now ἀποκόπτω, in Galatians 5:12. According to Craig Keener, "So Paul hopes that those wanting to "cut around" the Galatians' foreskins, who 'cut in' to make them stumble, will instead 'cut themselves off'—writers often displayed their rhetorical skill or even made arguments based on wordplays" (Keener, *Galatians: A Commentary*, 477).

his converts, as a protective apostle and pastor, hoping against hope that these imposters would remove themselves from such destructive behaviour.

This would have solved so many issues in the churches Paul had planted. Zealous Jewish Christians with a passion for law observance had followed Paul all over Asia Minor, trying to coerce Gentiles into a law-focused gospel.

LIVING IN FREEDOM

Paul comes back again to the freedom that was the people's in Christ, and he includes himself in this freedom by addressing them as his family members. His reminder is that freedom is not anarchy, a license to do as one wishes without accountability. This is the farthest thing from his mind as he points the Galatians toward the freedom that is in Christ, where the community devotes itself to Christ and is empowered by the Spirit to live out the basis of the entire law given by God to Israel: loving one's neighbour.

Paul addressed the Gentiles, who were knowledgeable concerning the passions and cravings of their fallen humanity, having come out of abusive and destructive living. The last thing Paul wanted was for their newfound freedom to take them back to such a life. His goal for them was to look to the future and live out their new humanity by living in the Spirit and expressing the love of Christ in all their relationships.

Life in the Spirit fulfills the nature of the community Jesus birthed in His coming. It is the fulfillment of the promise God made to Abraham, a future where Jews and Gentiles are able to live in harmony under the love and providence of the Triune God of grace.

Paul encourages the Galatians that if they walk by the Spirit, they won't give in to the flesh. The Spirit will push against the flesh and work to keep the flesh at bay.

Their turmoil, at the instigation of the imposters, was the flesh pushing against the Spirit and robbing them of their freedom. If they continued to let the Spirit lead them, as He had done from the onset of their conversion, they would avoid being enslaved by the law. Remaining in the Spirit would also keep them from the destructive acts of the flesh that created strife in their community and turmoil in their personal lives.

A law-focused gospel creates tension within any community living in the Spirit. With the law, the emphasis is placed on following rules, as opposed to organic relationship with God and others, which prevents God's community from living out the character of the Trinity in the fullness of their love for each other. Focusing on rule-keeping creates a culture of suspicion, with individuals looking to see if others are towing the line. Suddenly what was freedom becomes a fear of being excluded and judged.

Paul mentions that such an atmosphere prevents a community from living out their new humanity. Nothing in the exertion of human effort can replace the Spirit's empowerment. The Spirit will never lay a heavy burden that supresses the new humanity Jesus has given us.

I mentioned earlier in the book that present generations of believers try to maintain the spiritual freedom of previous generations by turning those previous believers' freedom into rules and requirements. By doing so, they destroy the freedom of the Spirit to work in the present, robbing themselves of the Spirit's desire to do something new, relevant, and timely in their generation.

Such communities stagnate, unable to move forward. They lose the voice of the Spirit to lead them into a greater relationship with the Father and others. The focus shifts from having a relationship with the Trinity to a fleshly focus on human effort. The result is hyper-legalism on one hand and a vulnerability toward sinful behaviour on the other.

Paul warns the Galatians that they are on a dangerous precipice. By focusing on their own effort to adhere to the law, they had created a contentious culture that pitted individuals against one another. Their focus was on adhering to the law instead of loving one another in faith. Only the latter can ultimately fulfill the focus of the law. Shaking off the shackles of such a law focus is crucial to maintaining the freedom to walk by the Spirit and embrace a forward-looking perspective that creates a thriving community.[293]

WALK IN THE SPIRIT

Paul lists the types of behaviour that keep one from inheriting the kingdom of God. It's always interesting to take note of the items he adds to such "sin lists," where envy and divisions are listed with behaviours such as orgies and witchcraft.

The point is that the behaviours are destructive, regardless of their nature or source. Such actions keep people away from God and their freedom in Christ. It also keeps them in a less-than-human state, far from the new humanity that is theirs in Christ, creating chaos and confusion. The reality is that a law-keeping gospel moves people toward the kinds of behaviours Paul listed, which are just

---

[293] According to Gordon D. Fee, "what is at stake in this argument is not the 'interior life' of the individual believer, but the 'behavioural life' of believers in relationship to one another and the world" (Fee, *Galatians: Pentecostal Commentary Series*, 206).

as dangerous to communal harmony as some of the obviously destructive pagan practices.

How much better it is to exhibit the fruit of the Spirit, with actions like love, joy, peace, kindness, gentleness, and patience bringing harmony and deep connection to a community. These actions speak of God, in eternal relationship as Father, Son and Spirit, sharing of Himself with humanity. The Trinity desires humanity to engage at every level of relationship in love, and it is the Spirit's desire to make the love of the Father and Son a reality.

No doubt Paul envisioned so much more for the Galatians than what they had been living before coming to Christ. The last thing he wanted was for them to give up their freedom and harmony for the confinement of living under the weight of guilt in a law-focused community. His fear was compounded by the knowledge that the weight of the law could also send the Galatians back to their old destructive lives.

The imposters were proposing a hierarchical, ethnically divided community that created the same strife that existed in communities that indulged in the flesh. Envy, jealousy, fighting, and division are the reality in both contexts.

In contrast, the community that lives by the Spirit and walks in the freedom of Christ has the potential to experience the kind of relationship that is shared between the Father, Son, and Spirit. Believers in such a community have the greatest chance of living out their new humanity in full.

Evil has a hold on humanity at the point of flesh. The law-focused gospel aggravates the fallen flesh and creates a destructive community, but those who have shifted to living in Christ have essentially crucified the fallen flesh. The desires that come with it have been put to death.[294]

What emerges is a life lived in the Spirit, apart from the flesh. It is a total devotion to the Spirit's presence and His empowerment. This is life lived in community. The gifts of the Spirit are shared and create a culture where people are restored and grow in their new humanity. It becomes a new discipline, a way of following Christ that doesn't give attention to the flesh.

---

[294] Take note of Gordon D. Fee's qualification of this statement: "At the same time this is not to be understood as some form of triumphalism, as the exhortation that follows in v. 25 makes clear. Rather this is to be understood within Paul's eschatological framework. Here is the 'already' of eschatological salvation; the death of the 'flesh'—the former way of life—has 'already' taken place through Christ's death and resurrection. But at the same time vv.25–26 bring one back to the reality that there currently remains a 'not yet' to this same salvation" (Fee, *Pentecostal Commentary on Galatians*, 226). One's dependence on the Spirit is predicated on one's need for help from the Spirit to keep the flesh at bay until the final consummation at the end-time of the transformation from mortality to immortality (1 Corinthians 15:42–44).

Paul uses a military analogy, using the action of marching to symbolizing "keeping in line" with a life lived with the Spirit.[295] As Paul mentions in Ephesians, there is a discipline to putting off the old humanity and putting on the new humanity.[296] The community focuses on serving one another versus enslaving one another, by exhibiting the fruit of the Spirit as a daily routine.

While Christ has crucified the flesh, the Spirit is present to empower the community toward building virtues, such as love. The community makes a conscious choice to walk and keep in step with the Spirit. Such a community does not agitate each other or live jealously. These behaviours aren't in keeping with living in the Spirit. This would be to fall out of step, or to march out of line, with the Spirit.

Freedom in Christ is ultimately ours through Christ. We can consistently live in this freedom by the Spirit empowering us to be free. But a community needs to want to be free and stay free.

Paul's encouragement to the Galatians to walk in the Spirit is the pathway to consistent freedom. If law-keeping takes centre stage at any point, the community will fall back into a flesh-focused life, living according to their own fallen behaviours and forsaking the Spirit.

In this chapter, Paul calls on us to stay focused on the Spirit and what the Spirit brings to our community, so that the love of the Trinity can reign supreme.

So far, the Galatians have shown a communal atmosphere that is in keeping with the flesh. Paul points out that this is incompatible with life in the Spirit. It will take a conscious effort and focus toward the things of the Spirit, and away from the things of the flesh, to restore their freedom in Christ.

---

[295] Timothy George says, "The verb translated 'keep in step with' is a military term meaning to 'be drawn up in line,' to 'stand in a row.' In Hellenistic philosophical circles, this word was used to mean 'follow someone's philosophical principles.' It suggests, therefore, the basic idea of discipleship: conformity to Christ under the leadership of the Spirit. Therefore, just as we put to death the old existence of the flesh in mortification, so too we move forward in the life of faith by keeping in step with the Spirit in our attitudes, conduct, and lifestyle" (George, *Galatians, Volume 30*, 406).

[296] In my previous book, I wrote, "What you learned was to put away your old way of living, which only made you worse because of the insatiable appetite for empty things, and to be renewed in the spirit of your mind. Put on your new humanity that has been created for righteous relationship and holy living" (Lombardi, *A New Humanity*, 83).

Chapter Twelve

REDEMPTIVE FREEDOM

Galatians 6:1–10

Family members, if anyone is caught off guard[297] by any moral slipup,[298] you who are Spirit people[299] should restore them [back to community again][300] in a spirit of humility. [While you're doing this] be careful so you too aren't tempted. Help each other with the load you carry[301] and

---

[297] The passive voice and subjunctive mood in προλημφθῇ gives this action a sense of the unexpected. Moulton points out that "to take by surprise, pass, be taken unexpectedly, be overtaken, be taken by surprise, Gal. 6.1" (Moulton, *The Analytical Greek Lexicon Revised*, 345). I've chosen to maintain this by using the phrase "caught off guard."

[298] We read in *The Lexham Theological Wordbook*, under the definition for παράπτωμα, "This is the noun form of piptō and carries the same connotation of moral failure. It can denote the greatest of moral failures, such as the sin of Adam or the totality of sin (Rom 5:20), as well as less severe lapses (Gal 6:1)" (Sigrist, Mangum, Brown, Klippenstein, Hurst, *The Lexham Theological Wordbook*). Compare with to W. Gunther: "*hamartia*, which with its cognates designates offences against morals, laws, men or gods. *Adikia* and its cognates cover a more specialized area, drawn from the legal world; as the opposite to—righteousness—it denotes unrighteousness, injustice, and unjust deeds. *Parabasis* and its cognates throw light on a further aspect: in particular they refer to transgression of the law. On the other hand, *paraptoma*, which is derived from *parapipto*, fall down besides, lose one's way, fail, means more generally a moral lapse and an offence for which one is responsible" (Gunther, "Sin," *New International Dictionary of New Testament Theology, Volume Three*, 573).

[299] I'm using Gordon Fee's translation. He wrote, "To be a person of the Spirit does not make one an elitist or a 'pneumatic' in the midst of others who are not so. As all the preceding imperatives imply, a Spirit person is not a perfect person, but one who by the Spirit's empowering lives in keeping with the life the Spirit produces (the fruit of the Spirit)" (Fee, *The Empowering Presence*, 462).

[300] I'm following Moulton again in his suggestion "to restore to a forfeited position, to reinstate, Gal. 6.1" (Moulton, *The Analytical Greek Lexicon Revised*, 229). Paul has written so far in a communal sense in terms of behaviour toward others. In Galatians 6, it's clear that he is encouraging the Galatians to help their fellow believers remain in community by showing them the restorative love of the Spirit. The opposite, of course, is the law-keeping gospel's focus on keeping the law to remain in community, which Paul critiques implicitly in Galatians 6:1.

[301] Paul's literal statement here is "bear one another's burdens." Each one of us carries the responsibility to pay attention to the weight of living in God's community, and to be there to share in the bearing of that load. W. Mundle tells us, "In Gal. 6:2 Paul encourages his readers to bear one another's burdens. They ought to come to the aid of one another, if overtaken by a fault. The joint bearing of suffering is not excluded. Such joint bearing does not do away with the personal responsibility of Christians" (Mundle, "Burden, Heavy, Labour," *New International Dictionary of New Testament Theology, Volume One*, 261). I chose the phrase "help each other with the load you carry," harkening back to the words of Jesus in the Sermon on the Mount in Matthew 5:41. Since Paul references the law of Christ, I felt it consistent to use such a phrase.

[by doing so] fulfill the law of Christ. You deceive yourself if you make yourself out to be more than you are.[302] Each one should examine their own efforts [whether they have "kept in line with the Spirit"],[303] so that their boasting will be only in themselves and not in their neighbour's [efforts] [like the law-keeping imposters do]. Everyone will have to carry their own load [regarding the keeping of the law of Christ].

The one who is taught the word should share all that is good with their teachers. Don't be led astray. Don't turn your nose up at God. Whatever you put out there will come back to you. If you put out from your [fallen] flesh, you'll get back destruction. But if you put out from the Spirit, then from the Spirit you will get back eternal life. So let's not get tired of doing good, for in time we will benefit[304] if we don't give up. In every chance we get, let's do good to everyone, and especially to those in our faith community.

HOW IT WORKS ITSELF OUT

Paul now describes what it looks like to put one's walk in the Spirit into practice. Since living by the Spirit is the focus of remaining in the freedom of Christ, he wants to give the Galatians a practical perspective on what that looks like, in contrast to the self-centred law-keeping gospel that was dividing God's community.

The theme of Galatians 6:1 is forgiveness and restoration. Paul describes the very real possibility of believers being surprised by a moral lapse of some sort. My translation describes this as a "moral slipup." This refers to those moments when someone is drawn into a morally questionable activity, compromising their ability to stay in step with the Spirit. Paul encourages the Galatians to restore

---

[302] Paul's literal words are "If anyone thinks they are someone, they deceive themselves." This comes on the heels of him encouraging those who are spiritual to help those who have fallen morally. Paul quickly reminds the Galatians to not put on airs about their ability to do so. The proof is in how each models the law of Christ and expresses it in love. This is then worthy of boasting, but only in oneself or else they would fall in with the imposters, boasting about others to bolster their case about the superiority of their law-keeping gospel.

[303] It's certain that the "works" mentioned here, translated as "efforts," relate back to the kind of behaviour that is consistent with walking in the Spirit. Paul focuses on this behaviour in Galatians 6, having established in the previous chapter that the pathway to freedom in Christ is to walk in the Spirit, keep in step with the Spirit, and produce the fruit of the Spirit. These are positive expressions of what it looks like to express faith in love.

[304] I strayed from the "sowing and reaping" analogy to render this thought in our vernacular. Ultimately, "to reap" is to benefit from what our hard work has "sown," or put out there.

such an individual to the community. The idea is to help pick them back up again in a spirit of humility, where those doing the lifting are aware that they could have been the one needing the lifting.

Paul calls on "Spirit people" rather than "you who are spiritual," which is how this is commonly translated.[305] The notion is not on finding those who at a particular time feel more spiritual or close to the Spirit than others. Rather, Paul describes what this looks like for people of the Spirit, which in this case is the Galatian community. It's more a description of how to behave in community as Spirit people than an indication of what some among the community can do because they are more Spirit-endowed than others.

Given the argument Paul has made throughout Galatians 5, in which he points out the arrogance of the law-focused imposters and how it has set the community at odds with itself, he means to point out communal behaviour rather than individual privileged behaviour.

As a Pentecostal pastor, I have seen no shortage of a few wanting to jump over other believers in the same community into an elitist existence of privileged Spirit empowerment. Such individuals have laid claim to spiritual gifts as though the gifts were an office they held, germane only to them. They self-proclaimed these positions to lead the community into hyper-spiritual activity that promotes their own spirituality and pronounces their authority over such matters.

These individuals don't want to hear what Paul has to say about their self-proclaimed spirituality. They've turned living by the Spirit into a personal spirituality that defines false notions of charismatic gifts, creating inequality in

---

[305] The focus here is not on whether someone feels especially empowered by the Spirit at that moment, exuding a level of spirituality that is superior to another. This would make the opposite point to Paul's. The point is that the Spirit community behaves in this way. Gordon D. Fee writes, "With this word he is not, as some would have it, addressing a special group within the community, who are, or think they are, 'spiritual,' who must restore the fallen one because both he and others in the community are (presumably) not 'spiritual.' Rather, Paul is addressing the entire community ('you [plural] who are Spiritual' = 'you who live by the Spirit'), just as he has with all the second person plurals that have immediately preceded the sentence" (Fee, *Pentecostal Commentary on Galatians*, 230). According to Longnecker, "But Paul has repeatedly spoken elsewhere in Galatians of all Christians as being possessed by and in possession of God's Spirit (cf. 3:2–5, 14; 4:6, 29; 5:5, 16–18, 22–23, 25; 6:8). There is, therefore, no reason to doubt and abundant reason to believe that Paul here uses this designation with approval in speaking about *all* his converts in Galatia. They are, despite their legal and libertine enticements, 'the true spirituals' simply because by being 'in Christ' they have become the recipients of God's Spirit. So, by reminding his converts of their status as πνευματικοί Paul calls on them to live up to that status" (Longnecker, *Word Biblical Commentary, Volume 41: Galatians*, 273).

the community. Such activity is just as damaging as the law-focused gospel of the imposters in Galatia.[306]

Those imposters evinced no spiritual humility. Their concern was strictly regarding the conduct of others and making sure they followed practices like circumcision and Sabbath-keeping. They arrogantly judged and excluded anyone who didn't observe the law. This spoke of their sense of separation from others; they had no real connection in terms of community.

In a law-based culture, when one slips up, the result is judgment and separation from the community. Rather than help pick people back up, law-followers instead keep their distance, as in the parable of the good Samaritan (Luke 10:25–37). This creates the kind of agitation and jealousy Paul mentions in Galatians 5:26.

Paul follows his example of restorative freedom for the Galatians with a statement about being careful not to be tempted by whatever causes a fellow community member to stumble. The reality of the people's need for the Spirit's help is evident in a Spirit-focused community.[307] In the same spirit that the Trinity demonstrated to humanity through the coming of Jesus, Paul encourages believers to offer forgiveness and restoration to others. It is an expression of the equality mentioned back in Galatians 3:28, with everyone being *"one in Christ Jesus."*

In such a community of equality, individuals seek to help each other live in the Spirit. Helping others carry their load is an act of faith expressing itself through love.[308] Those in God's community help one another carry the burdens

---

[306] Longnecker adds, "And while Paul was always against sin in whatever form, for him pride, aloofness, and conceit were also sinful, being often, in fact, far more damaging to the community of believers and the gospel message than overt moral lapses. So here in a practical manner he brings together his two lists of vices and virtues in 5:19–23, showing how in practice 'the fruit of the Spirit' overcomes 'the works of the flesh'" (Longnecker, *Word Biblical Commentary, Volume 41: Galatians*, 274).

[307] Ronald Y. K. Fung writes that "'each one of you' has the responsibility to exercise the strictest vigilance over himself, lest the would-be restorer become an offender himself. Such vigilance is necessary because 'anything can become a temptation and because no one is above the possibility of succumbing to temptation (cf. 1 Cor. 10:12)" (Fung, *The Epistle to the Galatians*, 286).

[308] We read from Longnecker, "Here τὰ βάρη has primary reference to 'the burdens of temptation' spoken of in v 1, though probably also has in mind more generally oppressive burdens of any kind (cf. Rom 15:1 and 1 Cor 12:26, though without the noun βάρος). It is doubtful, however, that Paul is using βάρος with any idea of 'financial support for Jerusalem,' as some have posited..." cf. James D. G. Dunn Epistle to the Galatians, pg. 322 "... Paul is probably thinking of a whole range of illnesses and physical disabilities, of responsibilities born by slaves or widows, scruples of fellow members (Rom. Xv.1—not sins), and so on..." (Longnecker, *Word Biblical Commentary, Volume 41: Galatians*, 274–275).

of everyday life as they move together along the pathway toward the coming kingdom that will arrive upon Christ's second coming.

Paul describes this practice of carrying each other's loads as observing the law of Christ. Based on what he has written so far in the letter, it's clear that the law of Christ focuses on good in the face of evil, letting love reign in community, and giving of oneself to help others.[309]

In the immediate context of the present passage, Paul is most likely alluding to the one aspect of the Torah Jesus proclaimed as being among the greatest commandments: loving your neighbour as yourself (Galatians 5:14; see also Matthew 22:37–39). Paul draws this from the teachings of Jesus and puts it front and centre as the chief expression of the community that "keeps in line with the Spirit."[310]

Where the mention of this command in Galatians 5 defines those who live in the freedom of Christ and live by the Spirit, it is represented in Galatians 6 by the example of helping those who have slipped up and those who need help with the weight of life they are carrying.

Being equal in relationship and identity in God's community results in a reciprocity where we help one another. This makes the Spirit the focus of the community. It also models how the Trinity supports one another in their redemption of humanity, with the Spirit empowering the Son to do the will of the Father for the sake of creation.

The persons of the Trinity give themselves to one another and together give themselves for humanity. As a result, there is no greater modelling of the character of Father, Son, and Spirit in God's community than the love they show one another.

In Galatians 6:3–5, Paul reminds the Galatians that each one bears the responsibility to keep the law of Christ as well. The goal isn't to achieve a level

---

[309] Gordon D. Fee writes that "'the law of Christ' is first of all an appeal not to some new set of laws or even to some ethical standards that the gospel imposes on believers, but to Christ himself, who in this letter has been deliberately described as the one 'who gave himself for our sins' (1:4) and who 'loved me and gave himself for me' (2:20). Thus, he has already served as the paradigm for the argument in 5:13–14" (Fee, *The Empowering Presence*, 463). Ronald Y.F. Fung adds that "here he speaks of 'the law of Christ' polemically, if not almost playfully, as an antithesis to 'the law of Moses.' It is as though he said to his converts: if you must observe the law (as the agitators say) do so—only make sure that the law you observe is not Moses' law, but the law of Christ" (Fung, *The New International Commentary on the New Testament*, 287). Finally, Scot McKnight notes, "The Christian's law is following Jesus, that is, living in submission to the Spirit" (McKnight, *Galatians: A Commentary*, 5544).

[310] James D. G. Dunn says, "In Galatians the climax comes by referring to the law of Christ at the equivalent point and with the equivalent function: fulfilling the law of Christ (Gal. vi.2) means following the example of Christ in seeking the good of the neighbour (Rom. Xv. 2–3)" (Dunn, *The Epistles to the Galatians*, 323).

of growth that sets one above another. Thinking too highly of oneself sets one at odds with a community that focuses on equality and loving one another.

Rather than compare our growth to someone else, we should keep close watch on our own walk in the Spirit.[311] We should boast in ourselves for achieving the fruit of the Spirit and refrain from applauding one individual over another.

The imposters promoted a community that followed the law-keeping gospel in which the achievement of keeping the law was acknowledged and very evident to all. This led them to the dangerous practice of measuring the success by each member of the community, boasting in those who did and deriding those who didn't.

In a community of those walking in the Spirit, each person bears the responsibility of carrying the load of keeping the law of Christ without it becoming a competition. After all, whatever an individual accomplishes as they walk in the Spirit is enabled by the Spirit.

I have noticed a trend where faith leaders often take sole credit for the communal efforts of those in their communities. They speak in terms of "I" rather than "we." This mentality implants a sense of hierarchy in leadership that doesn't exist in the Trinity's expression of their work in our world. The cooperation of the Father, Son, and Spirit in giving themselves to our conversion and restoration is betrayed by those who seek to promote themselves.

As leaders, we should be asking ourselves, "Have I fulfilled the law of Christ, as I walk in the Spirit, in the role that I play in my community?" Our acts of love and personal assessment of ourselves against the fruit of the Spirit should be front and centre in God's community. Anything we use to measure our success should be evaluated against God's character.

The temptation to acknowledge the efforts of the flesh should be avoided at all costs. It's far too easy to fall into the trap of boasting in our own human effort. This produces a culture of insecurity where leaders compensate by being controlling and authoritarian, while members of the congregation fall in line with unrealistic expectations.

In my experiences of working with churches and leaders, unhealthy faith communities exhibit a sense that something isn't right in their culture. The obvious places to look are their leadership and the behaviour of their members.

The first flag is assessing whether it's a law-focused community. Members of Spirit-focused communities exhibit more care for one another. Law-focused

---

[311] Craig Keener says, "Some plausibly suggest that the comparison with others here is a back handed slap at Paul's opponents, ready to boast in the Galatians' circumcised flesh (Gal. 6:12–13)" (Keener, *Galatians: A Commentary*, 117).

communities create cultures of insecurity and division. It's easy to turn a community into being law-focused by igniting our fleshly desire to excel above others. Such a culture promotes human effort to get to a place of elevated spirituality, which feeds into the desire for prominence and recognition.

Therefore, Paul makes a point of demonstrating what it looks like for a community and its leaders to keep in step with the Spirit. Paul presents a challenge to the Galatians, as well as a challenge to readers, concerning the measurement of oneself against the character and expression of Spirit-focused living.

To remain a Spirit-focused community, it is imperative that we examine ourselves. What would it look like if we carried our own load and measured our behaviour against the law of Christ? What would be the result if we did the hard work of being faithful to the Spirit, being preoccupied with loving others above all else? What would it mean to continually crucify the desires of the flesh that continually threaten to emerge?

Asking these pressing questions expresses the work of Christ in delivering us from the present evil age and leading us into the age to come.

There is no doubt of the passion of the Apostle Paul to start Spirit-focused communities among the Gentiles. If we could get our heads around letting go of all the petty works of the flesh and move into Spirit-empowered communities that extend the love of Christ to the world, we would truly be God's community, bringing the redemptive freedom of relationship with Christ wherein our new humanity, described by Paul as living in the Spirit, is front and centre.

GETTING BACK WHAT WE PUT IN

Galatians 6:6 brings home the argument about the importance of us carrying each other's loads. This scripture concerns the relationship that teachers like Paul should have with those they teach. The underlying thought draws on the previous five verses to reflect on how the two groups should care for one another.

Just as teachers care for the spiritual needs of those they teach, so should the students care for the teachers. Paul addresses the responsibility of those who receive teaching to share with those who teach. The reciprocity of the teachers carrying the spiritual load, while those being taught carry the financial load, represents God's community functioning in the Spirit.[312]

Although Paul rarely took support from the churches he planted, preferring to provide for himself so as not to burden the churches, there were times

---

[312] Ibid., 123.

when Paul did take support from specific churches to further his missionary endeavours.[313]

It is prudent to remember that Paul was a church planter. His self-support created opportunities for him to start faith communities throughout his travels. Not only did he raise his own funds, he was supported by other faith communities.

But his example is not the model by which a faith community cares for their ministry leaders. His words in Galatians 6:6 remind communities to be sure to carry the load of the leader financially, while the leader in turn carries the load for the people's communal spiritual development. This mutual giving causes everyone involved to thrive.

Paul moves into the metaphor of sowing and reaping to highlight the reality that certain actions in the present result in certain returns in the future. The idea is that what one puts in will be what one gets back. It is a law of reciprocal returns, and God has put it in place.[314] No amount of manipulating on our part can circumvent this principle at work in creation.

Like the analogy of turning up one's nose at God and attempting to defy the order of the universe, the law-focused behaviour of the Galatians doesn't contravene God's principle.

The example, of course, is that of the imposters. They tried to follow Christ by sowing the seeds of law-keeping and maintaining Jewish identity, the result of which was the community getting in return arrogance, agitation, and jealousy, where they were *"biting and devouring one another"* (Galatians 5:26, NLT).

The thoughtful, gentle, and loving actions of the Spirit reap a return of eternal life. Such actions allow the Trinity to move. The final hope is a restored humanity and world where evil is eliminated and peace reigns. God's community can leverage the principle of reciprocal returns in a way to bring about the restoration of our world through the Trinity.

Paul's concern was that the Galatians might be growing weary of doing good in a world where evil reigns. There was all kind of evidence during the early Roman period concerning the difficulties of life and the authoritarian control

---

[313] Read what Craig Ott writes on this subject: "Paul received financial support from the Philippian church while in Thessalonica (Phil. 4:16), although it was apparently not enough to fully support him, since he also laboured there to support himself (1 Thes. 1:9). Paul initially supported himself while in Corinth, but 'When Silas and Timothy came from Macedonia, Paul devoted himself exclusively to preaching, testifying to the Jews that Jesus was the Messiah' (Acts 18:3–5). The reason was that, as Paul states, 'the brothers who came from Macedonia supplied what I needed' (2 Cor. 11:9a)" (Ott, "Missions and Money: Revisiting Pauline Practice and Principles." *Evangelical Review of Theology*, volume 42, issue 1, January 2018, 9).

[314] N.T. Wright, *Paul for Everyone*, 78. See also John Stott, who speaks of the concept of "seed, time and harvest" (Stott, *The Bible Speaks Today*, 165).

of the emperors. Christianity was a small movement that lived contrary to the oligarchs who ruled over society. It was a tough go to express Christian love in such a violent culture.[315]

Yet Paul encouraged the Galatians not to succumb to discouragement. The principle of reciprocal returns will determine what one is rewarded. Those who exhibit the selfish desires of the flesh will reap its destruction, whereas those who exhibit the loving acts of the Spirit will gain eternity. This would have been the motivation of the early martyrs of the Christian community as they gave their lives for the faith.

At times, believers grow weary of doing good. They wonder if the hard work of doing good makes a difference in our culture, especially when the culture seems to reward other ideals that are contrary to the work of the Spirit.

The answer to this is found in what we "let in." It's easy to get discouraged by the barrage of daily news morning, noon, and night. The focus is always on the destructive actions of humanity and nature. Yet this is but one point of view. Yes, bad things occur daily. But much good takes place as well and we have the freedom to choose where we focus our attention. Humanitarian efforts that take place around the world, much of it in the name of Jesus, offer encouragement that actions in keeping with the Spirit result in the perpetuation of life.

When we exhibit the actions of the Spirit, time is on our side. Over time, consistent acts of love, both individually and as a community, create a benefit that outshines the evil in our world. This is true for the act of Christ's sacrifice on the cross and it is true for us as His community living according to the Spirit.

Because of this, Paul encourages the Galatians to take advantage of every chance to do good. He points out that doing good should be most evident in the community of faith, because for the Galatians their dividedness had put them at odds with each other, promoting evil among them. Paul tells them to get started doing good in their own community so that good would spill out to the world around them.

The Galatians had been handed flashlights and candles that couldn't withstand the onset of evil. This new faith focus had made them emphasize their own behaviour and put them at odds with each other. The imposters had kept their eyes on the law and taken them off Christ, making Christ subservient to the law.

The focus of God's community is on Christ and the strength of our relationship is found in the Spirit, which aligns us to Christ and the Father.

---

[315] See my book, *A New Humanity*, for a detailed commentary on the Roman Empire and its cultural heaviness during the time of the first century.

Making use of the gifts the Spirit gives us results in increasing returns that lead us into lives where we can thrive in relationship to the Trinity and one another.

This is the place Paul desires the Galatians to get back to. We would do well to respond to Paul's encouragement by making use of the gifts of the Spirit to perpetuate the growth of God's community and the coming of His kingdom.

I don't know about you, but I want to be part of a community that loves one another and helps carry each other's burdens. Knowing that my brothers and sisters in Christ have my back and are there to show me love and kindness in my worst moments gives me hope. It keeps me pointed in the right direction and focuses my heart on the restoration of all things in the end.

When I live in such a community, I am motivated to exhibit the things of the Spirit, which have a certainty of positive returns. It also brings freedom in Christ to others, like it came to the Gentiles who were lost in the destructive practices of the pagan cults.

Having known such freedom, my desire is that others share in it. I have no desire to return to a law-focused faith that obsesses about identity and rule-keeping. For that matter, I have no desire to perpetuate acts of destruction. The goal is to live in the freedom Christ has given us and not get tangled in the sordid life of exhibiting the flesh and reaping destruction.

If you're still hanging on to flashlights and candles of your own making, or those that were handed to you, I encourage you to lay them down and take up the freedom of living in Christ and expressing the fruit of the Spirit. This behavioural focus keeps us on the path toward eternal life.

Chapter Thirteen

FREEDOM TO SEE WHAT GOD SEES

Galatians 6:11–18

You'll notice the large letters I'm writing with my own hand. All who want to look good in the flesh, and who convince you to be circumcised [do it] to not be persecuted for the cross of Christ. The truth is those who are circumcised don't keep the law themselves, but they want you circumcised so they can boast in your flesh. But there is no way that I will boast[316] except in the cross of our Lord Jesus Christ, through which the world has been crucified to me and I to the world. For neither circumcision nor uncircumcision gives anyone an advantage.[317] [What matters][318] is a new creation. And for all who keep in step[319] with this standard, peace, and mercy on them and on the Israel of God. Now don't cause me trouble, for I carry on my body the marks of Jesus.

The grace of our Lord Jesus Christ be with your spirit, my family, Amen.

GIVING IN TO CONFORMITY

For reasons that are difficult to corroborate, Paul decides to point out at the end of the letter that he is writing with his own hand in large letters. Scholars are divided on whether Paul had written the entire letter by his own hand, and now made a comment on how large his writing was, or had at last

---

[316] Paul's literal words are *"But no, no way, me to boast..."* As you can see, it sounds awkward in English. I have chosen to massage it into *"There is no way I will boast..."* The phrase used here, μὴ γένοιτο, is a common one for Paul, and he uses it to respond emphatically to rhetorical questions. See Romans 3:3–4, where Paul responds to the rhetorical question of *"Will someone's lack of faith nullify the faithfulness of God?"* and Paul responds with *"No way!"*

[317] Paul's literal words here are "is anything." I have decided to use "gives anyone an advantage," since this is in keeping with the argument Paul has been making about the outward focus of the flesh and the uselessness of such a focus when considering one's relationship to the Trinity.

[318] I've added the words "What matters ..." This is an evaluation of worth tacked onto the previous mention of circumcision and uncircumcision, which continues in the sentence with the mention of "a new creation."

[319] This is the same word Paul used in Galatian 5:25 concerning "keeping in step with the Spirit." I have stayed consistent to make Paul's literary comparisons obvious to the reader.

taken over from a recording secretary and added these final thoughts personally. Or perhaps he was simply making these next sentences larger for emphasis.[320]

Regardless, Paul makes a point of bringing to a conclusion all that he had written by ending with a summary that left the Galatians with the essence of what it was he wanted them to take away from the letter.

Paul concludes in Galatians 6:12–13 that the reason the imposters showed up among the Galatians was to encourage their conformity to the law-focused Jewish gospel, perpetuated by a certain group in Jerusalem that was a part of the Jewish Christian community. Encouraging the Galatians to follow the outward adherence of the law—in this case specifically, circumcision—would keep them from being persecuted for their belief in the work of Christ.[321]

These individuals were concerned that they and other Jewish adherents to the gospel Paul preached would succumb to critique and persecution by their fellow co-nationals, unless they showed their adherence to the Jewish law. Giving witness to their Jewishness by their actions of law adherence would allow them to move freely in Judea as Jews, showing where their loyalties lay. As a result, they wanted to boast in other believers following the outward markings of the law.

Paul sums up his critique of the imposters by saying their desire is to conform rather than convert. Unconvinced of the sole work of Christ and the enabling work of the Spirit, they hold to their Jewish identity and ideals as a way of avoiding the violence toward them that someone like Stephen in Acts 8 suffered at the hands of other Jews.

What particularly bothered Paul was how they boasted about their fleshly markings when their focus on such markings proved that they weren't sold out to the Spirit, having not crucified the flesh altogether. This put the work of Christ in question and drew the Galatian Gentiles back into a fleshly focus.

Conformity is not evidence of conversion. In fact, Paul has built a case that evidence of conversion is a changed heart that lives out of love for the Trinity and others. He points out that this is the chief purpose of the law and is perpetuated by embracing the Spirit, who enables one to remain in such love.

Legislating conversion to a certain outward expression robs the Spirit of renewing a person from the inside out. Conformity focuses on the outside and is satisfied when those external changes are complete.

---

[320] For a comprehensive review of the reasons Paul writes in large letters, see what Craig Keener writes about Galatians 6 (Keener, *Galatians: A Commentary*, 1–93).

[321] N.T. Wright notes, "Under pressure themselves from fellow Jews to prove that they are not compromised by associating with Gentiles, they are passing on this pressure to the Gentile converts.—They are shown up as shallow and trivial" (Wright, *Paul for Everyone*, 81–82).

It's paramount that we acknowledge in our faith communities that conversion is the beginning of a relationship with Christ wherein one lives in harmony with the Spirit in the new humanity the Father has willed to all. Such expressions of love are as varied and unique as the character of those who come to Christ. There is no one way of ordering such expression, although Paul does mention some common behaviours that are in keeping with the descriptions of the fruit of those who live by the Spirit.

It would be good at this point to think of your own faith community and ask whether conversion is evidenced by the transformation toward loving God and others. Is there freedom to make room for the multiple ways people express their love? Is there unity that comes in the diversity of gifts and personality in a group of people who devote themselves to Christ and one another? Or are there expectations of conforming to some regimented behaviour that comes with a law-keeping focus?

I ask this because Jesus reacts to the religious leaders who sought converts with the sole purpose of conforming them to their ways. In Matthew 23, Jesus pronounced several warnings to the religious leaders regarding their focus on forcing others to conform to their ways while preventing them from embracing the kingdom of heaven.[322] Jesus had no time for people who sought out others to conform them to their version of a distorted gospel.

As Paul mentions in Galatians 6:5, the onus is on God's community to bear their load in keeping the law of Christ and leaning on the Spirit for the ability to love others. There is no conformity in the Trinity. The Father does not force the Son or the Spirit into a uniform expression. They live and love in unity but express themselves uniquely.[323]

Paul encourages the Galatians, and by extension us, to see that the Spirit enables us to stay faithful to the good news of Christ and live our lives in Him

---

[322] The phrase "kingdom of heaven" in Matthew is synonymous with "kingdom of God" in Mark, Luke, and John. Particularly scathing is Jesus's comment in Matthew 23:15: *"Misery on you, scribes and pharisees, [you] hypocrites! You cross sea and land to make one convert, and when he becomes one, you make him twice the son of hell as yourselves"* (my translation).

[323] Baxter Kruger writes, "Fellowship, camaraderie, togetherness, communion have always been at the center of the very being of God, and always will be. It is critical that we see this. And it is just as critical that we see that the shared life of Father, Son and Spirit is not one of sorrow and loneliness and emptiness. It is not about isolation or self-centeredness. It is all about fellowship. And fellowship means that God is not a lonely, sad, and depressed being. As Father, Son and Spirit, living in fellowship, God is essentially and eternally very happy. The Father, Son and Spirit live in conversation, in a fellowship of free-flowing togetherness and sharing and delight—a great dance of shared life that is full and rich and passionate, creative and good and beautiful" (Kruger, *The Great Dance: The Christian Vision Revisited* [Vancouver, BC: Regent College Publishing, 2000], 24).

by walking in the Spirit and letting our connection to the Trinity flow into living harmoniously with one another. Our maturity as God's community should move us to ask the hard questions of ourselves so we don't fall into the distorted gospel of the imposters but uphold the gospel of freedom in Christ lived out in the Spirit.

CHANGE IN PERSPECTIVE

Paul contrasts the boast of the imposters in a law-focused gospel to his one and only boast in the cross of Jesus.

As mentioned earlier, "the cross of Christ" is short-form for Paul's emphasis on the work of Christ in delivering humanity from evil and restoring them to their new humanity. For Paul, Jesus's story was a lens that transformed his fleshly view of the world into a redeemed view of the world. He no longer saw from a human point of view.[324]

In 2 Corinthians, Paul told his readers that he had once seen Jesus from a fleshly point of view, a dead Messiah who hadn't fulfilled His calling. Now that he had experienced conversion, he knew Jesus in a new way.

This shift in perspective changed how Paul saw the world. It was no longer a place that needed to conform to law-focused adherence, but rather a place that was loved by Christ and the object of the work of Father, Son, and Spirit for its transformation and restoration.

Paul's desire was to bring the transforming message of Christ to Gentiles and Jews across the Empire. He saw that God's plan was to renew His creation. The law had disadvantaged everyone so the Father could bring the advantage through Christ, by the Spirit.[325]

People were no longer expedient for Paul, but precious and valuable—and his animated, pointed words in this letter direct the Galatians back to this value. It upset him to see them behave like pawns in the plans of the imposters.

Paul lived in a culture where wealthy people used others for their own purposes and then discarded them when they were finished. This was a fleshly point of view, seeing others as instruments for one's own interests. The imposters were no different.

By the Spirit's perspective, every human being is a creation of the Trinity and destined to live in the new humanity Christ has brought to all. This is the focus of the Trinity, whose desire is for the affections of humanity to be aligned with

---

[324] "Therefore we, from now on, know no one in a fleshy way" (2 Corinthians 5:16, my translation).
[325] A pivotal parallel verse is Romans 11:32, which says, "For God has kept everyone under disobedience so that he could pour out his mercy on everyone" (my translation).

theirs and be expressed in the life-giving way that has existed between Father, Son, and Spirit for eternity.

In this cruciform perspective,[326] the symbols of a person's faith are not as important as the content of their heart and character. Circumcision was an obsession of the imposters, representing the defining outward mark of adherence to the law and belonging to the Jewish faith.

For Paul, it was immaterial whether one was circumcised or not. This outward expression had no significance. The fleshly markers did not speak of what was inside people. He knew that all too well as a religious leader who had persecuted those who followed Christ. The outward symbol of his belonging to God had been betrayed by the hate in his heart for those of the Way.

What mattered for Paul was whether a person had been transformed into a new creation, where the new humanity had taken birth and the Spirit empowered them toward love for God and others. It is this transformation he desired the Galatians to hold on to by walking in the Spirit.

This transformation is part of the greater work of the Trinity in restoring all creation to its identity and intended purpose.[327] Paul's forward-looking perspective anticipated that conversion and looked forward to its full transformation in the coming inheritance of a new world.[328]

In Galatians 6:16, Paul reaches out to all who desire to continue in the Spirit and live out their new humanity, encouraging them to keep in step with this way of living out their freedom in Christ. He calls it a standard by which to measure their affinity to Christ.

Letting the Spirit enable their new humanity and so live as a new creation, he calls for peace and mercy over the Gentile converts and the "Israel of God." This phrase is intended by Paul to identify the true Israelites who had come to faith in Christ and those who truly belonged to God.[329] These would be those who saw the promise to Abraham of the freedom that came through Christ, the ones who

---

[326] This term is the focus of Gregory Boyd's two-volume set, *Crucifixion of the Warrior God*.

[327] There is no better parallel verse than Ephesians 2:10, which says, *"We are his masterpiece, created in Christ Jesus to do good works in keeping with how God intended for us to live"* (my translation).

[328] Constantine R. Campbell's brief but excellent review of the salient passages in Paul addresses the new creation and gives a well-rounded perspective on Paul's view (Campbell, *Paul and the Hope of Glory: An Exegetical and Theological Study* [Grand Rapids, MI: Zondervan, 2020], 234–241).

[329] A parallel verse is found in Ephesians 2:14–15: *"Jesus is our peace, making us one by tearing down the wall of hostility. He did this in his flesh, rendering powerless the law with its commands and decrees by taking Jews and Gentiles and making them, in himself, one new humanity and so restoring peace. He did this so that he might reconcile both Jews and Gentiles into one body by putting to death hostility and division through his work on the cross"* (my translation).

were called to be sons of Abraham and sons of God over those who simply saw themselves as being part of the bloodline of the people of Israel.[330]

As a reader, you feel the burden of the battle Paul went through with the imposters and others who continually opposed his ministry and mission. He asked them not to cause him trouble, since enough trouble had already trailed him throughout his missionary journeys.

Having endured hardship, persecution, beatings, and punishments, his body bore enough proof of what he was willing to sacrifice so that others might come to know the freedom to be found in Christ. Like the stripes of the Roman lashes Jesus bore, Paul could show evidence on his back of the same suffering.

The imposters' degree of sacrifice paled in comparison. They were interested in avoiding controversy and strife by peddling their distorted gospel. It was time for the Galatians to stand their ground and withstand the weak onslaught of the imposters, holding on to their freedom in Christ and sending the imposters on their way.

Paul signs off with a pronouncement of the grace of Christ over the Galatians and the hope that Christ would remain with them. His affection in calling them his family members demonstrates his deep emotional connection with the Galatians as a spiritual father. His sincere and heartfelt desire was to see the Galatians continue in the Spirit and grow into their new humanity. Desiring that they remain close to Christ, he implores them to shed the law-focused gospel of the imposters who caused much strife in God's community in Galatia.

Paul then reminds them that it is far too easy to fall into false teaching that focuses on personal behaviour and adherence to certain rules and regulations. This stifles the life of Christ and the work of the Spirit. Any flashlight and candles that promise what only Christ can offer will weaken God's community and rob it of its true fellowship with the Trinity.

By withstanding the temptation to take over the work Christ has accomplished in us, we can become the loving community that brings peace and mercy to the

---

[330] James D.G. Dunn tells us, "But, in the light of his earlier argument, that would have to mean the Jewish people precisely in their covenant identity, 'Israel' rather than 'the Jews.' That is, an Israel understood in terms of the promise of Abraham (and Jacob/Israel), the very promise which included blessings for Gentiles (chs. iii-iv)—in other words, Israel understood not as excluding Jews as a whole, but as including Gentile believers (cf. Rom. ix. 6; xi.17–26; 1 Cor. x.18)" (Dunn, *Black's New Testament Commentary*, 345). Longnecker points out that Paul is using the "Israel of God" phrase in its truest sense, where Gentiles make up part of the people of God, along with Jews, who put their faith in Christ, unlike the imposters who demanded law adherence from Gentile followers of Christ to be part of the "Israel of God" (Longnecker, *Word Biblical Commentary, Volume 41: Galatians*, 298–299). Paul takes the "self-designation" of the Christian Judaizers and turns it into a proper designation of those who gather around Christ through faith.

world, introducing others to the love of the Father, Son, and Spirit so they might experience the transforming presence of Christ in their lives, and in turn live in such a transformed community. This is how we are to be the beacons of light Christ so desired of His followers.

CONCLUSION

Embracing Our Free Humanity

It's time to put down the flashlight and candles. There is no point in holding on to them. They are useless in battling the evil that seeks to keep us from living our lives in relationship with the Triune God of grace. Focusing on our own behaviour to stave off the onslaught of the evil one results in utter failure.

Christ has dealt the final blow to evil, and in the end He will crush evil permanently and purge the world of its presence. For the time being, He gives us the opportunity to enter into relationship with the Father, Son, and Spirit and find our identity in our new humanity so we can live in the freedom such relationship brings to us.

That kind of freedom brings equality and diversity, expressed in community, so that no one feels inferior or excluded. The goal of God's community is to take its collective unity and diversity and live by loving one another and sharing that love with others. As others taste the love of Christ in the freedom of God's community, they too will lay down their flashlights and candles and move to the rhythms of the sort of life the Spirit gives.

This will require us to carry each other's burden to live out the law of Christ. When we do, we will be unstoppable. People will find freedom and discover their identity in Christ. The world will look in awe at what God does in our midst. They will want what we have.

I know of no greater goal for any faith community than to be what the Apostle Paul encourages the Galatians to be in this pivotal letter.

I trust that if you've read this far, you will pass it on to others in your community. Determine to live in the trajectory of the Apostle's vision of a free humanity. Let the cross of Christ be the lens through which His compassion and love live through you to others. Lean on the Spirit and walk in the rhythm of the life the Spirit brings. See what He will do as you faithfully keep in step with His leading.

For those who may not be so convinced of the Apostle's argument, think of the reality of living out the law as described by the Lord Jesus. His encouragement to those who pointed Him to the law was to remind them that loving God and others is at the crux of what the law was about. Such a way of living and loving was only achievable when the Spirit was invited to empower us to live in and out of the love of the Trinity.

The Apostle assured the Galatians that *"only faith working through love matters"* (Galatians 5:6, my translation). If we stay focused on this, everything else will fall into place. God's community will settle into an equilibrium in which we seek to love and redeem. This perspective led the early church to work slowly but surely to influence the entire Roman Empire.

What might we accomplish if we stay the course as Paul encourages?

May the strength of Christ give us the freedom to live in love and harmony with one another, helping each other, to fulfill the Lord's desire that we respond to evil with good, to hatred with love, and to violence with peace, forgiving freely and loving lavishly until His kingdom comes and evil is no more. Amen.

WORKS CITED

_____, *La Sacra Bibbia Antico e Nuovo Testamento: La Nuova Diodati* (Brindisi, IT: La Buona Novella, 1991).

Abbot-Smith, G. *A Manual Greek Lexicon of the New Testament* (New York, NY: Charles Scribner's Sons, 1922).

Alland, Kurt, *The Greek New Testament* (Stuttgart, Germany: United Bible Societies, 1983).

Banks, Robert J. *Paul's Idea of Community: The Early House Churches in Their Cultural Setting* (Grand Rapids, MI: Baker Academic, 1994).

Bates, Matthew, *Salvation by Allegiance Alone: Rethinking Faith, Works, and the Gospel of Jesus the King* (Grand Rapids, MI: Baker Academic, 2017).

Boyd, Gregory, *Crucifixion of the Warrior God: Interpreting the Old Testament's Violent Portraits of God in Light of the Cross. Volume 1: The Cruciform Hermeneutic* (Minneapolis, MN: Fortress Press, 2017).

Boyd, Gregory, *Crucifixion of the Warrior God: Interpreting the Old Testament's Violent Portraits of God in Light of the Cross. Volume 2: The Cruciform Thesis* (Minneapolis, MN: Fortress Press, 2017).

Boyd, Gregory, "God's Akido Way of Defeating Evil," *Renew.* April 1, 2013. (https://reknew. org/2013/04/gods-aikido-way-of-defeating-evil/).

Brown, Colin, ed., *The New International Dictionary of New Testament Theology, Volumes 1–3* (Grand Rapids, MI: Zondervan Publishing House, 1971).

Burke, Trevor J., *Adopted into God's Family: Exploring a Pauline Metaphor* (Downers Grove, IL: IVP Academic, 2016).

Cahill, Thomas, *The Gift of the Jews* (New York, NY: Doubleday, 1998).

Caird, G. B., and Hurst L. D., *New Testament Theology* (Oxford, UK: Oxford University Press, 1995).

Caird, G. B., *The Language and Imagery of the Bible* (Philadelphia, PA: Westminster Press, 1980).

Craigie, Peter C., *The Daily Study Bible Series, Volume 2: Micah, Nahum, Habakkuk, Zephaniah, Haggai, Zechariah, and Malachi* (Philadelphia, PA: Westminster Press, 1985).

Danker, Frederick W, Walter Bauer, and William F. Arndt., *A Greek-English Lexicon of the New Testament and Other Early Christian Literature* (Chicago, IL: University of Chicago Press, 1979).

Dunn, James D. G., *Black's New Testament Commentary: The Epistle to the Galatians* (London, UK: A&C Black Limited, 1993).

Eastman, Susan G, "Cast Out the Slave Woman and Her Son: The Dynamics of Exclusion and Inclusion in Galatians 4:30." *Journal for the Study of the New Testament,* 28.3, 2006, 309–336.

Ellul, Jacques, *The Meaning of the City* (Grand Rapids, MI: Eerdmans, 1993).

Enns, Peter, *Inspiration and Incarnation: Evangelicals and the Problem of the Old Testament, Second Edition* (Grand Rapids, MI: Baker Academic, 2015).

Fee, Gordon D., *God's Empowering Presence: The Holy Spirit in the Letters of Paul* (Peabody, MA: Hendrickson Publishers, 1994).

Fee, Gordon D., *Pentecostal Commentary Series: Galatians* (Dorset, UK: Deo Publishing, 2011).

Fung, Ronald Y. K., *The New International Commentary on the New Testament: The Epistle to the Galatians* (Grand Rapids, MI: Eerdmans, 1988).

Gaebelein, Frank E., ed., *The Expositor's Bible Commentary, Volume 10* (Grand Rapids, MI: Zondervan, 1976).

George, Timothy, *Galatians: Volume 30* (Nashville, TN: Broadman and Homan Publishers, 1994).

Gundry, Robert H., *Commentary on Galatians* (Grand Rapids, MI: Baker Academic, 2010).

Gunton, Colin E., *Christ and Creation* (Waynesboro, GA: Paternoster Press, 1992).

Gunton, Colin E., *The Christian Faith: An Introduction to Christian Doctrine* (Oxford, UK: Blackwell Publishers, 2002).

Hahn, Scott W., "Covenant, Oath and Aqedah: Diaqhkh in Galatians 3:15–18." *The Catholic Biblical Quarterly*, Volume 67, 2005, 79–100.

Hays, Richard B., *The Conversion of the Imagination: Paul as Interpreter of Israel's Scripture* (Grand Rapids, MI: Eerdmans, 2005).

Hays, Richard B., *The Faith of Jesus Christ: An Investigation of the Narrative Substructure of Galatians 3:1–4:11* (Chico, CA: Scholars Press, 1983).

Hemer, Colin J., "The Name of Paul," *Tyndale Bulletin*, 36, 1985, 179–193.

Hendriksen, William, *New Testament Commentary: Galatians and Ephesians* (Grand Rapids, MI: Baker Book House, 1989).

Horsley, Richard A., ed., *Paul and Empire: Religion and Power in Roman Imperial Society* (Harrisburg, PA: Trinity Press International, 1997).

Hultgren Arland J., "The Ethical Reorientation of Paul: From the Law of Moses to the Law of Christ." *Currents in Theology and Mission*, January 1, 2019, 30–33.

Kaiser, Walter C., *Mission in the Old Testament: Israel as Light to the Nations* (Grand Rapids, MI: Baker Books, 2012).

Kruger, Baxter C., *Jesus and the Undoing of Adam* (Jackson, MS: Perichoresis Press, 2003).

Kruger, Baxter C., *The Great Dance: The Christian Vision Revisited* (Vancouver, BC: Regent College Publishing, 2000).

Kruger, Baxter C., *Patmos: Three Days, Two Men, One Extraordinary Conversation* (Jackson, MS: Perichoresis Press, 2016).

Keener, Craig, *Galatians: A Commentary* (Grand Rapids, MI: Baker Academic, 2019).

Lee, Chee-Chiew, *The Blessing of Abraham, the Spirit, and Justification in Galatians* (Eugene, OR: Pickwick Publications, 2013).

Lewis, C.S., *The Screwtape Letters: Letters from a Senior to a Junior Devil* (Glasgow, UK: Collins, 1987).

Lombardi, Luciano, *A New Humanity: A Walk Through the Letter of Ephesians* (Belleville, ON: Guardian Books, 2014).

Lombardi, Luciano, "Land and Judgment: Toward an Understanding of God's Wrath on Other Nations in the Old Testament," *McMaster Journal of Theology and Ministry*, Volume 8, 2007, 82–96.

Longnecker, Richard N., *Word Biblical Commentary, Volume 41: Galatians* (Grand Rapids, MI: Zondervan, 1990).

McKnight, Scot, *The NIV Application Commentary: Galatians* (Grand Rapids, MI: Zondervan, 1995).

McKnight, Scot, *The King Jesus Gospel: The Original Good News Revisited* (Grand Rapids, MI: Zondervan, 2011).

McKnight, Scot and Modica, Joseph B., eds., *The Apostle Paul and the Christian Life* (Grand Rapids, MI: Baker Academic, 2016).

Morgado Jr., Joe, "Paul in Jerusalem: A Comparison of His Visits in Acts and Galatians." *Journal of Evangelical Theological Society*, series 37, volume 1, March 1, 1994, 55–68.

Moulton, Harold K., *The Analytical Greek Lexicon Revised* (Grand Rapids, MI: Zondervan, 1977).

Newbigin, Leslie, *The Open Secret: An Introduction to the Theology of Mission* (Grand Rapids, MI: Eerdmans, 1995).

Nickelsburg G.W.E., "Jews and Christians in the First Century: The Struggle Over Identity." *Neotestamentica*, series 27, volume 2, 1993, 365–390.

Ott, Craig, "Missions and Money: Revisiting Pauline Practice and Principles." *Evangelical Review of Theology*, volume 42, issue 1, January 2018, 4–20.

Parry, Robin, *Worshipping the Trinity: Coming Back to the Heart of Worship* (Waynesboro, GA: Paternoster, 2005).

Porter, Gregory, "Be Good (Lion's Song) Official Video," *YouTube*. March 20, 2012 (https://www.youtube.com/watch?v=9HvpIgHBSdo).

Ridderbos, Herman N., *The Epistle of Paul to the Churches of Galatia: The New International Commentary on the New Testament* (Grand Rapids, MI: Eerdmans, 1984).

Sanders, E.P., *Paul, the Law, and the Jewish People* (Minneapolis, MN: Fortress Press, 1983).

Santala, Risto, *The Messiah in the Old Testament: In the Light of Rabbinical Writings* (Jerusalem, Israel: Keren Ahvah Meshlhit, 1992).

Schnabel, Eckhard J., "Jewish Opposition to Christians in Asia Minor in the First Century." *Bulletin for Biblical Research*, series 18, volume 2, 2008, 233–270.

Sigrist, D.J., Mangum, D., Brown D.R., Klippenstein, R., and Hurst, R., eds., *Lexham Theological Wordbook* (Bellingham, WA: Lexham Press, 2014).

Smith, Michael J., "The Role of the Pedagogue in Galatians." *Bibliotheca Sacra*, volume 163, April–June 2006, 197–214.

Stott, John, *The Bible Speaks Today: The Message of Galatians* (Downers Grove, IL: Intervarsity Press, 1968).

Thomas, Matthew J., *Paul's "Works of the Law" in the Perspective of Second-Century Reception* (Downers Grove, Il: Intervarsity Press, 2020).

Torrance, J.B., *Grace, Law, and Atonement*, Audio Course Lectures, Regent College (Vancouver, BC, 1994).

Torrance, T.F., *Atonement: The Person and Work of Christ* (Downers Grove, IL: IVP Academic, 2009).

Torrance, T.F., *Space, Time, and Incarnation* (Edinburgh, UK: T&T Clark, 1969).

Wenham, David, *Did St. Paul Get Jesus Right? The Gospel According to Paul* (Oxford, UK: Lion Hudson Place, 2010).

Westerholm, Stephen, *Justification Reconsidered: Rethinking a Pauline Theme* (Grand Rapids, MI: Eerdmans, 2013).

Wright, N.T., *Paul for Everyone: Galatians and Thessalonians* (London, UK: SPCK Press, 2004).

Wright, N.T., *Paul and the Faithfulness of God* (Minneapolis, MN: Fortress Press, 2013).

Wright, N.T., *The Challenge of Jesus: Rediscovering Who Jesus Was and Is* (Downers Grove, IL: Intervarsity Press, 1999).

Wright, N.T., *The Climax of the Covenant: Christ and the Law in Pauline Theology* (Minneapolis, MI: Fortress Press, 1991).

Wright, N.T., *The Day the Revolution Began: Reconsidering the Meaning of Jesus's Crucifixion* (San Francisco, CA: Harper One, 2016).

Wright N.T., *The New Testament and the People of God* (Minneapolis, MN: Fortress Press, 1992).

Young, Paul, *The Shack* (Newbury Park, CA: Windblown Media, 2007).

Zizioulas, John D., *Being in Communion* (Crestwood, NY: St. Vladimir's Seminary Press, 2002).